D1596086

ON MARRIAGE

ON MARRIAGE

Devorah Baum

Yale UNIVERSITY PRESS

NEW HAVEN AND LONDON

Typeset in 12.25/15pt Fournier MT Std by Jouve (UK), Milton Keynes.
Printed in the United States of America.

Library of Congress Control Number: 2023933820
ISBN 978-0-300-27193-5 (hardcover : alk. paper)

This paper meets the requirements of ANSI/NISO Z39.48-1992
(Permanence of Paper).

10 9 8 7 6 5 4 3 2 1

For Josh, in particular

'Away . . . into the unguessable country of marriage.'

Angela Carter, *The Bloody Chamber*

CONTENTS

Marriage as Religion

Marriage as Afterlife

Marriage as Philosophy

I

Are You Thinking About Marriage?

'There is something ridiculous about a married philosopher.'
Kathleen Nott, 'Is Rationalism Sterile?'

Writing about marriage wasn't my idea – someone eligible proposed it to me and I said yes. It wasn't long afterwards, however, that I started fretting over the wisdom of my decision. Is marriage really a suitable subject to get myself tied up with? Can it truly sustain my interest over a long engagement? And hasn't it been around so long anyway that it's already been done to death? Certainly, marriage is something you're supposed to *do* unto death. Maybe my cold feet were a sign of this; a sign that I feared losing myself in marriage, or feared getting buried in it. Yet the more time I spent thinking about marriage, the more wedded to the idea I became. Okay, okay, I hear you . . . I won't keep on making these marital puns, *I do* (ahem) recognize they're annoying – although the fact that marital puns should offer themselves up this readily is also one of the curiosities *about* marriage. Marriage is so fundamental to shaping our ideas about what it means to get attached that one often finds it invoked when thinking about all manner of other attachments as well.

All manner of attachments besides marriage itself, that is, which seems to be much harder to think about. Since committing (sorry) to this project, I've even found that raising marriage as a topic of consideration in polite company tends to provoke a wide range of

3

emoji-type facial reactions, and often a few expletives, but hardly any interesting reflections. War may be less contentious. And yet writing about marriage not only isn't hard to find, it's a veritable industry; one that, from Mills & Boon to self-help, fills countless bookshelves and endless column inches. Nor has there been any shortage of critics ready and willing to make vociferous cases for or against marriage. But since most of us descend from a history of marriages made or unmade, and most of us get married or attend, when invited, the weddings of others, we do seem to take marriage, as a concept, for granted. Whatever it is we think about it, we already know what we think. That, or we just don't think about it at all.

In my own case, for example, before getting married, I only ever questioned *who* I would marry not *if* I would marry. I knew and cared little that there were reasons to distrust an institution responsible for perpetrating and perpetuating a surfeit of historical abuses. Marriage was what I wanted. Not that it felt like a want exactly. Neither marrying nor having children felt like a want or even a need at first. If anything, these seemed more like necessary developments: if not this, if not marriage and children, then what? It's as though I saw marriage, a bit like death, as something coming for me, not I for it.

Besides, I was raised on a literature comprised almost entirely of marriage plots, and in a world that was, so far as I knew, full of happily married people. I had no call, therefore, to question the institution in the way children of divorced parents do. Children like my husband, who was much more wary of the contract than I. Nor was it clear to him, since we'd been living together for years beforehand, what possible difference, if any, marrying could make. We knew we were in love, he said, so what did we need marriage for? Wouldn't marriage imply that we didn't quite trust our love to sustain us? Wouldn't marriage even insinuate that we *weren't* really in love? Many a romantic has said the same. It's an argument that's created real headaches, in fact, for those who wish to see love and marriage as wedded terms.

Yet, once upon quite another time, the argument that love is

4

incompatible with marriage held water for altogether different reasons. Before romance claimed its rightful ownership over marriage (which was the winning argument, according to the historian Stephanie Coontz, by the end of the eighteenth century), if you fell in love, not only was that *not* a good reason to get married, it was a sign that you probably shouldn't. Marriage was a matter of convenience – convenient for your family and the wider community. Love was the whim of individuals who had lost all reason in the throes of their passions. Love was selfish, individualist, insubordinate. Marriage, meanwhile, as the foremost instrument of social reproduction, was too important to be left to lovers whose unruliness could only threaten it. So, if you wanted to marry someone with whom you'd fallen in love, you'd better make it look like a marriage of convenience.

Making their way through the eighteenth and nineteenth centuries, however, were new ideas about what's sacred. Where love once threatened the sanctity of marriage, now marriage was what threatened the sanctity of love. And yet love, by virtue of now *being* sacred, had become the only possible justification *for* marriage. So if you want a marriage of convenience today, you'd best make it look as though you're in love.

In early modern literature (by which I mostly mean Shakespeare) we already meet the insurrectionary force of modern love and its ideological takeover of marriage. The rise of the love match had its way paved by religious reformations, and specifically by the new Protestant emphasis on the importance of companionability and consent, and the subsequent effort to recapture civic duty by turning marriage, in the mid-sixteenth century, into one of the sacraments. This was under the auspices of a Church whose familiar wedding ceremony has barely changed its wording since. Romeo, named after a pilgrim to Rome, embodies some of these contradictions. After marrying, he does briefly show a Christ-like compassion for his fellow man and a strengthened awareness of his wider social responsibilities. But if Romeo and Juliet have remained literature's archetypal young, passionate and impulsive lovers, that's also because they appear to us as modern people; as people who disobey their elders to pursue their own desires; and people who find the justification for marriage only in what comes from their own hearts and imaginations. Juliet demands this explicitly of her Romeo. Whatever vows he makes her, she insists, should rest on no external point of authority. Which is how love becomes a social menace. For if love, to prove itself true, cannot afford to anchor itself to anything outside the beating heart of the lover, then love must be, in the purest sense, antisocial. In Romeo and Juliet's case, this is why their play ends in tragedy. The couple do marry in secret, but their marriage can't work without social sanction. Death comes for those who cannot go outside with their love. The most emblematic moment of the play is therefore not for nothing the balcony scene, that ideally romantic space between interior and exterior, where the lover yearns not only for unification with the beloved, but for a marriage between their private desires and public roles.

Yet nor does love elude crisis in Shakespeare's romantic comedies either. Comedy's affairs of the heart are indeed the playground of precisely the sort of fools who rush in where angels fear to tread. Although what we do at least get, with comedy, is a version of the happy ending that marriage is said to promise. Where fools rush in, after all, angels presumably have to at some point venture, even if they have a clearer sense of the risks involved. Both fools and angels are actors, doers. It's intellectuals who prefer to contemplate and consider before committing to act.

So, what do intellectuals think of marriage? Very little, from what I can gather. Writing at the start of the nineteenth century in his *Enquiry Concerning Political Justice*, William Godwin lamented the 'evil of marriage' as practised by a 'thoughtless and romantic youth' deluding themselves into a 'vow of eternal attachment', surmising that the 'abolition of the present system of marriage appears to involve no evils'. Somewhat embarrassingly, he then went on to marry

Mary Wollstonecraft. Although, fair play: Wollstonecraft's *Vindication of the Rights of Women* had already identified marriage as an area where sexual oppression had a habit of destroying that which, in her view, marriage ought to be – an ideal form of friendship based on equality.

Nor were Godwin and Wollstonecraft as unusual as they perhaps imagined. This pattern of denouncing marriage while also marrying is one that, if you look out for it, you can find everywhere repeated among the intellectual classes. The rule of intellectuals who marry is that they do so as exceptions to the rule. Later in the nineteenth century, for example, we find John Stuart Mill's searing denunciation of the subjugation of women via marriage; which was an opinion in no way modified by his marriage to Harriet Taylor. Yet Mill's own marriage was exceptional, he believed, because he actively sought to reverse the sexual dynamics of the master–slave relation. If anyone was to be a slave in his marriage, he commanded, it would be him! Both he and Taylor, moreover, seemed to think a largely chaste marriage unvexed by Eros was the best way to ensure their marriage remained a sensible as well as righteous one.

But laying these polemics to one side, there's more than one way for thinking people not to think much of marriage. And in the case of most post-Enlightenment philosophy (the schools of thought that, in seventeenth- and eighteenth-century Europe, privileged reason over tradition), there seems a remarkable dearth of engagement with the subject at all. It's a pretty strange lacuna to encounter when you consider that marriage is a formal relation that could arguably lay claim to being the world's most enduring and universal. Indeed, as far back as our history books go, we have no record of a time preceding marriage. Isn't that an extraordinary fact? On this basis alone, you'd expect marriage to have inspired more famous philosophical works. Yet when marriage does appear in the modern canon, it tends to be a subsidiary topic brought in to substantiate a thinker's wider philosophical claims; while those who've made marriage a priority aren't generally best known for these particular writings. So, could this relative lack of philosophic interest in the question of marriage be key to understanding what marriage *means* philosophically? Is marriage – for the philosopher who hasn't written a treatise against it – what you only do when you do not ponder it too much?

'Those engaged in the life of the mind have never seemed to think excessively highly of the institution of marriage', observes the humanist philosopher Kathleen Nott. And there's no denying that some of the main thinkers to have broached the subject – thinkers such as Kant, Nietzsche and Kierkegaard – never themselves married. In Nietzsche's case, whatever his other iconoclasms, he was broadly in sympathy with the traditionalists' view that marriage is a good that stands at risk of modern love's toxic influence. Meanwhile Hegel, though sharing these reservations, came to the conclusion that one *can* be married and a philosopher, but only so long as one's marriage is arranged for the sake of higher principles, leaving romantic follies for extramarital affairs. (A solution that seems to have been happily adopted by a number of other married philosophers as well.)

Well, perhaps that stands to reason. If it's only fools who fall in love, then philosophy can't afford to get mixed up with it. But nor is philosophy unrelated to love. Love, in the Western tradition, is both a part of philosophy's name (*philo*/love-*sophy*/wisdom), and the subject of Plato's *Symposium*, one of its foundational texts. Read today, the *Symposium* presents unusually as a philosophical work. Not only does it contain as much of what we would now consider literature as it does reasoning, but its ideas about love are formed in dialogue with others. In these dialogues, Eros does go through some rigorous questioning, finding itself considered from various angles – including the sexual and (as we would now say) the platonic. Ultimately, however, what appears as true love for the Western philosopher – as in a love worthy of a lifetime's commitment – is the love of knowledge.

And it's this love of knowledge that, according to the Lithuanian–French philosopher Emmanuel Levinas, puts the Western philosopher directly at odds with another character – a character that Levinas calls angel. For 'the secret of angels', he says, is to upend the order of philosophical priority – think first, act later. The angel is someone who agrees, in the first place, 'yes', and only after that fact do they then begin to reflect on their decision. So it's not that the angel *doesn't* think, it's just that the angel thinks things over a little later than the philosopher, i.e. after a decision has already been made. To the rationalist, this can only sound like madness. And yet anything else, argues Levinas, leaves one hanging in a state of sublime distraction, tempted by all the temptations, but never really entering into the world in all its murk, muck and confusion. Which is why the philosopher has often appeared as someone who rarely, if ever, gets moved *into* action. Like the serial seducer, the philosopher generally prefers to keep their options open. To determine upon any course of action, after all, one must accept beforehand that every decision (*de-caedere*, from the Latin, to cut off) murders all other possibilities.

So is this – the spectre of violence inherent in the madness of decision-making – what haunts the 'man of reason'? For that, surely, must be the lesson to be learned via Romeo's tragic example: that acting without thinking risks consequences that are unpredictable and potentially fatal. To which lesson, how should the angel respond?

The angel, being no fool, must recognize these risks. Likewise, the covenant entered into must recognize that a certain propensity to violence lurks within its original institution. Indeed, if not monitored carefully, this constitutive violence risks certain ripple effects; ones that could cause its symbolic violence to morph into actual violence. As such, the violence within the vow, if it's to avoid transforming into more than merely a propensity, ought never to be disavowed. As its history unfolds, the foundational violence will have to be processed rather than denied. But then, isn't inaction an equally perilous course? And doesn't the temptation towards inaction that Levinas considers the great temptation of Western philosophy risk its *own* propensity for violence? If every decision murders all other possibilities, surely indecision murders *all* possibilities.

The marriage contract is, unquestionably, a fearsome one that commits its parties 'unto death'. Marriage, in fact, may be one of the only things most people do that they vow, on point of entry, not to get out of alive. More than merely offending against the priority of thought ahead of action, therefore, marriage could also be viewed as a direct competition *for* philosophy. For philosophy too, particularly in its existentialist modes, has represented itself as a commitment unto death. To philosophize, said Montaigne, is to learn how to die. The life of the mind, agreed Heidegger, is one of being-towards-death. The only real decision we have to make, Camus cheerfully counselled, is whether or not to commit suicide. To be or not to be – that *is* the question of philosophy.

So much, you want to say, for reason. Indeed, rationalists, Kathleen Nott remarks of her colleagues, can express 'a great deal of the obsessional anxiety which we nowadays describe as neurotic'. She mentions the philosophers Descartes, Kant, Nietzsche and Schopenhauer as cases in point (all, incidentally, unmarried). But what's perhaps *more* to the point is one of the directions such reasoning out of all reason can sometimes take. 'This need for certainty or finality', ventures Nott, 'might partly account for the suicidal wishes of many neurotics. Death is inevitable – so let us have done with it.'

It's Hamlet, literature's foremost man of inaction (diagnosed by Freud as a 'neurasthenic'), who made the fundamental thing we have no choice over such a decisive matter. To be or not to be is *his* question. Perhaps because, as life's one certainty, death can also sometimes appear as a source of mastery. A prince, to be fully possessed of his sovereignty, must wield the power of life *and* death. Although this can feel no less true for those without such worldly power as kings, but who still wish to be able to lay claim to having such power over themselves. It isn't his death, Freud intimated, that man necessarily dreads or resists. It's the idea of somebody else interfering with it. What man wants above all is to die in his own fashion. Which might help to explain the strangeness of the death drive; if to choose one's own death is also a means of becoming the hero of one's own life or the author of one's own story. Despite the indecisiveness upon which his reputation hangs, after all, Prince Hamlet ultimately dies in a bloodbath of his own making. Though what leads him unto his premature death is the maddening uncertainty aroused by a social world organized by marriage; and his strong but unproven suspicion that his mother may have committed adultery. Is there then, with all these philosophy bros, something of a pattern emerging?

Ophelia dies by her own hand too of course, when the marriage that was to be her future is denied her. And her tragedy foreshadows the numerous later narratives featuring female protagonists for whom the marriage plot is no less decisive than the death plot, and no less determining of the meaning of their lives. That isn't only true, though, for the heroines of tragedies. The American writer Ralph Waldo Emerson once railed against the comic novels of Jane Austen precisely on account of their narrow obsession with 'marriageableness'. He'd rather die, he protested, than submit to such vistaless horizons. But what Emerson misses in his critique of Austen is how, for the female characters in such novels, that really *is* the choice they face: marry or (you may as well) die. The response of many of these female protagonists isn't necessarily to deny or avoid the marriage that dominates their life choices, however. Rather, like Freud's man facing death, what they seem to want is to get there in their own fashion. Or better to say, what they want is a share in their own life stories. Unlike the lonely and heroic Thanatos (Freud's Greek name for the death instinct), driven to destruction in a bid for mastery, the story of Eros centres on a subject who is dependent and may *have* dependants, but who reveals that it is no less difficult nor any less heroic to live with love than it is with death.

So it's hardly surprising, then, that the most sustained reflections on marriage within modern philosophy come to us from one of its more literary corners. In the second part of *Either/Or*, the major work of the Danish nineteenth-century thinker Søren Kierkegaard, marriage is very much a matter to be taken seriously. Taken seriously, that is, not by Kierkegaard himself, but by Judge Wilhelm, one of Kierkegaard's fictional personae. The fact that Kierkegaard mostly avoided stating positions in his own name tells us that Prince Hamlet wasn't the only Danish philosopher plagued by such doubts as to render him afeared of commitment. But where Hamlet asked to be or not to be, Kierkegaard had another existential question: to marry or not to marry. In *Either*, this question is said to be unresolvable since neither choice – neither marrying and forgoing all others nor embracing all others and forgoing marriage – leaves one without regret.

But in the end, of course, indecision does become a form of decision. And in Kierkegaard's case, having been engaged to Regina Olsen, he failed to make the leap of faith into an actual marriage with her. For that reason, he must have suffered his regrets. Whereas, approaching the marriage question from a different axis entirely, it's the curious claim of Kierkegaard's Judge Wilhelm that 'I have never passed myself off as a philosopher . . . I usually appear as a married man'. Kierkegaard and his judge would thus appear to be foils for each other: Kierkegaard couldn't marry because he was a philosopher, the Judge can't philosophize because he's married.

In what sense, though, is the Judge unable to philosophize? Well, for one thing, what he claims for marriage is a testament not to logic but to conviction. Yet this conviction is one he nevertheless pitches as a resolution to the problem my husband alluded to before we got married: the problem for erotic love once it's been commandeered into a form of legally enshrined obedience. For what the Judge believes is that the marital vow is the *realization* of erotic love. The decision to marry, he charges, made in the flush of 'first love', is the decision of someone who knows, just as a visionary knows, that their love is eternal. Their faith is that the fullness of their love as experienced in its first manifestation will not degrade or lessen over time.

First love is assumed, on the contrary, to initiate a history that works to conjure the future – a position in no way palatable to the type of thinker seeking to settle a case rather than allowing it to generate new horizons of possibility.

In what sense, then, is Judge Wilhelm able to judge? In the sense, it would seem, that he can make positive decisions even in the absence of reasons. Reasons, on the other hand, are by no means hard to arrive at for those seeking to oppose his decisions. You don't need to spend too long reading his purple prose, for instance, to find him alternately conceited, buffoonish, smug, sentimental, moralistic, petit bourgeois. Most intellectuals would surely consider the Judge a clown, if not a fool. Wilhelm is the sort of guy you find abundantly depicted in comic novels, cartoons, sitcoms, adverts – the very image of the hapless husband. And yet despite all his preening, isn't he also akin to Levinas's angel?

It was Levinas's contention that the Western tradition of philosophy may have its priorities the wrong way round. Rather than ontology (the nature of being), the philosopher's primary concern ought, in Levinas's view, to be ethics, the nature of human relations. While philosophy's true translation, he suggested, isn't the love of knowledge, but the knowledge of love. Although this knowledge, to really be considered as knowledge, would have to be more than merely theoretical. It would have to begin – as the *Symposium* begins – with an invitation to others to enter into a relation whose meaning can then only be discovered intersubjectively. Treatises cannot easily play host to such a knowledge. If you take the book currently in your hands, for example, you'll notice how the knowledge it aims at is forced to begin its journey rather abstractly, as an idea, or as a series of ideas, but over time you'll find that the journey gets much more up close and personal, and hopefully, too, with experience, it should get easier as well. A bit like a marriage. Or like some marriages, at any rate. So if it's knowledge of love you're after, you may, having read your fill of treatises, be better advised to move on to literature as a tradition largely organized and dominated by the marriage plot. For marriage – as the quintessential philosophical novelist George Eliot once claimed with regard to her major marriage epic, *Middlemarch* – is nothing if not a practical way of finding out what love is. Or as Taffy Brodesser-Akner puts it in a more recent novel, *Fleishman is in Trouble*, 'only when you're actually married, once this need is fulfilled, you can for the first time wonder if you even want to be married or not.'

And it's in literature too that we can follow the sentimental arc of thinkers such as Hamlet, whose crippling uncertainties made him a poor lover to his fiancée. Literature allows for this immersion in the subjective character of experience precisely because what literature doesn't compel us to jump to, necessarily, are conclusions. As Freud noted of dreams, literature isn't a field of either/or. If not always in reality, then in its very idea, literature permits itself the freedom to conjugate disparate and even contradictory elements. Just this, in fact, is the conjugal freedom whose significance the Algerian-French philosopher Jacques Derrida once described in relation to the most subtly subversive of all words, at least from the vantage of rationalist philosophy: 'the conjunction "and" brings together words, concepts, perhaps things that don't belong to the same category. A conjunction such as "and" dares to defy order, taxonomy, classificatory logic, no matter how it works: by analogy, distinction or opposition.'

The word 'and' makes a real mess of philosophy. Whereas, via literature, we can observe how, if Hamlet and Ophelia are dead by the end of their play, so are Romeo and Juliet by the end of theirs. And yet Romeo appears as the very antitype of Hamlet – no less the passionate adolescent, but driven by impulse, decisiveness and a distinct lack of reflection. Romeo, by not thinking before acting, exhibits the fatality of recklessness. Hamlet, by overthinking, exhibits the fatality attending the philosophical lust for certainty. Nevertheless, for all they differ, Romeo and Hamlet are both alike in being tragic heroes in whose fates we can see that *the course of true love never did run smooth* – although that's a line not from tragedy, but from comedy.

A Midsummer Night's Dream is the comedy, and it's very much a conjugating play: a play about coupling and the question of who gets together with whom. And it's a play as well that puzzles whether or not the lover's eyes are seeing clearly, and what seeing clearly, when it comes to love and marriage, even means. Love is variously described in the play as folly and madness. While the idea of 'true love' is often invoked, with different theories competing no less than they do in Plato's *Symposium*, what love seems to lead to, primarily, is the quarrelling itself. In *Dream* we again encounter the same historical tensions regarding arranged marriage versus modern romance that led Romeo and Juliet to their tragic ends – the consequence of young people disregarding what fathers and rulers want, to pursue their own desires. And we see again too how choosing for oneself whom to marry threatens, even in the world of comedy, generational conflict, social unrest, and women taking on a role they feel ill befits them – that of the wooer, not the wooed. Meanwhile, everybody gets soiled in the process; including, in the middle of the play, the Queen of the Fairies, who gets loved up with a human ass. Since this *is* a comedy, however, it ends with a (triple) wedding wherein social stability has been restored as the lovers have all conveniently married within their class.

Still, despite its concluding revelry, we end the play not necessarily any more conclusive about what constitutes true love; nor has every social relation been repaired. The failure of Hermia to honour her father's wishes as announced at the start of the play when he drags his daughter before the sovereign of Athens, asserting that 'she is mine, I may dispose of her; Which shall be either to this gentleman, or to her death', haunts the finale. The fact that this father makes no appearance at his own daughter's wedding shows how a happy ending can nonetheless hint at a social order coming unstuck, even as it tries to marry its various parts back together. Nor, for all its mirth, does the comic mode save us from having witnessed patriarchy's merciless power. When, at the start of the play, both father and sovereign are at one in dictating to Hermia whom she must marry, those scenes would be hard to play for laughs. And if you want to know how that looks in the tragic version, you need only consult the brutal threats made to Juliet by *her* father.

Romeo and Juliet's conjugal tragedy, in fact, casts a subtle shadow over *Dream*'s conjugal comedy. We sense this particularly in the final wedding party where the just-married couples watch amateur actors perform scenes from *Pyramus and Thisbe*, a romantic tragedy whose lovers, like Romeo and Juliet, are driven to early deaths by a world that won't sanction their love. But while Shakespeare's major handling of that tragedy produces pathos, in *Dream* the tragic play within the comic play provokes only ridicule. Is *Dream*, then, less besotted with love and marriage than its audiences are wont to imagine? How otherwise should we interpret the three couples laughing on their shared wedding day at the spectacle of a play about a couple loving each other unto death – when that's precisely what they've just contracted for themselves?

Dream is at once a romantic comedy, a satire and a proto-bedroom farce – one in which liberated youths, seeking to defy patriarchal authorities, find themselves the playthings of woodland spirits instead. The mythic idea of the soulmate derived from the philosophers' *Symposium* has in this play a kind of ridiculous farcical fungibility whereby the lovers pursue with the same passion and conviction a new lover much as they had a completely different one just moments before. Nor is it clear to the play's audience why each lover prefers whoever it is they prefer – to the outsider, all the young lovers appear much the same. (Even in his tragic rendering, Shakespeare was hardly inconsistent in this view: Romeo was head over heels in love with Rosalind before Juliet crossed his path.) So it is that, in *Dream*'s woodlands, reason comes undone as we're led to discover that there are more things in heaven and earth than are dreamt of in our philosophy.

But now I'm back to quoting *Hamlet* again. And indeed, the existential question for Hamlet, tortured as he was by his suspicions and doubts, was never purely philosophical either. For it isn't simply a choice between living with outrageous fortune or taking up arms in a fight until death. What Hamlet finds tantalizing in death, after all, isn't death as such, but the opportunity 'perchance to dream'. His dream of dreaming, in other words, is the dream of an alternately comic sphere of fantasy and play; a sphere where ends can appear as new beginnings and nobody need fear being taken for a fool. Or a sphere of lovers rather than fighters where *everyone* is taken for a fool.

And nowhere is this clearer than in *A Midsummer Night's Dream* whose standout fool is Nick Bottom. Yet Bottom is also, it might be argued, the play's image of the true lover. Albeit he clearly isn't one of the highborn whose aristocratic conjugations are celebrated at the end of the final act. He's a mere weaver, in fact, there at the wedding party to entertain the newly-weds with his real passion – acting (which passion Hamlet, a fellow thespian, could surely appreciate). As an *amateur*, Bottom is therefore a lover by very definition. And if you were to ask Bottom who is the romantic lead of *Dream*, he'd undoubtedly step forward. It's even he who describes *A Midsummer Night's Dream* towards the end of the play as 'Bottom's Dream'. Nor does he think himself an unworthy protagonist. Amongst the group of players to which he belongs, not only does he instantly say yes to whichever part he's given, even before he knows what part it is, but he puts himself forward for all the other parts too. It's what makes him so funny. His is the folly of the egoist: that person who doesn't seem to know their proper part. But then, isn't that true of all dreamers and all dreams – where we never do quite know our place or our part, or where every part in our dream turns out to be a part of ourselves? As with all of Shakespeare's fools, therefore, we have to wonder if Bottom is really such a fool or whether he's the character in the play who could teach us something about the nature of true love.

For if Bottom is the comic inversion of Hamlet's thespianism on the one hand, we can equally see how Bottom, in performing the part of Pyramus, shows himself to be a comedic variation of Romeo on the other. Certainly Bottom, no less than Romeo, is prone to rush in passionately, without thinking. And yet however much we're invited to mock Bottom and his fellow players, it's no less the case that these are amateur actors in a dangerous situation, performing at the wedding of a sovereign who holds the power of life or death over them. If they fail to entertain the Duke, they may not live to see a new morning. Much like the fatal lovers Pyramus and Thisbe or Romeo and Juliet, these actors are risking all for what they love. And it's by so doing that they produce the play's 'happy' ending, delighting the Duke not because he's been moved to the tears warranted by their attempt at tragedy, but because he's been moved to a laughter elicited by their accidental comedy.

What, then, does this curious comic conclusion of *Dream* suggest regarding how the play views marriage? Early on, Hermia declares that it is 'hell! To choose love by another's eyes'. Since, by the final act, she has married whom her heart chose, she might well feel vindicated in her decision to rebel against arranged marriage. But what are we to make of the fact that Lysander only loves Hermia because a magic potion has altered his vision? In his case, love *has* been chosen by another's eyes, thus implicating Hermia in a new marriage already halfway into hell. The play would thus appear to mock the dreams of mastery of both the sovereign (Duke) *and* the sovereign individual (Hermia) when it comes to love and marriage. If we consider for instance the moment when the beauteous Queen of the Fairies awakens from her drugged slumber to fall in love with Bottom, a human ass, this scene is clearly obscene and ludicrous. And yet the first thing Titania asks upon sight of him, 'what Angel is this?', could equally have been posed by a Levinas scholar. Contrary to tragedy's descent into a final and fatal self-knowledge, in comedy we find characters whose ignorance of themselves deprives them of any such self-knowledge, but may yet put them in the way of a different kind of knowledge: the knowledge of love that's proper to literature – a knowledge of love that can *only* come to us through another's eyes.

As a case in point, consider the tales that comprise *One Thousand and One Nights*. In this legendary epic of Arabic literature, it's his first wife's infidelity that provokes the King to hatch his macabre take on the marriage plot: wed a new virgin every day, deflower her at night, and behead her the following morning. His is a brutal lesson in fidelity – an uncompromising vision of marriage till death doth part. Within the strictures of this marital set-up, there's no suspense, no uncertainty, no possibility of a second betrayal. Nothing, not even death, is left to chance. The purest of marriage plots is thus the one that knows the future in advance with all action bent towards that end. As such, a spouse, to be fully determined as a spouse, must be a dead certainty. But while that might well have seemed like a good plan on paper, there remains within it a potential flaw that threatens to undermine the King's tactics: because if someone's a dead certainty, there's always the risk that you'll lose interest. So it isn't clear that 1,001 different but identically fated brides will keep eros aflame night after night after night any more than could the same returning bride.

Enter, therefore, Shahrazad (Scheherazade), with a marriage plot to rival the King's. Albeit hers is a high-wire act. For she weds her groom willingly, knowing and never doubting the gruesome terms of his contract. But though it's death she risks, it's life she wants, as she makes clear, in Hanan al-Shaykh's striking rendering of her story, in her initial proposal: 'Father, I want you to marry me to King Shahryar, so that I may either succeed in saving the girls of the kingdom, or perish and die like them.' She marries, that's to say, in order to save the girls of the future from death by marriage.

There's no doubt, then, that Shahrazad is a worthy heroine. She's courageous, she's gifted, and she has one helluva historical mission before her. But even these talents and virtues are insufficient in themselves. She still has to pick her moment. She has to figure out when the King has been through enough virgins to be getting a vague inkling that marital bliss continues to elude him. And she has to propose marriage when she senses that her would-be groom is tiring, becoming bored, and secretly wanting, the way cynics always deep-down want, to be dazzled, disproved, surprised. So it must have been tempting for Shahrazad to suggest herself as the surprise he believes he's after: a sort of Schrödinger's wife; someone who can be both alive *and* a dead certainty at the same time. Whereas what Shahrazad does is quite the opposite. She tells stories, and her stories, which are mostly about marriages, are often erotic and frequently adulterous. They even occasionally feature storytellers who, like Shahrazad herself, tell their tales to seduce sovereigns with the power of life and death over them. Sometimes, too, her stories are of women and their mistreatment at the hands of cruel and jealous men. Although there are also stories of mistreated men and the adulteresses who wronged them. What her stories do not forecast are their own ends. In fact, they never *do* seem to end.

Given this endlessness, lots of Shahrazad's stories also begin to resemble each other. So why doesn't a man as obsessed as King Shahryar is by the concept of the virginal and the new accuse his latest wife of getting repetitive? And why doesn't he take issue with the way she so conspicuously turns her tricks – by means of the breakaway, the cliffhanger, the cheap thrill, the predictable uses of suspense? Has his sensibility perhaps taken a literary turn? You could say of Shahryar that he arrives upon this conjugal scene in the mould of a philosopher-king. For he's clearly a man with a firm logic; a man who has his way of knowing things, and making sure of them. But then with Shahrazad his logic starts unravelling. He can no longer quite establish for himself what causes things to happen in the various ways they do. Indeed, for all that he, listening to her for so long, must be attuned to her literary devices, something in the energy of her storytelling keeps him interested. He may have heard a version of a story before, he may have heard it 1,001 times before, but he still tunes in each night, wondering what will happen next. It's as if, when it comes to Shahrazad, nothing is a dead certainty. Even if it *is* the same night with her 1,001 times, a night with Shahrazad feels to him more original than would many legions of new wives.

Perhaps, therefore, we can speculate that what's in the storyteller's gift, which might not be in the logician's, is the singular power to reframe the terms of the contract – and specifically, the contract that marries unto death. For while death may be depended on as life's only certainty by a philosopher, or by a king who would like to make of his wife another instance of the same dead certainty, death becomes, in Shahrazad's telling, the existential condition of life's *un*certainty – and thus the knife's edge upon which she can compose new worlds. And so, by the same token, she can also proffer her alternative vision of marriage – one whose erotics can only be sustained by inventiveness, liveliness, and the looming possibility of running into an unscripted silence where nobody knows what will happen next.

So it's important not to underestimate the risks Shahrazad is taking. If she ever does run out of inspiration and dare to meet her King on the grounds of her own emptiness, that's when the suspense really could kill. Yet it's also just here, in the pause of the narrative, that the King might glimpse how Shahrazad has used the open horizon of her story to overturn the closed fist of his plot. And so he might glimpse as well how this could be the means to a different kind of 'happy ending' – an experience of marriage that can only be as fulfilling as the couple are prepared to entertain doubts, and a spouse who finds that there may lurk between the lines of the marriage plot an unspeakable love story that's all his own. It's the King himself, in other words, who turns out to be the unwitting romantic lead of Shahrazad's love story. As the listener to the story, by making himself permeable he puts *himself* at risk of unexpected things happening, and of his own character changing. Meanwhile, Shahrazad wagers, by changing the character of the King she can change the kingdom for herself, and for the girls of the future as well.

'I am Gimpel the fool. I don't think myself a fool. On the contrary. But that's what folks call me.' So begins 'Gimpel the Fool', one of Isaac Bashevis Singer's best-loved stories. Gimpel is undeniably gullible. Is there nothing or nobody he won't believe? All the townspeople mock and sneer at him. He's so easily deceived that few can resist making him the subject of their cruelties and pranks. He marries Elka, known to everyone but himself as the town prostitute; she's five months pregnant at the time, but tells her husband that the baby born prematurely is his. He certainly loves the child that way, even when, later on, he's put in the picture. By the end of the story Elka has six children via various infidelities, admitting as much on her deathbed to a husband who still loves them all as his own. It's not that Gimpel is beyond suspicion of the tall tales he's told: 'If I ever dared to say, "Ah, you're kidding!" there was trouble. People got angry. "What do you mean! You want to call everyone a liar?" What was I to do? I believed them, and I hope at least that did them some good.'

The hope that believing people might do them some good isn't far off the approach taken by psychoanalysis, not least in the interpretation of dreams. And indeed, by the end of the story, Gimpel does emerge more in the mode of the wandering sage than the fool: 'After many years I became old and white; I heard a great deal, many lies and falsehoods, but the longer I lived the more I understood that there were really no lies. Whatever doesn't really happen is dreamt at night. It happens to one if it doesn't happen to another, tomorrow if not today, or a century hence if not next year.'

Gimpel is comedy's character. You're invited to laugh at him, not with him. Yet he's right, it turns out, not to think himself a fool, though he sees very clearly that he's regarded as such. Compared with his outwitting neighbours, his relationship to the truth would not be considered logical, or in any obvious sense philosophical. He does not share King Shahryar's lust for certainty. But then, his is a world in which there are no lies. Or you could say, his is a world of conjugations instead of contradictions or conclusions. Gimpel's idea of truth is one that explicitly includes what happens at night (dreams) and what happens a century hence (the future). In this sense, his approach is not dissimilar to that of Judge Wilhelm, who invokes the same tenets of faith to underpin his belief in the vow and commitment to love within marriage. For even though this commitment hangs on a version of fidelity that others might consider gullible, it proves sustaining for the likes of Gimpel. As if marriage, rather than being opposed to philosophy, could be viewed as the condition and testing ground of an alternative philosophy – the one that Levinas might likewise subscribe to as 'ethics first'. Philosophy not as the love of knowledge but as the knowledge of love. For one thing's clear: however much Gimpel's marriage is rife with adultery, his love remains unadulterated. And that isn't because Gimpel is incapable of suspicion and doubt. It's because these aren't his preferred methods of reasoning. You could say of Gimpel that his life is the life of marriage *as* philosophy: the philosophy of the 'yes' and the 'and'. And marriage as philosophy can cover every kind of life, including that of the individual who isn't – as Gimpel isn't by the end of his story – actually married.

2

The Veil
(a cover story in seven parts)

'When is marriage an honourable estate?'

Stanley Cavell, *Pursuits of Happiness*

1. The Veil of Ignorance

Not really understanding why I wanted to get married, I cast around for a story to cover my ignorance and quoted, in my wedding speech, some lines from Yehuda Amichai's poem 'Instructions for a Waitress':

> Don't clear the glasses and plates
> from the table. Don't rub
> the stain from the cloth: It's good to know
> people were here before me.

Marriage, I think I was suggesting, is my way of reassuring myself that I am not alone – not only by tying my life to someone else's, but by tying myself to past lives as well. Or to put it a little more philosophically: the world arranged by marriage is, fundamentally, a shared world. It's a sentiment that, a good number of married years later, still makes sense to me. But it does now bring to mind certain questions that I was less conscious of at the time. Who, for instance, really *has* a share in the world arranged by marriage? And whose common sense does marriage really reflect?

2. The Veil of Normality

Writing in the early eighteenth century in repudiation of some of his contemporaries, the Italian philosopher Giambattista Vico claimed that the social contract is founded on the marriage contract and that it's thanks to marriage that our very 'democracies arose'. Marriage functions this way, he says, by becoming 'the school in which we learn the rudiments of all the great virtues.' It produces social norms and expectations, telling us both what a person is and what a person should be.

Stated so baldly, such a view can only sound antiquated to contemporary ears. Yet it's not clear either that this moral mandate for marriage has ever entirely expired. In America in the mid-twentieth century, for example, we can find the psychoanalyst Edmund Bergler making marriage the proving ground of one's mental health. Neurotics, he instructs, are fantasists who can't manage to make their marriages work. Normal people, by contrast, are realists who can.

The idea that coupled people are normal people and that it's by coupling that people can create norms finds more recent if less effusive corroboration in Sally Rooney's novel *Normal People*. In this fiction, an awkward pair of young neurotics negotiate the various obstacles obstructing them as they strive to form a normal couple. Their neuroses are psychological, but they're also very clearly social, rooted in norms of class and gender – and so it's the social solution that appears to them as the ready cure for what shames and isolates them as individuals. To become normal people together, these two must become bourgeois people together, beating their neuroses by transforming themselves into the purveyors of social norms.

In American singer John Legend's hit 'Ordinary People', he takes the unusual step, in a pop song, of hymning to a love that's moved beyond the infatuation stage. He and his girl have been going through some rough patches, but they can figure out a way to make their love work, he assures her. It's a curious kind of song in which passion isn't spent exactly, but love has turned into labour. In Diana Evans's novel *Ordinary People*, named after the song, ordinariness is signified by marriages between people who are honestly trying to do that work. But while the novel acknowledges the satisfactions to be derived from working at an ordinary marriage, it also explores how such work can sour very easily into resentment as passion gets twisted into dullness, disappointment and, finally, betrayal. None of which makes for an ideal marriage, although nor does it dramatically depart from what would count as a normal one.

In her exuberant polemic *Against Love*, cultural critic Laura Kipnis points to the sorry state of erotic lives subjected to the capitalist work ethic. Recalling psychosexual revolutionary Wilhelm Reich, she charges that 'the only social purpose of compulsory marriage for life is to produce the submissive personality types that mass society requires.' A spouse, according to Kipnis, is that poor soul in need of liberation but too bludgeoned by domesticity to be sexually or intellectually curious, and too waylaid by vows to rebel. Thus, in a way quite distinct from feminist arguments regarding woman's exploitation as the unpaid labourer of social reproduction, marriage as a private space colonized by the injunction to 'make it work' is here said to be what de-fangs and de-politicizes *all* parties to marriage. Their values may be bourgeois, says Kipnis, but the married person is more essentially aligned with the oppressed worker.

So, if marriage is what makes normal people, as well as ordinary people, does it also make common people? In Pulp's Britpop anthem 'Common People', a rich woman aspires, via her relationship with someone from a lower social class, to commune with the masses. But if her aim is to cover up what singles her out as different by getting hitched to a core humanity, her proposal is rudely rebuffed. To be truly wedded to her fellow man, she's informed, she would have to harbour no such ambitions.

It's in 'Common People', then, that the couple is firmly rejected as the basis of a wider social contract. In this version, if you like, Titania may be spellbound by fantasies, but Bottom, however happy he is to receive her passing attention, ultimately knows what's up. As the social machinery for manufacturing a world of rules, norms and expectations, marriage is a model for conventionality rather than radicalism, for law rather than romance. Viewed thus, who wouldn't prefer to shirk the (unpaid) work of the ordinary people, or shun the values of the normal people, in order to 'dance and drink and screw' with the common people? To establish common grounds, such people can still, if they wish to, marry, but private lives and interests can't be prevailed upon to form the bonds and binds of a world that would truly be shared. For all its modern marketing as a love match, in other words, the common world envisaged by marriage remains, on this reading, a world of privilege shored up by private property and passed on through orderly inheritance.

Whereas, back in the eighteenth century, here's Vico again: 'Moral virtue began, as it must, from a conscious *effort* . . . the giants checked their bestial habit of wandering wild through the earth's great forest . . . Instead, each giant would drag a woman into his cave and keep her there as his lifelong mate. In this way, they practised human intercourse secretly in private, which is to say, with modesty and shame.'

The type who dance and drink and screw are too vulgar for Vico's liking. In fact, marriage came along precisely in order to deal with such shameless scenes as this, by founding not only society, but humanity itself. But what then are 'people' if marriage is what makes them so? Says Vico, humans are those peculiar creatures who can't always appear decent to each other. The institution of marriage is thus conditional upon the revelation of a moral law whose paradoxical meaning it is to make of marriage a place where humankind can afford to be a little less angelic. Marriage, that is, takes what's bestial when it roams at large in the world and then sanctifies the same under its own covers.

So, while the idea of dragging a woman into a cave and keeping her there in perpetuity might not sound particularly progressive to your ears, for Vico this is precisely the moment when progress – the power to improve upon reality – takes root. It's when the woman gets dragged that humanity is born, and born into marriage, because marriage brings to the world a remarkable new idea: that humans have a need for privacy. Indeed, by affording humans the chance to withdraw from the social world, marriage has the paradoxical effect of simultaneously *creating* that social world – a world into which humans can then re-enter, but now *as* humans rather than brutes. People are only people, in other words, once they feel they have things to hide, and marriage is what offers them such cover. Nuptial, from the Latin *nubere*, even means this: 'to cover'.

3. The Veil of Sex

The best-known story of human beginnings, that of Adam and Eve, presents an interesting parallel to Vico's. As the original couple to become conscious of a need to veil parts of themselves, their demand for privacy occurs at the point when they lose paradise. As such, we might envisage the fall of man and woman as the moment of their true creation: humans are not humans unless or until they self-fashion. And with this impulse for fashion comes also the impulse for marriage – at a strange moment in time. For the first couple's decision to, in Vico's sense of the word, marry – a couple who've presumably been able to frolic without tying themselves up in such knots before – is what they only do once the solidarity between them begins to fracture. They cover themselves after they fail to invent cover stories for each other. Specifically, it's Adam who, facing God's interrogations, fails to cover for Eve, blaming her instead for his own transgressions. And so it's on that basis that a complicated picture emerges. For what Adam covers himself with is what he's persuaded himself is the truth. *She made me do it!* And yet the fact that man is now someone who feels such a wish for concealment also seems to have a curious effect on his truth. When truth gets paraded as an alibi, as it does when Adam blames Eve, it becomes its own kind of cover story.

The 'beginning of history', writes the American philosopher Stanley Cavell, is the beginning 'of an unending quarrel. The joining of the sexual and the social is called marriage.' We can ask, therefore, how marriage transforms the sexual and the social by virtue of conjoining them. For Vico, as we've seen, to marry the sexual with the social is to marry nature and culture. Man, as a giant grown conscious of something bestial about his nature, develops a sense of shame that mandates culture – and culture, in the first place, means doing what comes naturally to him only behind closed doors. This not only comprises marriage's morality, but its spirituality. It accords, for instance, with the Catholic injunction that sexual intercourse should take place only within marriage, and for the sake of procreation rather than recreation. Inventive is what sex should never be. (The irony of the Church's position here, as the Slovenian Marxist philosopher Slavoj Žižek points out, is that it thereby maintains sex as something wholly animal: socializing sex hasn't altered it, it's only hidden it.)

It's tempting to contrast a moralist like Vico to the type of romantic figure, such as Goethe, who regards the union of the sexual and the social via marriage as to the detriment of the former by making of its native vigour a source of boredom, obligation and deathly destruction. However, despite the very opposite evaluations which the moralist and the romantic each gives to sex, these two figures are not, in the most significant sense, all that different. Both, after all, understand sex as primarily a force of nature to be either contained by or emancipated from its civilization. While they disagree about the *virtue* of marriage, they at least seem to agree on what marriage essentially is.

Meanwhile, other theories of marital sexuality are surprisingly hard to find. For it's not untrue, I think, that most married people are pretty discreet about their sex lives – so much so that confidences told about marital sex automatically place these confidences outside the spectrum of marriage's normal people. Which isn't to deny that there are various assumptions abroad – whether it's that marital sex is just nature doing what it does, no different to unmarried sex; or whether it's that marital sex is still sex, but turned into something dull and dutiful; or whether it's that marital sex is still sex, but on a timetable; or whether it's that marital sex is a contradiction in terms because marriage, as everyone knows, is where sex goes to die, etc. But do these clichés really stand up? Or are we with such clichés covering for a marital sexuality that is its own distinct form of relation; a relation that remains enigmatic even for those involved in it, and not least since it operates in part through its own veiling?

When Adam and Eve exit the Garden of Eden and enter history as the perpetrators of marriage's long quarrel, what they've been exiled from, on one account, is the state of nature. Man becomes man when he's no longer natural. And what triggers this is the taste of a knowledge that would appear to be, since Adam and Eve specifically cover their genitals, coded as sexual. What's distinctively human, in other words, is sexuality denaturalized. Says Žižek: 'Far from providing the natural foundation of human lives, sexuality is the very terrain where humans detach themselves from nature: the idea of sexual perversion, or of a deadly sexual passion, is totally foreign to the animal universe.' It isn't human nature, in other words, but its perversion, that sends humanity indoors. Whence marriage must be, quintessentially, an institution of and for the perverse.

Perverse creatures that they are, what makes humans recognizable to themselves are the signs of their own concealment. Humans enter their history wearing clothes. While what's no less perverse is that, by covering something, clothing, like marriage, also *discovers* something. What both marrying and clothing mutually reveal is that they can only socialize the sexual by simultaneously sexualizing the social. For however much Adam and Eve may wish, through their veiling, to insinuate that what they're hiding is the naked truth, what fashion shows is that the veils that cover up our sexuality also have the odd effect of magnifying our sense of it. Few things, after all, are sexier than a veil – least of all what lies beneath it. And nor do you need to watch a seven-veiled dance like Salome's to perceive how the interplay of dressing and undressing teases us with the promise of a sexual knowledge that can never be entirely stripped – a knowledge whose status, in the biblical story, is forbidden.

Although it's not only in religious thought that that's the case. In some strains of post-Enlightenment thinking there are also things that are *not good to know*. Immanuel Kant's concept of the 'noumenal', for example, alludes to what humans not only don't know, but can't know, or can only drive themselves mad with wanting to know. And in both these traditions, the pursuit of sexual knowledge seems to be fraught with moral risks as well as punishments. Indeed, for the couple at the beginning of the human story, these punishments include what could even be construed as a beginner's guide to not only humanity, but marriage too: the traumas of exile, the disorders of desire, the birth pangs of maternity and the intimations of mortality.

4. The Veil of Labour

In Buchi Emecheta's novel *The Joys of Motherhood* (1979), set in Nigeria in the first half of the twentieth century, our heroine is Nnu Ego, a young woman who knows it's her destiny to marry and give birth to sons. Abandoned by her husband when she fails to provide any offspring, she leaves her small village and heads to Lagos to marry another man from her tribe; a man she's never seen before. When she first encounters Nnaife, he repulses her. He isn't a farmer, as a man should be, but a laundryman whose job it is to wash the underwear of a white lady whose contempt for her husband Nnu Ego perceives, though Nnaife seems not to. But despite this and his many other failings, she learns to love this man because he helps her to fulfil her destiny as a mother. Indeed, Nnu Ego goes on to have many children; children whom she feeds, clothes and partially schools with barely any support from her husband, whose consideration becomes even more scant when he takes on other wives and has even more children with them. Nor is it easy for Nnu Ego to maintain the traditions of her 'people' in a city undergoing massive upheaval due to colonial changes. When one of her daughters declines her father's choice of mate to decide for herself whom to marry, for example, Nnaife is so enraged that he heads out into the night with murder on his mind. As he's later dragged off to prison, Nnu Ego, noticing that the cloth he was wearing is about to fall off, begs to be allowed to tie the knot around him more securely. 'We shall always try to hide your nakedness, Nnaife', she calls after him as he's strong-armed away.

It's a vexing scene. Nnaife is a man whose fate is being determined by a law and judgement that are inexplicable and alien to him. He might well appear to us, therefore, in the guise of tragedy, as someone more sinned against than sinning. But to be a tragic hero he would have to have arrived at self-knowledge, or have the capacity for such self-knowledge, whereas there is no grandeur of revelation in this laundryman's undressing. And nor, for all that he's been an ass throughout the book, is he comedy's merry fool. It's as if he's been dispossessed of sense entirely, with no identity left at all.

Hence, watching the fall of her man, Nnu Ego acts quickly, retying the knot on his night cloth in an effort to shield her husband from the eyes of a world that envisages, in a man's nakedness, his whole truth. It's a moment that calls to mind the psychoanalytic conception of a phallic power that only works by veiling the fallibly fleshy organ its fantasized potency alludes to. Because unveiled, the phallus looks to be merely a penis. Yet Nnu Ego, though she clearly grasps what's at stake here, still wins no praise for her labours. No less than Adam blamed Eve, in fact, Nnaife blames Nnu Ego for his own actions. Where he blames, however, she defends. At his trial in Lagos, she swears he's 'the best husband a woman could wish for', but then finds the words of her testimony twisted by the colonial court in such a way that she condemns him where she'd hoped to save him. It's as if, in this court, not just Nnaife but her entire people are standing trial.

So why does Nnu Ego choose to cover for a man who's so often and so miserably failed her? Is her defence of him down to some sort of arrested development on her part? You'd have to assume so if Nnu Ego had no inkling of what she's missing. But she knows perfectly well the abject conditions of her daily existence. Yet she's a woman, too, who knows not only the narratable pains but the unnarratable joys of motherhood. And when she reties her husband's knot to conceal his nakedness, she also reties the knot of their marriage, as if discovering, in her marriage, a locus of resistance to a colonial usurpation of what feels proper to her and her people, even if these are people who fight bitterly amongst themselves.

As with the biblical story, then, Emecheta's modern tale is one in which man's fall becomes the catalyst for women's labours to multiply as they strive to keep their families and communities together and alive. But what isn't so clear is what man can be said to have fallen *from* exactly. Paradise, evidently, is nowhere to be glimpsed in this picture. Yet there are hints here as to what any paradise worth having (be it marital or social) would have to be. It would have to be a place free from the imposition of a law and language determined by those with whom one does not share one's reality; people who might well promote an idea of what's decent or human, but who fail to treat one's own people as if they really were. And it would have to be a place where one feels free to make one's own sense, and to share or not share the sense one makes. And it would have to be a place where one feels free to enjoy not only one's leisure but one's labour. And it would have to be a place where one could feel free as well to fall in such a way that the consequences of falling aren't, inevitably, tragic, but are also, potentially, comic. Although to fall comically may depend upon maintaining access to the familiarity of a tradition (one's own) that has already laid down a safety net to assure the one who falls that *people were here before me.*

5. The Veil of Knowledge

While marriage can be the handmaiden to one's oppression, it can also be the site of resistance to one's oppression. And since it can be both these things at once, marriage isn't easily knowable by means of rationality. So is marriage knowable *at all*?

Here's Kant's touchingly romantic definition of marriage: 'the reciprocal use that one human being makes of the sexual organs and capacities of another'. The formulation is axiomatic of his famous moral maxim that people must never use each other as they would objects. Because of the contractual nature of marriage, he saw the marital institution as the only moral means of managing human sexuality and thus avoiding the temptation of exploitative relations ('reciprocal use' works as a get-around, from the perspective of universal law, of the issues that might otherwise arise on account of sexual difference). Yet a quick glance at his definition tells you that Kant wasn't writing from either observation or experience. Kant's narrowly genital definition, let's face it, suggests very little imagination for what it might be like to actually *be* married. Long-term married people, at least, would surely have been able to reassure the moral philosopher that marriage isn't chiefly about constant reciprocal sex. But if Kant's definition narrows marriage into being little more than an instrument for sanctioning sex without being sexist (no bad thing were it so), his definition also manages to narrow sex itself, whose object it seems to have presupposed, meaning the only thing left to consider is how best to organize its relations. But is this really an area of human relations that can be summarily solved, or don't genitals also symbolize something else; something that overwhelms practical reason's assignation of their utility or identity – namely, the existence of desire as that which exceeds all reason by putting us more in the dark than in the picture?

Slavoj Žižek has various things he wishes to say about genital knowledge. Taking specific aim at Hegel's haut-Enlightenment moral model of marriage, the European tradition, he charges, 'dissolves passion in its cold utilitarian understanding, reducing it to a patho-logical excess to be properly cured'. Hegel stands here for the normative and bourgeois marriage that e.g. Reich and Kipnis con-demn as so lethal for politics. Opposing this, Žižek wants to speak instead for marriage as a site of the passions, and as the social acknow-ledgement of an excess that threatens the dominant order in a manner distinct from but not wholly dissimilar to the excess of the 'rabble' (aka the common people).

What Žižek believes about human sexuality is that, as 'the excess that is neither culture nor nature', it's the place where physics becomes metaphysics. It's a useful observation if we're seeking other ways to understand what marriage veils – no longer, on this reading, man's bestial condition, but his uniquely metaphysical one. Veiling is still necessary, however, because a site of excess can have no public role in a conservative world striving only to reproduce itself. Yet import-antly for Žižek, while marriage is accordingly private, and therefore disjoined from politics, it is not incompatible with the revolutionary struggle. Indeed, by exceeding the parameters of what's strictly required for the social contract, both metaphysical marriage and revo-lutionary struggle have their propensity for excess in common. Hence even though Bolshevik lovers who were totally dedicated to the revo-lutionary cause were 'ready to sacrifice all personal sexual fulfilment to it', says Žižek, their readiness to sacrifice didn't imply these lovers

were any less devoted to each other: 'The lovers' passion was tolerated, even silently respected, but ignored in the public discourse as
something of no concern to others.'

This rumour of a barricades-ready Bolshevik love respected but
ignored by one's political allies is presumably intended as a warning
to the bourgeois proclivities of any reader tempted to wonder about
Žižek's own private passions – though that happens to be the direction
I find myself going in (and I note that Žižek explicitly mentions
rumours of Lenin's private life to back up his own thinking too). For
I can't help noticing that Žižek publishes this critique of Hegel on
marriage somewhere between the end of the third and beginning of
his fourth marriage. Yet this is a piece of writing on marriage that
firmly rejects any association with the kinds of compulsive repetition
that would make of the love object something essentially impersonal
because infinitely replaceable. Instead, Žižek employs Hegel against
Hegel to claim that metaphysical sexual passion undergoes its own
dialectical movement – i.e. 'in order to arrive at the right choice, one
has to begin with the wrong choice'.

Hmmm, that argument sounds rather convenient. But does the
self-justification hinted at between its lines really matter? Even if
Žižek *has* left something veiled, that isn't necessarily to weaken his
case. His point is precisely that his personal life, while irrelevant to
his public discourse, is nevertheless a kind of animating force that
shares features with it. And as it happens, I'm quite seduced by this
revisioning of marital sexuality as metaphysics, which strikes me as
an idea that helps to preserve the sense that there's something enigmatic about the marital bond lying in excess of Enlightenment reason
or easy description. Where I'm less persuaded, however, and where
I think Žižek may be more in the dark than in the picture, is where
he, by arguing for the formal disjoining of lovers' private passions
from their political ones, ignores feminism's part in the quarrel that
comprises marriage's history – 'the personal is political' ring any
bells? – and thus the various ways in which the strict separation of

the private and public spheres can allow bourgeois values to creep back in.

And I wonder too at his choice of words regarding the sacrifice Bolshevik lovers are said to have made for the cause, i.e. 'all sexual fulfilment'. Would all said lovers frame their sacrifice that way? Would most married people forced apart for whatever reason see it primarily in such terms? Even if we do now recognize this sexual passion as a peculiarly metaphysical one, it's still, shall we say, quite a genital way to put it. Where, you want to ask, is the love? Indeed, for all Žižek sings a sublime song of perversion the better to distance himself from the bourgeois moralists, one comes away from his metaphysics with a no less narrow sense of what marriage is ostensibly good for. Hence even for the rabble rouser, it seems, shame at one's own naked desires, attachments and excesses could turn out to be, with regard to marriage, the motivating factor. To wit, if this is indeed the case, it suggests that marriage must always to some extent involve donning the garb of the normal people and doing the work of the ordinary people, however much one wishes to forge some alternative marital state ideally suited to the needs, demands and visions of the common people.

So I think we probably do, in the end, have to acknowledge that there's likely to be some validity to Vico's thesis about humans getting shamed, normatively, into marriage – even if what marriage becomes behind its veil is a radically different object on account of its concealment; an 'object' perhaps closer to Žižek's postulation of a sexual metaphysics. On that basis, therefore, instead of viewing the veil as a sign of the coming into consciousness of sexual knowledge, what if we view it, on the contrary, as the sign of the coming into consciousness of sexual ignorance? We're ashamed not because of what we now know, in other words, but because of what we've discovered that we don't know – or can't know. As shame, that's an experience that could well feel isolating. But insofar as our shame remains tied to the antisocial excess that grounds human universality, it might also have the potential to be a source of what could become emancipatory as well. Veiling, after all, needn't only be the procedure of those who are minded to perform their most private acts beyond the range of prying eyes. What shames people no less is to be left out in the open, not nakedly *doing* but nakedly *wanting* – and this may be particularly true for those who, powerless to assert any control over their lives (whether because they lack property, fluency or the means of self-determination), have nothing *but* their wants. I'm thinking again of Nnaife, but I'm thinking too of Nnu Ego. And I'm also thinking of just how often shame has flooded my own mind and body whenever I've sensed that something of my desires and my perplexity about desire has been unmasked in public, leaving me with no place to hide. So it's really myself I'm reminding when I stress that wanting to conceal one's desire needn't entail regarding desire itself as shameful.

While the intention to cover up may well originate with the sense of abjection that comes from feeling oneself an object for others, to feel shame isn't necessarily to agree with the definition these others have imposed. Garmenting one's desires, in whichever way one sees fit, can also, if we're being dialectical, be a progressive movement; one that can transform shame at the impotence of wanting into the potency of reimagining what it is one wants; such as, for instance, a world of one's own dreaming and making.

6. The Veil of Celebration

It's Vico's belief that the woman's wedding veil symbolizes 'the origin of the first marriages in a sense of shame'. What marriages originally veil, he argues, or what they've found reason to be ashamed of, is man's attachment to woman – aka she who gets dragged along. And if that was true at the beginning of the institution, it's proved a remarkably enduring trope. In the opening scene of 1980s teen comedy *Mystic Pizza*, for instance, we watch a very young woman who can barely see anyone from behind her veil holding on to her father's arm for security and orientation as she gets dragged along the aisle in a dress designed to trip her up. Eventually she joins the young man she's about to wed and as they stand there together, the priest lays out the terms of a covenant that 'may never be broken without risk of eternal damnation . . . for as long as you both shall draw breath on this earth.' All around she can dimly make out the wide smiles on the faces of the wedding guests. But hearing these priestly words, she teeters on her feet and faints. It's as if the veil's dimming of her vision has worked to fine-tune her hearing. And what she hears, as nobody else seems to, doesn't sound like much fun. Unless she isn't the only one hearing these words . . . are those smiley faces perhaps concealing something more sadistic? Could it be that they're not happy for her so much as they are for themselves, for the chance to repeat their own eternal damnation on a new and unsuspecting generation?

One fairly common view of marriage suspects just this: that what marriage veils is the misery of those it has never ceased to ensnare by offering a cover story of respectability under which the historic and unequal distribution of patriarchal power and its abuses can continue unabated. When the early self-help author Marie Stopes stunned polite society by lifting the covers on matrimonial sexuality, what her readers found especially scandalous was the contention that most outwardly happy marriages are secretly 'unhappy'. This she presents as 'an astonishing and tragic fact.'

But if, in 1918, marriage's outward show of happiness provided a cover story for the marital misery hiding behind closed doors, today that revelation is unlikely to be considered astonishing, or even tragic. If anything, we might speculate that the cover story now works in both directions. For while there are undoubtedly still many married people leading lives whose miserable reality they feel unable to disclose, behind the scenes too, a lot of married people might be getting on very well together – or at least, doing much better in private than the world is doing in public. A widespread presumption of marital misery might therefore provide a cover story for those who are currently, secretly, enjoying happy enough marriages. I say secretly because why should it be any less shameful to have found an oasis of comfort in an unjust and unequal world, and via the very institution that has founded and cemented so much of that inequality and injustice?

But nor, on the other hand, is the idea that marriage can help to cover up one's happiness anything so new. It's an idea that can even be identified within another well-worn interpretation of the wedding veil, which in some traditions is considered symbolic not of the need to blind the bride to the truth of her impending doom, but as a source of protection from the evil eyes of those wedding guests who cannot see the good fortune of others without wanting to trash it. What needs concealing from the world via marriage in this scenario is thus the happiness secured by the very institution that has granted this right to concealment. For if marriage does offer a moral cover of respectability, it stands to reason that it might well conceal other things besides just abusiveness or cruelty. It might cover up alternative arrangements for living together, for example. Or, in a slightly different style to Žižek's Bolshevik radicals, it might cover up radical experiments in sexuality, power, gender, family, language, utopia, identity.

7. The Veil of Difference

When I got married, in the Jewish tradition, a short ceremony took place just before the wedding itself. This ceremony was based on the biblical story of Jacob who thought he was marrying one sister, Rachel, only to discover, postnuptially, that he'd gotten himself hitched to her older sister, Leah. To avoid any similar mishap, my groom checked under my veil to see if it was really me. The veil in this case deliberately evoked questions of identity by dramatizing the sense that you can never be entirely sure who it is you're marrying. But does lifting the veil really help to resolve the issue? I don't think it has resolved it for my husband. While the person you're marrying today may be familiar to you, who she'll be however many years hence is of course impossible to know. And the veil, 'a blur worn as a garment' as literary critic Tony Tanner describes it, stages this uncertainty beautifully. But it also stages something else regarding the identity of the one who, under her veil, may be, as Tanner writes of Madame Bovary, 'deliquescing, not only socially but ontologically too.'

In *The Argonauts*, Maggie Nelson's experimental memoir partially lifting the covers on her marriage to video artist Harry Dodge, she quotes the philosophers Gilles Deleuze and Claire Parnet: 'Nuptials are the opposite of a couple. There are no longer binary machines: question–answer, masculine–feminine, man–animal, etc.' What they're expressing is a paradox: the nuptial as that which allows a couple to cease to be one, of which Deleuze and Parnet's own writerly collaboration offers an instance; a co-authored book is one wherein each author has contracted to cover for the other. Depending on the state of the relation and the powers at play, that dispossessing of one's ownable authority has its potential dangers. But it also has potential pleasures. And for Nelson, it's the latter she confesses to in her memoir, along with a certain fear: 'The happiness police are going to come and arrest us if we go on this way'. Hers is thus the scandal of a happy marriage exposed. And this, she recognizes, makes for a risky confessional, not only on account of the envious outsiders who could wish her ill, but because it risks as well the whole concept of a happy marriage as a space of privacy and concealment. 'Poor marriage!' Nelson writes of her own: 'Off we went to kill it (unforgivable). Or reinforce it (unforgivable)'. The married happiness that Nelson dares to report on thus seems to have been derived from this sense that she and her spouse have granted themselves the licence to please no one else with their union. As a queer and trans couple who can pass, when they wish, for a conventional heterosexual family unit, they have the illicit pleasure of imagining who, across a wide spectrum, they may be offending as they indulge their own interests and desires under cover of the straightest of institutions. Which is a lesson that marriage's normal, ordinary and common people all presumably, at some point, have to learn: that the happily married are the ones who have accepted their own ignorance and learned to play as they did during their infancy; and that the happily married are the ones who've simultaneously killed and reinforced the institution by making it suit themselves. Or in Cavell's words, to turn 'marriage itself into romance, into adventure . . . means to preserve within it something of the illicit, to find as it were a moral equivalent of the immoral.' You could even say that it's this that gives marriage its best bet of being an honourable estate, albeit not one that marriage's moralists would likely approve of. Still, when all's told, isn't this what Vico's myth also suggests – that marriage, as a respectable hideaway, was created to offer a 'moral equivalent of the immoral'? Although if that really is the case, it isn't hard to see why marriage could be for better *or* for worse.

Marriage as Creation

3

Natural Selection

'This strange coexistence of two, its impertinent validity'
Susan Taubes, *Divorcing*

1. The Couple

In the biblical story, everything God creates is 'good', except one
thing: 'It is not good for man to be alone'. Man needs a helpmeet.
Hence woman. Hence the couple. What good is goodness, after all,
if it can't be shared? God looks upon His own creation and concedes
that mortals also need good company. It's possible that God even
created man, with whom He later enters into a more formal, coven-
antal relationship, motivated by a similar impulse. Although in
addressing the issue of companionship, God also appears to have
inadvertently created some other *not good* things: the pathologization
of single life for example; the relegation of womankind to act as a
service provider for man for another. And yet presumably the solution
to man's existential loneliness didn't *have* to be a couple. Certainly,
one could imagine various other forms of community to mitigate his
solitude just as well. History shows that utopians of various stripes
have indeed since experimented in any number of such alternative
directions. But this, it seems, wasn't God's view. Perceiving that a
world of more than one could entail serious problems for man, God

chooses to make creation more populous only by increments. For paradise to remain paradise, He surmises, a couple, in the first place, is what's required.

The happy hazy wedding season is usually spring to summer, with many marrying couples seeking to celebrate outdoors in order to buoy themselves with the thought that the world itself is shining upon their nuptials. To marry in the open is to grace the occasion with a sense of liberty. To marry outside is to come out with your love. And if the weather is clement, then nature itself can seem clement too, as if it possessed sufficient bounty to sustain the marriage on leaves and berries alone. Those with the purchasing power will often curate their nuptials in some kind of beauty spot: a grove where fairies might frolic, fauns amongst the flora. Grove was the name of the place where I got married, in fact, in the grounds of a once stately home. The grove aesthetic insinuates this idea that a marriage between two people is also, implicitly, a marriage between nature and culture, between the real and the magical, between the lower and the upper worlds.

But the grove aesthetic insinuates other things too. Taking wedding guests out of their regular humdrum surrounds into a fairy-tale woodland is also a way of inviting the wedding party to step, symbolically, *into* the romantic orbit where the couple first granted themselves the latitude to fall in love. The grove, in other words, is the mythic place where lovers can be with each other like Adam and Eve, in a world where there's no one else whose needs or points of view have to be taken into account. Which is precisely what renders the wedding so peculiar. Because other people *are* invited into its grove – invited, that is, to bear witness to a union between people who seem to be calling upon the law to sanction their right to be a law unto themselves.

What, after all, is really being celebrated amidst the floral arrangements and waterfalls? A wedding is essentially a procedural and practical event, however dressed up with frivolity. But while contract law doesn't sound too romantic, nor is the contract unrelated to the grove and its magic. The law is even the magic itself: the speech act that imitates divine creation as the couple, by means of marrying, create themselves anew within the social world.

To fall in love, Stanley Cavell once suggested with reference to Hollywood's golden era of romantic comedies, lovers need to return to or invent a shared childhood together. They need, that is, to recapture the playfulness of infancy by regaining the sense of a time before they *had* any sense of time. Lovers, in order to be lovers, must inhabit their own original time; the time of creation. 'With thee conversing I forget all time', Eve tells Adam in *Paradise Lost*. She knows she's in paradise because she's in a place where history leaves no trace; a place where everything, regardless of who did or said it before, feels original to her.

To be fair, that feeling of originality was likely a lot easier to come by for the first couple at the very beginning of the world. But what about us – can *we* recover nature and bypass history too? There's certainly a history of humanity trying to do so. In the post-industrial period, for instance, it was the turn of the Romantics to seek to reclaim nature's authority from the perversions of a history envisaged to have divorced humankind from natural forms and feelings. And it's a history that continues. Thus while you'd assume that nature during the period we now call the Anthropocene would have a less enchanted status, today, as numerous recent memoirs and fictions attest, nature is often regarded as both what we must save and what we must turn to in order to be saved from ourselves. In fact, nature's salvific role has rarely appeared more manifold. Not only does it point the way to transforming global economic and political relations, it promises to transform our intimate relations too. In Esther Kinsky's novel *Grove*, for example, a widowed woman who finds little to console her in social life recovers herself from grief through minute observations of the natural world in particular. While in C. J. Hauser's virally popular short story 'The Crane Wife', a younger woman breaks off her engagement to her fiancé and then joins a biological expedition only to discover, amongst a crane population, evidence of the kinds of mutual dependency that her own relationship had lacked – and thus evidence as well that, contrary to her fiancé's admonishments, her own needs for mutual dependency are, likewise, natural ones.

Of course, when it comes to a biological expedition, we're in the realm of Darwin's creation story rather than the biblical one. Although in terms of the literary use writers make of these creation stories, it doesn't much seem to matter whether man originates in Africa or in Eden. And certainly the biblical account has never ceased to hold sway over even our secular imaginations. In American author Norman Rush's long novel *Mating* for instance, the biblical and biological appear as if they've laid their old quarrels aside and grown ever more happily wedded together.

Mating follows the journey undertaken by a couple of Westerners, both intellectuals, who fall in love in a way not easily divorced from where they find themselves – the veldt in Botswana. And that veldt turns out to be the ideal space in which to originate their own love story; one they dream might be undisturbed by history, uncorrupted by society, and untroubled by original sins. Our narrator is a woman who forensically analyses her own reactions as she falls head over heels for Denoon, an anthropologist who appears to her to be a great man. Denoon has come to Africa to build from scratch a new community – a utopian project looking to create a paradise on earth founded on the precepts of feminism, Marxism and anticolonialism. The irony of an American seeking to create a new world in Africa in order to reverse the devastating effects of earlier Westerners who had come to the continent with the aim of imposing their own ideals isn't hard to spot. Still, notwithstanding its knowing nod to its hero's white saviour complex, in this comic novel there's also a serious inquiry taking place – an inquiry into the question of whether or not one *can* begin the world anew without repeating the sins of the fathers. And for the couple wandering across the veldt together, this political question also gets tied up with their romantic quest. What hope can there be, after all, for the utopia Denoon intends to build if he can't even make a peaceful and happy relationship of just two? Aye, there's the rub: alone together on the open veldt, can this woman and this man arrive at 'love manifest', without succumbing to the master–slave relations inscribed within patriarchy, capitalism, and other such historical iniquities? Denoon, we learn, is divorced, so a marriage to him will already be a repetition of a historical experiment that he's tried and failed at before.

So, there's a lot for our protagonists to thrash out as they traverse the land of our beginning humanity. They argue, a lot. One thinks again of Cavell's notion of the couple who begin human history as the history of marriage, and of marriage as, essentially, a long quarrel. For what these two argue about is what an ideal relationship should be, and what an ideal society should be. One might well ask, therefore, whether these ideals aren't already compromised by the fact that, even as a society of just two, things between them prove so argumentative. And yet clearly this is a couple who enjoy arguing no less than the sparring couples do in Hollywood's romcoms. Indeed, their happiness seems to reside precisely in this: their very effort to figure out what would make them happy together. What, for each of them, *is* utopia?

What our narrator hankers after, she says, is refuge. But this is emphatically not the case for Denoon, who denies wanting any such hiding place. Instead he accuses her of succumbing to woman's principal fantasy: the idea of marriage as refuge. Marriage, on this account, is symptomatic of a psychological, social and political weakness that plays no part in his revolutionary vision of the world as it should be. And yet for all his vaunted transparency, Denoon has things in his history he wishes to hide too. And these private shames and humiliations, our narrator tacitly understands, are ones that, as his lover, she mustn't necessarily always confront, but must learn to help him conceal by pretending she hasn't even noticed them. So if her utopia *is* as he charges, then it's one she herself begins to create by providing, in the first place, refuge for a man who claims no such need.

Not that refuge is all she has to offer. For a man who finds himself alone in the world, there's no doubt that she's extraordinarily good company. So good, in fact, that as a reader you just want the novel to go on and on (and it does go on for a long time), simply in order to be able to spend more time with her – with her voice, her humour, her insight, her sensibility. When she's conversing, you forget all time. She's certainly a worthy candidate for Milton's ideal of the wife: the wife as provider of a 'meet and happy conversation'. Although not, it should be noted, in every respect. For Milton, a wife ought never to be quarrelsome, and nor should marriage be a relationship of equals, neither in status nor intellect. Argument, Milton supposed, is what happens to love in the fallen world – in a world fallen prey to the type of woman who wants and demands more. Whereas part of the pleasure of arguing for the couple in *Mating* is because their arguments prove, to them both, that they really do believe in progress. Our narrator even views herself as a creative project to be perfected by someone who takes a tutelary (but not masterly) attitude towards her. Her real idea of utopia, she says, is 'equal love'. And this utopia begins to seem like a human possibility in the state of nature, where 'love manifest' looks attainable because they've found themselves outside the social order of ranks, classes and economies dictating all values and terms.

But then, something appears to bedevil this paradise too – and it's not human law, it's nature's own. For nature, as we learn from Darwinism, is not without its hierarchies and values. It's these that our narrator laments:

> One of my most imperishable objections to the world is the existence
> of assortative mating, how everyone at some level ends up physically
> with just who they deserve, at least to the eye of some ideal observer,
> unless money or power deforms the process . . . Why can't every

mating in the world be on the basis of souls instead of inevitably and fundamentally on the match between physical envelopes? Of course we all know the answer, which is that otherwise we would be throwing evolution into disarray. Still it distresses me. We know what we are.

It's certainly a distressing thought for a romantic. But just this recognition, that even nature has ideas about who and how we should be, causes our narrator to lean even more heavily on the couple's own efforts to create themselves anew by living as if they *don't* already know what they are. And their method for this attempted originality is conversation – an endeavour about which they're both equally scrupulous, and both equally determined to avoid prejudgement, repetition or cliché:

> I was agitated because what we were both trying to do, I think, was arrive at love manifest – that is, love being established between us to both our satisfactions without anyone having to go through the horrible bourgeois ritual of declaring love, he for his reasons, I for mine. He was sensitive and knew that the last thing I wanted was a horrible sotto voce I love you and then on into a flurry of hungry kisses to bury the robotic nature of what he'd felt he had to say.

The problem is that not only 'I love you', but avoiding 'I love you', belongs to the index of romantic cliché. ('I love you' is a cliché, reckons Roland Barthes, that has only ever flummoxed the language of love.) There's nothing original about lovers wanting to prove their love by being original, after all. Romeo and Juliet were much the same. Nor, however, does the existence of lovers' clichés present the only inconvenience for a couple seeking to build a marital utopia conversationally. Getting out from under the master–slave relation and starting anew on an equal footing isn't just about avoiding pat phrases. Sometimes history repeats itself in silences too. Exactly this is what our narrator perceives in Denoon's occasional silences, for instance, which seem to betoken his belief that some sort of ideal communion has been reached between them – for which reason, these are precisely the moments when she suspects that a sort of smug complacency may be at work. For there is, it goes without saying, always *more* to say. Silence, when it comes to love, is thus the ultimate cliché. And this feels especially true for our narrator because her idea of happiness is inextricably linked to a situation of fluency – a situation of unimpeded creative flow that allows words, sentences and passages to pour forth, both from one's mouth and from one's pen.

The condition of creative inspiration, then, is another dream of utopia. Although what this creative utopia doesn't and shouldn't admit space for, our narrator cautions, are manipulators or fabricators such as telltales and liars. Which could turn out to be a problem because Denoon *has* lied to her. Early during their courtship, he tells her he's read *Middlemarch*, but later he confesses he's only ever read part of it, until finally he admits he's not even begun to read *Middlemarch* – but, he vows, he will now. It's the very making of a vow that intimates Denoon may have begun to move from love towards his own dream of marriage. Reading *Middlemarch*, you could say, is also the novel's idea of a novel marriage vow. Although what's novel in this vow, at least for Denoon, is the implicit acknowledgement that one can't always *be* novel. However much a sense of originality may be intrinsic to the fantasy of falling in love, when it comes to marriage, couples look around for precedents to reassure them that there are ways and means to make the contract work.

For many readers, *Middlemarch* is the key literary source for any postnuptial investigation. The author and critic Rebecca Mead even claims to have modelled her own life and marriage on what she's learned from her repeated readings of that one novel. In the prelude to *Middlemarch*, George Eliot indicates that her book will show how even the most inconspicuous existence can conceal an 'epic life'. The word 'epic' is a Miltonic hat tip; a hint that this novel's epic will be obliquely knotted to his. Indeed, the most memorable marriage in *Middlemarch* – that of Dorothea and Casaubon – occurs in part because Dorothea, like her author, is a Milton fan who picks Casaubon accordingly. She wishes to be the helpmeet of the author as great man; a woman created to provide domestic peace, pleasing conversation, and support for his vocation – that's *her* vocation. But over the course of the novel, it appears that Casaubon does not reside in a marital utopia of creative inspiration. What we see instead is how his blocked state, his failure to prove to himself that he really is an original, drives him towards the destructiveness of an envy that draws further and further away from Milton's original man, Adam, towards a much closer approximation of Milton's Satan.

Meanwhile, arguably the best marriage in *Middlemarch*, Mead suggests, is the one – between Fred and Mary – that we might have been tempted to barely notice at all, precisely because it looks, from the outside, to be wholly unoriginal. This happily married couple aren't artists or adventurers. They seem, if anything, to be content to repeat their parents' lives pretty much to the letter. But despite these two following the lines of the predictable marriage plot without twist or turn, what they've found is a way to remain with each other for ever in the grove, dwelling at the beginning of their lives all their lives. For these two, who spent their infancy together, look to be as made for each other as Adam and Eve. Though it was only in her own maturity and rereading of a novel she rereads every year that Mead says she began to acknowledge and appreciate their love, and their marriage.

For Phyllis Rose, the most eagle-eyed critic of marital disharmony between writers in the marriage-obsessed nineteenth century, George Eliot and George Henry Lewes possess the only utopian marriage she can identify. And that, she supposes, is because they were a couple not simply capable of enjoying their meet and happy conversation together, but a couple no less willing to support each other's creative endeavours, untrammelled by competition or envy. So what was their secret? Could it be that the illicitness of their relationship played a part in this unique achievement of marital happiness? By being married in spirit, but not legally (Lewes never divorced his first wife), it does appear as if the fact that they lived together in what the world considered 'sin' is what allowed these two to retreat into domestic bliss. For in the case of Georges Eliot and Lewes, the utopian gleam of their marriage really was a form of refuge from the onslaught of constant judgement. Indeed, what they created together, as social pariahs, was a situation not dissimilar to that of Adam and Eve before the fall: a grove with no real others in it.

2. The Third

'Two's company, but three's a couple.'

Adam Phillips, *Monogamy*

If, for both George Eliot and her heroine Dorothea, Milton is the foremost figure of the great man, the same may be true in Rush's more contemporary novel, *Mating*, where Milton's influence is subtly invoked via the figure of Denoon, whose journey to greatness has to go by way of reading not *Paradise Lost* but *Middlemarch*. It's in *Mortals*, however, Rush's follow-up novel to *Mating*, that Milton's example is explicitly invoked. And it's in *Mortals* too that we observe how a happy couple can lose their paradise.

Mortals introduces us to a different couple of Westerners in Botswana – a couple already mated and married, who enjoy not only a meet and happy conversation, but an excellent sex life to boot. The husband, certainly, seems content with his lot, and in such a way that Milton would surely have approved: his wife is helpful, attractive, conversationally adept, and she even explicitly subscribes to the 'great man theory of marriage'. She's gone so far, in fact, as to marry a Milton scholar – although that, it turns out, is just his cover story:

he's also a CIA agent with a quite different purpose in Africa to that of the Marxist-feminist Denoon.

If the earlier novel drew parallels between building a radical political utopia and a radical marital one, in the second novel the happily married husband is working in the opposite direction: he's on a mission to suppress all radical elements and conserve the status quo. And he's got his work as a double agent cut out for him, for he pursues his cause not only out in the world but on the home front too, where, using his espionage skills, he spies on his wife. So this is a postnuptial novel in which the marriage plot is an ongoing conspiracy. Although what isn't so clear is what exactly this happy husband is plotting. For here we find a married couple whose erotic life, both in bed and in conversation, seems enviably interesting, energetic, sexy. Nor do they have any kids to undermine their exclusivity (it's the reason he doesn't want them). All, however, is not as it seems. Under cover, this is a husband listening in suspiciously on his wife's discourse for evidence of her dissatisfaction or betrayal. And as a professional he can draw, from the scantest evidence, the widest inferences. By listening so intently to his wife, this Milton scholar/CIA agent begins to grasp how the intimacies of his private life could have a larger political significance, sensing that his wife's dissatisfaction within the walls of her gated garden could be manifesting a much more general malaise – one that threatens not only his marriage, but the whole order of patriarchal society. Both in his capacity as a Milton scholar, then, *and* in his capacity as a CIA agent, he perceives that the emancipation of women and women's desires is a distinctly undesirable outcome for the 'great man'.

If paradise is what gets lost when woman wants more, then there must all along have been a problem in paradise. And in *Mortals* we see how, as 'meet and happy' as their conversation may have been for him, it clearly lacked something for her. Although this thought only becomes conscious for her when she encounters the man she'll leave her husband for – a man who offers her something he doesn't.

What is that thing? Her husband at once assumes a sexual motive, and yet, she assures him, she and he have much better sex than she does with her new lover, who she finds relatively boring in bed. It's in conversation that the new man proves superior – an extraordinary claim, since she and her husband have scintillating conversations too. What sort of serpent can this new man be, then, to have thus found a means to come between two perfectly functional spouses? He's a shrink, of course. And so someone, in many ways, not all that dissimilar to a CIA agent. Both are men, after all, who listen intently to what she has to say, seeking clues within her discourse for her hidden misery and undisclosed desires. Yet there is, she feels, a vital difference to their modes of listening: when the shrink uncovers her secret desires, it's not to manage but to liberate them. Her husband, on the other hand, loses his paradise in the very effort to keep his wife happy – which is a strange way to fall, but something about the happiness he aims at seems to have already been lost in the proprietorial notion of 'keeping his wife'.

My husband sometimes grows impatient with me when we're alone and not speaking much. He's haunted by the idea that we've turned into one of those couples you see saying nothing to each other in restaurants. And even though he's not got a sword over my neck, and even though I'm not so gifted a storyteller as Shahrazad, I do occasionally try to come up with something to entertain him. Or else what I do is try to persuade him that our silences are a sign of our contentedness with each other – evidence that we have no need to speak to be assured we're in good company. This too is Denoon's fantasy in *Mating*; a fantasy that induces his lover to sense that history's master–slave relation is once again poking through. In *Mortals*, the CIA spy/ Milton scholar, overtaxed by his life as a double agent, would much rather relax into quietude of an evening, but suspects that a wife with a 'great man theory of marriage' won't be happy unless he has an endless supply of stories to tell. It is he, therefore, who plays the part of Shahrazad, albeit he talks not to save his life, but to keep his wife.

It's when Shahrazad finally stops talking that the King discovers he's fallen in love with his wife. Here, however, the husband talks so much in order to prevent his wife's discovery that she isn't happily married after all.

No surprises if one lover's original take on listening trumps another lover's cleverness at talking. Who are you going to fall for if not the person who shows you how to find even your own company more interesting than you did before? But if that implies the most seductive lover is the one who can split your own person in two, it also implies that the third whose vacillating role it is to at once divide the couple and marry them together needn't even appear in the guise of another person at all.

Romance is a genre for outlaws. Paradise is paradise for Adam and Eve, for Romeo and Juliet, for George Eliot and George Henry Lewes, for the Madonna and her child, when these sweet twosomes feel the need of nobody besides each other. They may stand guilty before the law, but the outlaw inhabits the purest of relations. Indeed, theirs is a situation that evokes the vision of ethics we get from Emmanuel Levinas: the idea of just two people in a state of absolute responsiveness towards each other. Paradise, in other words, as a place where we can attend wholeheartedly to each other in a relation of infinite responsibility. Albeit it's precisely this dream of unadulterated goodness that the intervention of a third undoes. For in a world grown more populous, there are decisions to be made regarding whose needs and demands should be prioritized. When there are more than two, metrics, economics and politics gain a foothold in paradise.

On such a retelling, the story of how paradise gets lost is the story of how politics comes along to adulterate a couple's blissful belief in the world's essential goodness. Politics, then, as a name for the real world that interrupts the fantasy of life outside the world and its history in a realm where insiders can enjoy nothing but playfulness, liberty and the pleasures of a lasting infancy. Politics is what causes lovers to lose their ethical innocence. For in reality there are always more than two people in the world, which means ties, relations and obligations will be tested by calculation, adjudication and judgement. Paradise is no longer paradise once questions of justice arise. And while these are the sort of questions that lovers, in order to fall in love, strive to remain innocent of, it's in the real and fallen world that marriages are made. As such, marrying people cannot for ever ignore matters of justice, nor the part played by the third in their couple formation. Nor can the real world ignore the part played by the married couple in its own formation either. As vehicles of social reproduction, what married couples confer upon others is the very identity of the social and political world as the world of competing needs, interests and demands. Couples are consequently creative not only with respect to themselves or their own progeny – they create us *all*, by bestowing upon us our social meaning and identity, which they do not so much by allowing us in, but by seeking to keep us out.

Thus described, the third is a rather abstract figure: a figure for language itself, or for the world as such. Though if we were to give this figure a less abstract appearance, we might note Milton's interpretation of what happens when a paradise of two becomes a world of three. For to consider, say, the guest at the wedding in Milton's terms is to envision the witness to a couple so seemingly satisfied with each other that they find all others dispensable; a witness who accordingly becomes possessed of an envy that can grow to satanic proportions in its will to destroy that from which he feels himself excluded.

Viewed in that light, it's little wonder that weddings so often prove provocative events. At a wedding, the couple not only parade their separation from others, they also invite these others to consecrate and give the seal of approval to their union. As such, it can be hard to attend a wedding without triggering feelings about one's own part in all of this – one's own history of love or marriage, one's own experiences of desire, loss or exclusion. If to be the third is to be positioned as a political subject, then to be witness to a wedding is to bear down on the paradise of mutual vows with news of a world in which other interests vie.

And as anyone who has ever sought to organize a formal wedding can vouch, there's no limit to how political these occasions sometimes get. A wedding brings together different and often conflicting or feuding families and friends, and involves the iniquities of the guest list, the table plan and other such incendiary items. In Alison Light's marital memoir, *A Radical Romance*, she describes how these dynamics played out when she got married to the Marxist historian Raphael Samuel and hosted, at their wedding, a retinue of guests armed and ready with their critiques of the couple's sell-out to marriage's bourgeois values. Although even with more mild-mannered attendees, no wedding, I think, could satisfy all possible objections. 'Does anyone here object to this marriage?' is sometimes asked formally by the officiant at wedding ceremonies. And bar in the movies, few guests ever do decide to 'speak now or for ever hold their peace'. But mightn't that be because (here's my hunch) *everyone* at a wedding is a conscientious objector, whether they're conscious of their objections or not? Caring little for politics, after all, and possibly even caring little for the *fact* of social inequality is arguably in the very nature of the wedding invitation as an invitation extended even to those who might feel they're politically against marriage as an institution. Just as it's extended to those who feel marriage has only ever hurt them, or who feel they would like to be married but have been less lucky in life and love than the marrying couple. Weddings don't take place in a world where all other things are equal – they take place in a world *as if* all other things are equal.

So, if the guests don't for the most part object to the marriage, even in the secrecy of their own hearts, that may be because weddings, insofar as we invite others to celebrate our own, invoke a different idea of generosity than one that could be easily measured or quantified. And this alternative idea of generosity is also a radical one.

Indeed, it's one which, by ignoring comparisons, extends to all guests the generous belief that they *will* be capable of feeling happy for the happy couple, regardless of their own situation. And one that assumes, moreover, the guests will agree to become a formal part of forging and protecting the couple's union. In a world of competition, it *is* unusual for people to come together in that spirit. Weddings may be the only real occasions. For what the marrying couple are essentially asking of their witnesses is to help them naturalize their romance by making of their love's origins in fantasy something that can also work in reality. It's in this sense that the wedding aims to turn the fallen angel back into one of the heavenly host, by treating somebody who might be inclined to destroy my bliss as somebody who I will instead invite to help me sustain it.

4

Creative Accounting

'There were three of us in this marriage.'

Princess Diana to Martin Bashir

1. Arranged Marriage

That Adam and Eve's marriage was a match made in heaven just goes to show: even two people who are *literally* made for each other can find themselves in disarray when a third character appears. And that's before they go forth and multiply. The couple is thus the unit of a strange sort of singularity. Not only is it impossible to think of the couple without calling forth their thirds, but even when we *speak* of the couple we tend towards some rather creative accounting. When we pepper our talk with the phrase 'a couple of others', for instance, we're often enough smuggling in a few extra souls under cover of that modest calculation. Why do we do this? Is the couple then a unit of our bad faith?

In Goethe's novel *Elective Affinities*, we meet a bourgeois couple, Charlotte and Edward, whose marriage, a love match, has the good fortune to enjoy the pecuniary benefits of an arranged marriage, both spouses having previously been married to partners who left them with significant inheritances, including the house and ample gardens where they currently reside. The fact that Edward's father had such an 'insatiable craving for property' that he first tied his son to a wife he wouldn't have chosen for himself has worked out for the best, therefore. By means of such calculations, it looks as though Edward's second marriage can experience love and property as values harmoniously bound together.

When we first meet Charlotte and Edward wandering around their grove and lounging in their arbour, they're considering whether their domestic bliss could use any further company. Contemplating such a prospect, Charlotte presages the danger of another's intrusion upon their present 'plans and arrangements'. 'Nothing', she warns her husband, 'is more significant than the intervention of a third party. I have seen friends, brothers and sisters, married couples, and couples in love whose relationships have been wholly altered and their circumstances entirely reshaped by the fortuitous or chosen advent of somebody new.' The point she's making appears less an emotional than a mathematical one. She fails, however, to carry her point. Now that 'somebody new' has been introduced into their discursive algebra, it proves curiously difficult to keep them at bay – although she does what she can to defer that eventuality, 'believing perhaps that the best way to blunt a purpose is continually to discuss it.'

The use of talking continuously to suspend a fatal decision of her husband's was Shahrazad's method too. But unlike Charlotte, the Queen's gambit was to enthral her husband with adulterous talk of what he most fears. In this she resembles less the bourgeois wife than she does certain aristocratic guests who show up much later in Goethe's novel, alarming Charlotte with their chatter: 'There is nothing more dangerous than an over-free conversation which treats a culpable or semi-culpable situation as if it were usual, general, and even praiseworthy; and surely anything that attacks the marriage union comes into this category.'

Since free speech is the sort of speech to wind up attacking the marriage union, Charlotte tends towards censoriousness. Where Shahrazad talks to whet her husband's appetite, Charlotte talks to arrest it. As such, while Shahrazad and Charlotte both talk to save their married lives, when it comes to blunting a husband's other purposes, the bourgeois wife would do better to take a leaf out of the Queen's far more exciting book. For as unimpeachable as Charlotte's wifeliness surely is, she doesn't sound like much fun. Not in Goethe's estimation, anyway. I feel differently. I can well understand wanting to preserve the idea of one's marital home as a safe space of seclusion away from worldly intrusion, even if – it's true – things between my husband and me can deteriorate very quickly when I regard sexuality as something to be tamed and domesticated, or when I seek to deny whichever libidinal purposes lurk within our household towards objects outside our household. Still, Charlotte's concerns aren't such a far cry from my own.

Poor dutiful Charlotte hasn't got much of a leg to stand on, though. Try as she might to provide her husband with a meet and happy conversation, it's conversation itself that intervenes to adulterate her paradise. And this occurs, thanks to language's own incalculable logic, *before* she admits into her happy home the outsiders who will soon enough wreck it. The tragedy that subsequently unfolds is not necessarily on account of her marriage's adultery, however. Rather, tragedy is what strikes when Charlotte strives to *blunt* the adulterous purposes that have arisen in her midst. By twisting her marriage from its origins in passion into the traditional shape of a marriage by arrangement, what she effectively demonstrates is that marriage's *most* blunted purpose is love itself. Love hasn't got a fighting chance in a marriage with property – or propriety. Which is precisely what Goethe was inviting his readers to ponder: how their idealized vistas of bourgeois respectability could very well be a death trap. Not that it's clear how *any* character could liberate themselves from a world so utterly wedlocked. For a social contract so tightly bound to the marriage contract appears knotted in such a way here that *everyone*, be they a bourgeois or a worker, be they a moralist or a romantic, be they a parent or a child, finds themselves similarly intruded upon by a state of discourse that overwhelms and subsumes every drive and aim. Goethe published his novel at the start of the nineteenth century when marriage had firmly established itself in the European imagination as the sine qua non of all human virtue, happiness and ambition. Yet it's a still life in lieu of real life, he was warning his readers, that's the truth of the world created by marriage.

So, if marriage is what speaks *through* everyone, who does marriage speak *for*? The married person is in the quite invidious situation of someone who is supposed to be, from the moment of her betrothal, 'spoken for'. The phrase assumes a reference to that person's removal from the marriage market, i.e. *s/he is already spoken for*. Whereas what Goethe's novel hints at is a marital discourse so much larger than any of its constituent parts that what look to be essentially private relations are mediated by the 'invisible hand' of a third party whose role in any couple formation cannot, it seems, be gainsaid. No surprises, therefore, that such powerful organizations as the Church and the State have moved, historically, into the intimate spaces where marriage is supposed to reside – all the better to profit from it. Could it be, then, that when we're 'spoken for' by marriage, it's the law, or the clergy, or the government, or indeed the market for whom we really speak?

In her egalitarian defence of the marriage-free state (a state not vested with power in matrimony), the philosopher Clare Chambers argues that marriage has for too long wielded the social capacity to shame, punish or render illegitimate those who have no share in the institution – whether because they're unmarried, or single, or divorced, or because they enter the world as the 'illegitimate' children of unmarried parents. She lays the blame for these damaging effects on the State's direct role in marital relations. Not only does State-sponsored marriage provide rights, privileges and legitimacy to some while denying these to others, but the State's control of who we make our private arrangements with is also a way of promoting and enforcing its own preferred system of 'family values', such that long-standing legacies of exploitation and entitlement have been preserved well into the present era despite whichever ideological changes marriage is supposed to have undergone. But what *are* these family values? Why, the economy, stupid. Successive studies have shown, for instance, that women do more housework when cohabiting than when single, and still more when married, and still more when a mother. State-sponsored marriage, disdains Chambers, is 'the main mechanism for maintaining the gendered division of labour . . . He works, she cooks and cleans; his work is paid, hers is not; his work is borne of power and entitlement, hers of love and duty.'

Love, historically, has been highly seductive for women, agrees sociologist Eva Illouz, 'precisely because it concealed as it beautified the deep inequalities at the heart of gender relationships.' Love, in other words, once it gets tied up with marriage, can be co-opted in such a way as to capitalize on interests that may be very different to those of the lover. As such, the liberalization of marriage to accommodate individual passions and preferences, as well as the more recent adaptation of the institution to other cultural shifts – e.g. the legalization of interracial and gay marriage – doesn't mean the inequalities enshrined within marriage's traditional arrangements have themselves been rearranged. For Chambers it rather suggests the opposite: that marriage will elasticate itself as necessary to protect the interests of its key beneficiaries. Her proposal to effectively divorce marriage from the State thus strikes me as convincing for the purposes of social justice she lays out. Albeit the legal withdrawal of marriage from management by the State, the Church or any other sanctioning authority cannot in itself liberate marrying couples to tie their knots in such ways as to speak only of and for the values they profess themselves. One might be able to create a marriage-free State – but not a marriage free of outside interference. A couple's private relation, as we find repeatedly in literary sources, speaks not only for itself, but for the social world that marriage has never ceased to reproduce, no matter how variegated its historical forms. And that includes the case of those egalitarians who reject the legal bond of marriage, but who nevertheless appear to the world to be, in however loose a sense, 'married' – even if only by virtue of the public-facing aspect of their commitment. Indeed, the curiously common desire to publicize one's personal attachments could hardly find better illustration than in the numerous books that reject or critique marriage written by authors who tend to dedicate these works to their significant others, 'without whom . . .' etc.

It's because love's fierce privacy, once rendered public, must enter the world of arrangements ('love is an arranging', writes Thom Gunn in 'Unpacking', his poem about first moving in with Mike Kitay), that the history of modern marriage has been consistently vexed by this perennial question: can love, in its antisociality and rejection of social values, and marriage, in its accession to sociality, ever be truly wedded, or entirely divorced? Clichés can have little purchase here. It's by no means certain, for instance, that love and marriage go together like a horse and carriage – nor, at the level of metaphor, is it even clear why love, pictured as the libidinal driving force of social reproduction, should have been yoked and burdened to such pragmatic ends anyway. You don't need to be an animal expert to deduce that horse and carriage aren't likely to be in the most unimpeded of relationships. So are we then forced to assume that love and marriage can never be happily hitched? Or would the perfect match have to be one wherein an arranged marriage matures into love? You'd think so. But if marriages have been traditionally arranged on the basis of economic interest and social convenience, love is surely too unruly in its passions to ever be so bridled. When love bucks within an arranged marriage, therefore, it could be doing other things besides simply confirming the wisdom of the arrangement. Indeed, to the extent that love reviles social interference, its arrival upon the scene might even work to critique the social values that married the couple together – who may now find they love each other *despite* the fact that they're already married.

It's not for nothing, after all, that our most passionate love stories are set in a world unwilling to make such necessary arrangements as might accommodate the lovers. Romeo and Juliet's love is as exorbitant as it is precisely on account of its unworldliness. Although if, for the sake of argument, we imagined a situation whereby their feuding families *did* accept their love, wouldn't it then be possible, or even likely, that continued conflict between the Montagues and Capulets could, in subsequent years, come back to haunt their marriage? For as we see no less today, couples can often find themselves surprised by the way in which social and political issues unsettle their peace, or when conflicts at home begin to mirror those outside it. The fact that many choose to marry within their 'tribes', even when they show little other interest in practising or representing the values and beliefs of their communities, perhaps signals this unconscious registration that, should history take a tumble for the worse, their private lives could risk being assailed by the return of whichever aspects of themselves they've maritally repressed. Indeed, for those who do marry across what others may see as enemy lines, it can be acutely painful, particularly when the news is full of escalating conflicts over race, class, nation, religion and ethnicity, to experience these worldly conflicts, however much one may disapprove of them, as triggering of one's own. If love is what whispers sweetly into your ear that you're your own person, marriage can tell you otherwise.

In her short-story cycle *Arranged Marriage*, Chitra Banerjee Divakaruni depicts a number of marriages, some of them between young girls uprooted from their homes and families in India to be married to men completely unknown to them – men who are already living and acculturating amongst even stranger strangers in America. As you'd expect, not all these fictional marriages are happy. But there are, too, examples of marriages where a surprised tenderness emerges between the couple, or a strength of togetherness develops that belies any outward impression of incompatibility. And it's in one such example that we encounter a cruel irony that surfaces within the marriage alongside love. For while the marital arrangement may have been formally based on socio-economic rather than personal considerations, it's a different set of social values that ultimately binds the couple when their social similarity becomes the only solace they can find within a racist environment that endangers them both. What truly weds this couple into a tenacious solidarity, in other words, *is* a condition of the social, but it's one that flies in the face of the social logic that originally bound them.

Likewise, though differently, American racism is what underlies matrimonial possibilities and impossibilities in Tayari Jones's contemporary novel *An American Marriage*. The novel's heroine is Celestial, a woman as determinedly independent as America's own Declaration. And it's because she's so committed to her own life, liberty and pursuit of happiness that she disregards what others think about who it might be sensible for her to marry – Andre, her childhood friend and neighbour – and marries instead for love. She does so as a bougie and avowedly feminist African-American woman, who will never, as she stipulates ahead of her wedding, vow to 'obey' her husband, any more than she'll obey any other iniquities or inequities whose legacies happen to intersect in her person. Roy, the African-American man she marries, may be from the wrong side of the tracks, but he is, she believes, just as she is, someone going places. Together these two feel special enough to make something epic of their lives. But it's on their honeymoon that Roy finds himself falsely accused by a white woman of rape. The only place he was going, it turns out, was prison. And who knows when he'll get out? Celestial's adventure has thus barely begun before she's required to press pause on her own life in order to wait for her husband's return, just as Penelope waits for Odysseus. Do so for the sake of all the black men betrayed by America, her father tells her.

Waiting is of course the ultimate romantic gesture for war-torn lovers, be these lovers separated by the Trojan Wars or the American Civil War that separates Rhett Butler and Scarlett O'Hara (plus her other lovers) in *Gone with the Wind*. There's nothing like a war to marry one's personal romance to the national one. But then, waiting is a lot easier if what separates you is a struggle you can both believe in, as Scarlett and Rhett both evidently believed the slave plantations were worth fighting to save. For the slaves themselves, however, marriage was officially prohibited because the state of bondage proscribed their entering into a legally enforceable civil contract. And though some slaves *did* get married (unofficially and overlooked by their masters), what they swore aloud to each other in these ceremonies was a commitment not 'till death do us part', but 'until distance' do us part, or in one recorded case, 'until the white man do us part'. Hence what we find in *An American Marriage*, whose title explicitly connects the marital state with the national state, is how the white man still, even over 150 years after the Civil War was lost by the Confederacy, wields that power to force apart those who would come together. It reveals, in other words, how bound our private contracts are to our public and civic contracts – and why it might be that someone who has been given little reason to believe in the vows made to her on a national level may then find it much harder to keep faith with the vows she enunciates for herself. Celestial, in fact, in a move at once tragic and pragmatic, eventually detaches from her wrongfully convicted husband and reattaches herself to Andre, the neighbour who has all along been hoping to capitalize on such an opportunity. This, though, isn't your typical novel of adultery. Celestial's trajectory isn't that of the romantic heroine forsaking marital propriety for a no-holds-barred adventure with an amorous outsider. On the contrary. Where her marriage was passionate, its adulteration is a matter of convenience. Celestial betrays her husband not because he's betrayed her, and not because she's fallen head over heels for another, but rather because she no longer believes in the American Dream, or in the American individual's manifest destiny to live her own life in pursuit of liberty, happiness and love. For a couple of lovers like Celestial and Roy, that romantic calculus just didn't add up.

The power of marriage to cast some children as legitimate and others not, and some relationships as legitimate and others not, helps to explain why, despite the popular view of marriage as a way of limiting personal freedoms, the history of marriage has been no less tied to that of human emancipation. What emancipation ostensibly granted the freed slaves, for example, was the severing of bonds in such a way that they might now, if they wished to, legally form their own bonds. Marriage after slavery was thus, for some, a means of expressing their personal autonomy, although it was also, for that reason, a means of testing the social contract and the degree to which historical conditions post-bellum really had, or hadn't, changed. *An American Marriage* suggests a bleak conclusion to that historical inquiry. But a conclusion that's also revealing of who marriage has primarily served. Should we take it, then, that creating a working marriage out of a love match is the luxury of those for whom the national context is so conveniently arranged that they can assume whatever quarrel they're having must lie strictly between themselves?

Stanley Cavell's *Pursuits of Happiness* is a philosophical investigation into the possibilities of marital happiness as a way of also reflecting on America's own promise of happiness. Whereas in *An American Marriage* social relations have the power to predetermine marital relations, in the oneiric landscapes of the Hollywood romcoms which Cavell's book analyses it seems to be the other way round; marital relations appear as the experimental chamber of what could then, potentially, become public ones. So in a film like *The Philadelphia Story*, we're invited to consider what makes for a happy marriage in order to further consider the question of whether or not America itself has fulfilled its promise. To that question, the resounding answer of the characters in *An American Marriage* would have to be no. That the genre of Hollywood romcom Cavell identifies as 'comedies of remarriage' largely features well-heeled couples who have more latitude to play with than most is no accident, therefore. The dream realm of erotic delights where these lovers pursue each other in a burst of creativity that requires their temporary escape from the society to which they will later return in altered form is, he says, 'a medium of magic, call it money'. Money – and the privilege it conjures – is what makes the marital magic possible.

As theories go, you have to admit that that one's pretty cynical. Why then, we might ask, do so many of us seem to fall for these fantasias, hook, line and sinker? Are we just masochists, or could it be that, as Cavell intimates, what looks cynical may veil something else, i.e. the fact that royalty and aristocrats are the subjects of so many of our fairy tales and romcoms is not necessarily because these people are different from the rest of us – it's because they have the good fortune to pursue happiness more freely than we do. In that sense, they *can* appear as the vanguard of our own dreamt-of futures. The 'natural aristocrat', writes Cavell, 'is not inherently superior to others, possessing qualities inaccessible to others, but, one might say, is more advanced than others, further along a spiritual path anyone might take and everyone can appreciate.' When the likes of Katharine Hepburn and Cary Grant pursue love and marriage on our screens, they act as if this is a world in which all other things are equal. We know, of course, that it isn't. But as unequal as we cannot fail to feel we are to these stars, we're happy enough for them to proceed in that spirit because they're the ones who can find out for us what it would take to make a marriage of equals – if other things really *were* equal. Since, that is, they can persuade us that they marry each other for love, and only love, they might also point the way to how love, never mind its inconvenience, could finally be arranged into a happy marriage.

And yet, even as we find ourselves falling in love with a love that looks to have successfully rid itself of all outside interference, here we are, the spectating audience, called upon to celebrate the on-screen couple's union – a celebration proven in the first place via ticket sales. So what does that tell us about reality? Perhaps this: that *even* in fantasy, those who are left out can never be entirely excluded; and that it takes a minimum of at least three parties to create the conditions wherein what looks magical now could become the common sense of the future.

2. Matchmaking

The third party interposing themselves between a couple needn't only appear post-facto after a couple have already merged. Celestial knew Andre before she knew Roy. King Charles knew Camilla Parker Bowles before he met Diana. Katharine Hepburn (as the character Tracy Lord) had married and divorced Cary Grant (C. K. Dexter Haven) before she got tied up with John Howard (George Kitteridge) and James Stewart (Mike Connor). And the lingering likes of Andre, Camilla and Cary Grant all eventually assume or resume their positions as *the* most significant other, as if to demonstrate this cardinal rule of couple mathematics: that when it comes to marriage, you can't always rely on the simple sum of one plus one equalling the even number you'd expect them to.

Moreover, it sometimes takes the active intervention of a third person to make a match in the first place. In one of Alice Munro's more unsettling short stories, two young girls on the verge of puberty play Cupid by inventing a game that treats adults the way adults often treat young girls – like dolls. The girls, who intend only to make mischief, write love letters from a man to a woman whom they see as a joke. Neither girl imagines this dowdy spinster could inspire anyone's real passion, nor do they think her capable of love, or marriage, or of even wanting such things. But it happens that their mischief does lead to a real match, and to a marriage whose devious origin is never discovered by the happy couple. A baby is also born from this match, leaving the young girl who first plotted it with the vertiginous sense that she's been a hidden co-creator in a new life.

Thanks to her, a new soul is making its way through the world with its own existential loneliness and its own romantic longings.

Anyone who has had a hand in any match could feel the pinch of this story. The role of matchmaker is a strange part to play. Although, as Munro represents that part, the match has really been made by the persuasive power of a writing that works to conjure the fancies of the letter's addressee. Receiving such a love letter is enough to motivate this woman into dramatic – romantic – action, leaving the letter's true author disturbed more than entertained at the discovery of her own creative powers. In matchmaking, that is, she learns to recognize the potency of words to cast spells, which power she finds all the more unnerving given that she really is still a child with limited autonomy of her own – yet with her words she can actually do things; she can add numbers to the world. But while it's true that her love letter reaches its formal destination, what this girl dimly perceives is that her letter's addressee was never its real target. She came up with her letter-writing scheme, in fact, to make sure of her own preferred couple formation – her relationship to her best friend and co-letter-writer, another girl her age, but one who already seems to be straying into pubescence and sexual awakening. The real love story hidden between the lines of the fake love letter was thus the author's wish to bind herself more closely to a love she already has but fears losing – a friendship that seems threatened by the sexual adventures of impending maturity. She's turned to writing, in other words, to take revenge on the early indicators of a biological destiny that's beginning to adulterate the paradise of her own first love.

More simply, Munro's story is just one of young girls in a small town experimenting with others where they fear to venture yet themselves. In this respect, they might be said to share meaningful ground with the rather less flattering image we tend to have of the matchmaker – the matchmaker as someone risible; an unlovely woman or old maid, not unlike the spinster whose match Munro's girls magic into being. For isn't the traditional matchmaker also she whose creativity has been thwarted by a world that has restricted her powers to very few domains? And so mightn't she, too, by becoming a professional marriage plotter, be taking a kind of revenge on what the marriage plot has dictated of her own sexual destiny?

If popular culture imagines the matchmaking urge as stereotypically a feminine one, then this is a femininity assumed cleansed of anything so threatening as a woman's sexual desire. For the late-nineteenth-century misogynist critic Otto Weininger, matchmaking is one of the traditional domains where feminine sexuality is sublimated. Not only does the female set a 'supreme value . . . on pairing', he charges, but 'femaleness and match-making are identical'. The dowdy matchmaker of the stereotype, whatever libidinal investment she might have in trading on other people's affairs, is thus seldom viewed as a figure for Eros herself. Far from it. She's paid to be practical rather than romantic, with her zeal always for the social rather than the personal. Indeed, as a source of data, information and calculation, she's lately been converted into an online algorithm.

Matchmaking, thus rendered, is more science than art. The business of coupling channelled into the digital economies of binary coding: a business wholly statistical and numerical, with all people and values viewed in strictly market terms. And yet for all that matchmaking may be calculable by computing engineers, marital mathematics has never ceased to evoke a more occult numerology – one that bestows upon numbers the significance of letters, and which makes positive integers look rather blunt tools for a proper accounting of social reproduction. Consider, for instance, how the additive sum of two ones into two is supposed by romantic logicians to turn two into one, which one, if it then combines with another one (a third), risks reverting into its original plurality of two or more. Unless the two who've become one create their own third in the form of a child, or multiple children, in which case, depending on how you view the family, these numbers can either be counted up as numerous units, or represented as additions that work merely to bulk out and extend the family as a single substantial unity of its own. Albeit *then*, parts of this unity are to be later subtracted, added to others and driven onwards towards new calculations and multiplications.

With such unwieldy tallies, you can't but wonder what value, positive or negative, the couple's formation confers on those they draw into their sum. What value does the couple parley for the single person, for instance, or the erstwhile singularity of their own married person? And how should the couple count their thirds, or count or discount the matchmaker, whose role may have been critical in turning two into one, but whose own calculating is not always calculated as a part of the sum she makes? Is she just the chilly personification of market forces – less cute like Cupid than cold-hearted like cupidity – or could her accounting turn out to be more creative than it looks?

In senior school, I studied two novels for my final exams in English Literature: Jane Austen's *Emma* and Henry James's *Portrait of a Lady*. Both were novels featuring female protagonists caught up in marriage plots. Both were by authors who did not marry themselves. And both novels also featured heroines who were intelligent, attractive, and of means – young women who could potentially lead a life free of any financial dependency on a man. Women, in other words, who could afford, or imagined they could afford, to show no interest in the facts and figures of their lives. Proto-Katharine Hepburns. For neither Emma Woodhouse nor Isabel Archer, strictly speaking, *needs* to get married – and in the case of Emma, she's the only heroine of Austen's you can say that about. But marriage remains the only future that we, their readers, can imagine for them. And marriage was the only aspect of the future I could imagine for myself back then as well.

The big question in the case of Isabel Archer is which one of her suitors she'll pick. Wanting an interesting life, she picks badly by alighting, much as *Middlemarch*'s Dorothea does, on a fraud. Her choice, Gilbert Osmond, is a vain man playing the part of a bohemian. It's because she herself is a rare soul that she makes this mistake – an error of her imagination rather than its absence. But having discovered her error, she shows no inclination to correct it. When, towards the end of the novel, another suitor appears and offers Isabel the chance to renege on her marriage vows, she prefers to double down on her original decision, resigning herself to an unhappy marriage as her fate.

It's via Isabel Archer, therefore, that we might perceive how not only matchmaking but even falling in love can be considered the sign of a frustrated artist at work. For if it's true that love, once railroaded into marriage, can be easily co-opted, then more things besides just exploitative labour may get underwritten by it. Isabel, after all, isn't expected to be creative. If anything, she's regarded wherever she goes as the artwork: the portrait of a lady whose image, from the opening pages of the book, we see constantly framed. So, if she uses real people to be imaginative with, then her motive, even if it's her own match she's making, may not be so dissimilar to the playfulness of Munro's meddlesome girls. Albeit Gilbert Osmond turns out to be far from the creative talent Isabel has used her own imagination to ascribe to him. He's just a man, in the end, who wants for himself only what everyone wants. As such, what Isabel's choice of Osmond marks isn't his originality, it's her own. 'I call people rich', aphorizes Isabel's cousin Ralph Touchett so memorably, 'when they're able to meet the requirements of their imagination.' In the crudest economic terms, Isabel is undoubtedly rich and Gilbert is undeniably interested in that fact. But to be rich in the way Ralph describes is far easier for a copyist like Gilbert than it is for a creative personality such as Isabel's, who chooses Gilbert precisely because, of those who propose, he's the least obvious candidate. So while one can find her refusal of her own freedom to leave a poor choice of husband dismaying, she has no wish to replace him with a more conventional option. The suitor who would liberate her, Caspar Goodwood, is a wealthy American businessman and a wonderful template of a lover. But despite his obvious attractions, he belongs to the standard marriage plot; one Isabel would never have authored for herself. The Goodwood addition is one that could only ever subtract from Isabel's singularity. By continuing with Osmond, on the other hand, Isabel remains wedded to her own creative endeavours – obscurely decoupling herself from Osmond precisely insofar as she stays married to him. Perhaps that was the best sum available for a lady who wished to try her hand at self-portraiture in the latter part of the nineteenth century.

If anyone is a frustrated artist, though, it's Jane Austen's Emma – literature's most famous, if failed, matchmaker, and the character Austen admitted to feeling herself closer to than any of her other creations. Emma, too, is the only Austen heroine to entitle her own book, and it's her first name, not her father's name, and not, like another eponymous Emma – Bovary – her married name. Her title belongs instead to an individual, and one who does indeed turn out to *be* an individual, with both a strong sense of entitlement and the lack of self-awareness that entitlement so often implies. Indeed, the fact that Emma meddles with other people's love lives rather than her own would seem to make her quite a different narrative proposition to both Isabel and Dorothea. And yet her chief problem, like theirs, comes down to the same thing: the problem of being an imaginative woman in a social world whose occupational horizon has been limited to what she can make out of marriage. Fortunately for the reader, however, Emma remains, for most of her novel, in the dark about the marriage plot lying in store for her. By repressing what's obvious about her fate, she can have some fun, as can we.

Jane Austen's style, an extraordinary eruption of creativity in the early history of the novel, is usually described as one of the earliest narrative instances of free and indirect discourse. This was a style born of necessity, suggests critic D. A. Miller, who believes Austen had the peculiar style of someone seeking to disentangle herself from the very marriage plotting her novels nonetheless did more than any other writer to establish as the absolute mainstay of the narrative arts. What 'lies at the close heart of Austen Style', he reckons, is 'a failed, or refused, but in any case shameful relation to the conjugal imperative'.

Once more then, we find conjugation linked to shame. And in this case, marriage has the power to shame because of its embeddedness within a moral law whose *truth is universally acknowledged*. Austen herself might even be deemed the proof of this law, for though she never married, it would be hard to find a writer more married to marriage than she. But while a philosopher such as Vico posits that we are quite rightly shamed into marriage in order to conceal our bestial desires – desires he seems to envisage as universal, even if not always universally acknowledged – what Miller finds in Austen's narration is something else: that those who get shamed into marriage may be attempting to escape from the sense that they conceal within their breasts different or even deviant desires. And these queer desires could include the desire not to be married. The desire, that is, to have desires that are unbound, untied, free and indirect.

So with Austen we get an alternative theory of marital motivation, which may be inferred from Emma, suggests Miller, because she's the one shamed into marriage precisely on account of her style itself. With all her flair, after all, Emma isn't quite the social norm. And what this makes her is an unusually attractive presence on the one hand, but an unusually disturbing one on the other. If someone like Emma remains unmarried for too long, she could threaten to desta-bilize social norms. After she marries, therefore, one assumes there's no novel to be written of her postnuptial existence. The end of *Emma* is, to all intents and purposes, the end of Emma; which ending is bound to the moment of her humbling – 'I was a fool' – and to her dawning recognition that: 'With insufferable vanity had she believed herself in the secret of everybody's feelings; with unpardonable arro-gance proposed to arrange everybody's destiny. She was proved to have been universally mistaken.' At the end of *Emma*, morality, decency and normality are thus restored. When Emma comes plus one, she's subtracted from the picture entirely.

What of Austen though? If she also turns to marriage plotting to elude the inevitability of her own marriage plot, then why does she succeed where Emma fails? She's the one who *succeeds* by means of her style, argues Miller, which is 'the utopia of those with almost no place to go.' As a bid for another, better world, utopianism is well served by style's subversive power to dent social reality without officially seeming to. To the extent that it makes itself felt as such, style proffers evidence that the world is made up not of normal people but rather singular people with singular desires. The 'happy ending' awaiting Emma is the duty of her husband, a moralist, who must now make of his free and indirect wife someone unfree and directed; a storied lesson for those who are wont to observe the irony of how often we fall in love with someone for one reason and then marry them so as to put an end to the very same. Whereas it was Austen's singular genius to never let marriage force her to become what Emma must become – namely 'a person', or someone clearly identifiable, whose needs, wants and desires are presumed *universally* known. Instead, Austen becomes not someone, but no one . . . the unhitched author as the serpent dwelling in the deviance of a creativity that lashes out at the very same conjugal imperative whose command over our narrative trajectories she did so much to ensure. English literature's foremost marriage plotter, in other words, may be no less the writer who teaches how marriage cramps one's style, and who reveals how, in the time it takes to suspend a marital commitment, the world could gather within itself new possibilities, including those that might, between the lines, admit queer desires into the creative accounting of marriage itself.

'Haunted always by shadowy thirds – the affair, the ex, the second husband, the sister-in-law, the child, the co-editor – the couple, it would seem, far from merging into one, easily multiplies into three or more.' So write the co-editors of 'The Ontology of the Couple', a special issue of *A Journal of Lesbian and Gay Studies* that considers 'the increasingly central role of the couple in queer life' and asks, 'Can one be queer and coupled?' The editors' hope is to bypass both the demand to legitimize couple ideology, and the contrasting demand to resist it, even if the couple 'seems to be the least queer of all relational forms'. Rejecting the conventional fault lines of these arguments, 'a queer theory of the couple' is solicited to respect 'the radical *twoness* of the couple – that is, what it means to encounter another as *an other*, rather than absorb that other into a narcissistic fantasy of oneself or dialectically synthesize into a third.' In so doing, they also reflect on what inspiration might be gleaned from being counted not up but down – as a zero.

What haunts is a spectral presence, at once there and not there. And if marriage is a haunted institution then it's haunted not only by the human face of various individuals such as those the editors list, but also, more abstractly, by – you name it: history, religion, society, sexuality, the State, the law, politics, economics, geography, language, or whatever it is one thinks of as 'the world'. All of these have been invoked to make marriage possible, or repressed to make marriage possible. Meanwhile, Miller's reading of Austen's style as a sort of third character in the marriage plot – a character who casts a queer shadow, but who is also no person at all – is a profound instance of how fundamental yet strangely elliptical this haunting of the couple can be. The third presents a figure whose value for the couple is incalculable. In much of queer theory, say the co-editors, 'the Queer is a shadowy third that simultaneously troubles and constitutes the Couple.' Lee Edelman represents queerness as 'the negative force that threatens to undo the Couple, and thus which the Couple must always "positivize" through its dialectical synthesis into a third – the Child.' These projections of the Queer versus the Child can be viewed as the conventional couple's 'family values' in their negative and positive form. And yet every third who gets positioned as such must surely include within itself both of these as their own ambivalent possibilities – as the rather unsettling figure of the child we find alternatively wrecking and matchmaking couples in Goethe and Munro's stories also seems to demonstrate. (It's no coincidence that the child in both stories is likewise portrayed as a nascent writer.)

So there's a vacillating relationship here. Just as the third *always* troubles and constitutes the couple, the couple troubles and constitutes its thirds. You could even think of the couple and the third as another couple; a couple who may not get along, but who would be very hard indeed to put asunder.

Yet notwithstanding these various creative collaborations, the couple still appears for the most part as a conservative unit of the reproductive order. And so creative personalities, especially if they think of themselves as such, frequently claim to be suspicious of couples. And that includes, very often, creative personalities who *are* coupled. The French writer Philippe Sollers, for example, while extolling his marriage to the writer Julia Kristeva, insists: 'One word I dislike is the word *couple*: I've never been able to stomach it. It implies a whole literature that I loathe.' It's a suspicion of the couple as that which could restrict one's freedom to be creative – with creativity understood as a sort of byword for being unlimitedly oneself. For even if we lay bromides about prams in the hallway as 'the enemy of good art' to one side, there are few things artists profess to fear more than the kinds of coupling that could put a curb on their creativity – marriage would be one example, or, as one hears nearly as often, psychotherapy would be another.

The psychoanalyst is of course liable to resist this implication. Your shrink, suggests the psychoanalyst and writer Adam Phillips, is 'the one person in your life who isn't speaking for you.' No need, therefore, to fear that the one you meet alone in the consulting room will subsume you into a couple that in any way resembles the sort of marital commitment that renders you spoken for. But by the same token, the shrink's invitation is perhaps to think of the space of psychoanalysis, not unlike the grove, as a kind of magical realm outside the world in which terms are dictated and marriages are made. Since both the lover in the grove and the analysand in the consulting room must eventually return from these magical realms, however, you can see why both the analyst and the spouse could similarly arouse the fear of the artist who, like Austen's Emma, say, or Shakespeare's Bottom, can only remain imaginative for as long as they are capable of being fantastical or fooled. Whereas what a coupled relation seems to threaten, in the eyes of those running shy of it, is to render them dangerously demystified, transparent, known – whence the fall into conventionality, or worse, contentedness. The artist who feels they cannot afford to be so satisfied will accordingly avoid any framework – such as marriage or such as psychoanalysis – that could certify them by telling them who exactly it is they are. A clever dodge if what impels creativity is a wish to escape reality, or if creativity is the half-desperate act of someone so deprived of herself that she invents one – or postpones the necessity of having to be a person at all.

And yet there are, too, examples of writers and artists whose creative partnerships work in the opposite direction, in such a way as to undermine discrete structures of property and ownership (as Deleuze professed he was doing with his co-authorships), or which queer how we imagine the coupled but not necessarily romantic relation (as one finds in the works of the collaborative art duo Gilbert and George). Nor is it necessary or even accurate to insist that what takes place in marriage, or psychoanalysis, is the intentional conversion of the queer, creative or singular self into that which is fixed, bound and categorical. It was the poet Czesław Miłosz who coined the oft-cited aphorism, 'When a writer is born into a family, the family is finished.' The writer, in other words, is the essential adulterer. But the writer, too, is the essential child, inescapably, according to the logic of this formulation, born of the very family they leave behind in pieces. Without marriage, as the French writer Roland Barthes once put it, 'what would be left for us to *tell*?' The adventurousness of narrative might have no condition of possibility *without* the regulatory force of marriage as its organizing principle and idea. The intimate relationship between the family and the writer, or the familiar and the novel, is thus a close even if ambivalent one. There would *be* no reproductive history of the family, after all, if the child didn't rupture its unity to break away and create its own variations on the theme. So, the child whose role may well be, according to convention, to confirm the couple's identity by naturalizing their relation and proving its profitability according to the accumulative logic of capital (multiplication), also represents, within the same social order it reproduces, a chaotic and creative presence – a plus-one that subtracts from the unity of the whole by adding its own difference and making a case for oddness rather than evenness.

Marriage as Conversation

5

What We Talk About When
We Talk About Marriage

'They flaunt their conjugal felicity in one's face, as if it were the
most fascinating of sins.'

Oscar Wilde, *The Picture of Dorian Gray*

1. Talk About Marriage

To think about marriage is to think a lot about conversation. Conversation, etymologically the act of living with or keeping company with another, sometimes appears, particularly in its more utopian iterations, as a sort of synonym for marriage. There's Shakespeare's 'marriage of true minds', for instance, or Milton's claim, in his tract on divorce, that a marriage that does not provide a 'meet and happy conversation' can reasonably be annulled. And there's the curious fact that even Nietzsche regarded 'marriage as a long conversation. — When marrying you should ask yourself this question: do you believe you are going to enjoy talking with this woman into your old age? Everything else in a marriage is transitory, but most of the time that you're together will be devoted to conversation.' This was all speculation of course, since Nietzsche never did find a woman he could imagine talking to for that long. But many a married writer has said similar. 'You marry to continue the conversation,' explained Ford Madox Ford.

Marriage as a means of continuance. Writ large, this has also been the view of those who deem the marriage contract the natural basis of the social contract. Without marriage, said Vico, nothing would make sense and people would not be able to make sense of each other. With marriage, on the other hand, enduring communities have been built. As such, any threat to marriage as an institution risks a descent into a Babel-like confusion of tongues. When marriage is in crisis, the world itself is in crisis, because no one any longer can be held to their word.

If marriage lays the foundations of the communicable world, then the walls of this room, the chair on which I'm sitting, and the coffee cup from which I'm presently drinking are none of them exempt from, not just my marital state, but *the* marital state. My coffee cup was a wedding gift as it happens, but that's beside the point if *all* objects, persons and relations inhabit the state of marriage. Such, at least, is the intimation of the bourgeois novel that rose into prominence in the latter part of the eighteenth century. What animates a novel like Goethe's *Elective Affinities*, Tony Tanner suggests, can even be paraphrased by the following question: 'What is the bourgeois family going to talk about? What can it afford to include; what should it work to debar?' What the novel was showing its readers, in other words, was how their private lives, and specifically their married lives, could be construed as a continuation of their public lives. Hence, says Tanner, the novel of adultery, whose mixing and pluralizing of relations outside the law brought into the novel the greatest challenge to its semantic universe. Take, for instance, the adulteress Madame Bovary. 'The crisis of the meaning of marriage, which she experiences,' writes Tanner, 'is inextricably involved with, and indistinguishable from, a crisis in the language in and by which she is formed and rent.' A crisis beginning with the takeover of her identity by her husband's name, whose stupefyingly bovine associations are hardly coincidental. If Madame Bovary was the harbinger of a much deeper crisis, therefore, this was because what her experience revealed was that marriage, upon whose foundations the very world is built, is *not* as good as its word.

So, what sort of word is the word of marriage? And what would it take to make this word good?

It was the philosopher J. L. Austin who referred to speech acts such as the wedding officiant's 'I now pronounce you' to demonstrate how words can actually *do* things. By such verbal means, states and statuses are actively changed as the officiant bestows upon the marrying pair a first-person plural that's legally recognized and distinguished from all other instances of the pronoun 'we' (in some contexts, legally wed spouses do not even have to testify against one another in courts of law). The marrying word is thus a word that ascribes alchemical power to language. Just this, in fact, explains Maggie Nelson, is what attracted her *into* the nuptial contract; because pronouncing a couple married is the sort of pronouncement that can also work to relieve the married couple of pronouncing the individuated pronouns by which they're ordinarily known. Through marriage's pronouncements, the couple can gain entry into the intimate arena of the unpronounced.

And yet, as intimate as these changes surely are, the word of marriage, as portrayed by Austin, is social rather than personal. Everyone present at the wedding – the couple, the officiant and the witnesses – is required to act as if reality really has been altered when the person with the power vested in them has decreed it so. A rather enigmatic situation is thereby set up: what can it mean to remain faithful to a word so openly theatrical, and so avowedly dependent on the willing suspension of everyone's disbelief?

This, to me, is what's so interesting about the word of marriage; that it seems to fly in the face of how discourses tend to function. For discourses (*pace* the French philosopher Michel Foucault) are in the habit of making their objects appear natural by covering up the role that language has played in creating them. Yet what we find with marriage is a discourse that actively exhibits its own processes of naturalization, as it were. Marriage shows us its veils. Marriage stages for us its pronouncements. Unlike sexuality, then – a discourse Foucault claimed could confer a natural status upon its object by pretending not to be rooted in discourse at all – and unlike love – which discourse Barthes claimed always falls between the cracks of mutual exchange – marriage is a discourse that not only aims to positively establish what passes for common sense, but owns up to itself as such. It's as if marriage, in its eagerness to construct the social, takes the unusual but demonstrative step of showing its own method of social construction. By pronouncing pronouncement itself, what marriage really pronounces is the silent part out loud.

None of which is to deny that, behind marriage's official discourse – its 'I do's – there are many other marital discourses, including those that aren't said out loud, but are whispered, in confidence. At the end of the eighteenth century, for instance, the Irish author Maria Edgeworth published her very funny essay 'On the Noble Science of Self-Justification'. Purportedly addressed to wives or wives-to-be, the essay discloses the secrets that women share with each other from behind their nuptial curtains. The essay is undoubtedly satirical, yet it's written by an author who, like her contemporary Austen, never herself married, and whose insights into the state of marriage may have been all the more penetrating for that reason. For her essay is primarily concerned with what you might call 'best practice' for wives involved in the husbandry of their husbands. To which end, clear instructions are given. Use your stereotype as the weaker sex for a weapon. If you are deemed inferior, plead inferiority at every opportunity. If you have been labelled irrational and overly emotional, then be even more irrational, even more emotional. If you are too stupid to do anything for yourself, then do nothing for yourself. Carry on like this until it becomes clear to the men who have degraded your sex that a presumption of sexual inequality is less of a boon than a burden for them. Which, I have to say, still makes for sound advice (and I'm speaking here as a whiz at learned helplessness). Although

Edgeworth's neatest trick was to reclassify these whispers or old wives' tales as a 'science', for when the world as arranged isn't particularly reasonable, irrationality does start to make a certain kind of sense. Hence, though the official audience of Edgeworth's essay was wives, the unofficial one was no less their husbands. Being published, after all, these whispers are effectively stage whispers – as if what their author was really drawing attention to was the very existence of such a whisper network, or the very need of it.

This need, no doubt, goes some way towards explaining why it is that – for all marriage has historically expressed the interests of men – the expressive discourses of and surrounding marriage have for the most part been associated with women. The world Austen depicts, for example, is one in which women's talk is what seems to glue society together, even as, via the confidences whispered between sisters or trusted friends, we also meet the suffering souls who find themselves hemmed into a social script so unoriginal that it seems to restrict all other possibilities. Earlier I mentioned D. A. Miller's interpretation of Austen's conjuring a vision of marriage as moral punishment for the sin of individuality; an interpretation that places all the talking Austen's most distinctive individuals do between invisible speech marks – speech marks whose hanging presence, for the individuals themselves, is acutely self-aware. For in a marriage-obsessed society, what singles these individuals out as different is their sense of ironic distance between who they feel they are and the words they're impelled to speak. Yet even within these narrow confines, marrying for the sake of better conversation does seem, for such characters, to be a real and maybe even realizable goal. And so it seems too for Austen's readers, who have never ceased to thrill at the chemical charge of would-be lovers making their way towards each other through thorny thickets of etiquette and even tilting the scales of social respectability by risking a few unscripted words.

Nor, within this purview, are romantic parries the only conversational risks to be taken. There's also gossip. And gossip, though it may not convey such daring as a passionate confidence whispered in desperation, is not without riskiness – and it isn't polite either. Even still, as it ventures off the permitted tracks into what's forbidden, gossip is also, for many, just a form of due diligence. In the proto-Facebook world of the Austen novel, even before meeting someone new, you likely already know if they're married, or what their marital prospects are, or what kind of income they have per annum. Talk of marriage is thus talk of hard material facts: history, housing, economics. So if marriage is the official discourse of polite society, that doesn't mean it's an uninteresting one. It wouldn't be the reliable source of gossip it is if that was true. In her reflections on famous marriages from the nineteenth century, Phyllis Rose notes the sad fact that still sustains the gossip industry today: a terrible moral quandary for me is a source of entertainment for you. But while a loose tongue doesn't sound like it has much purchase on what's moral, gossip wouldn't be gossip if it didn't grasp what's respectable. To be an effective gossip, one must be something of a moralist as well. Indeed, for all we disparage it, what often gets us gossiping, remarks Rose, is 'the beginning of moral inquiry . . . We are desperate for information about how other people live because we want to know how to live ourselves'. And marital gossip is the ideal terrain for this sort of investigation precisely because marriage is at once the norm and what can only really exist under cover. As such, the fact that the gossip, in her many indiscretions, knows her practice requires a degree of stealth and hiding, betrays something of this hidden seriousness of intent with which she compulsively probes her subject.

Meanwhile, if gossip is the kind of impolitic (or realpolitik) talk that can expect to get belittled by those with big and better things on their minds, there's another kind of talk, call it small talk, that's considered the very hallmark of politesse. Gossip and small talk are two kinds of talk that sometimes appear so alike that they often consist of the very same questions, if not always the same responses. Although there does tend to be an important difference in the motive of the person doing the asking. With small talk, marriage isn't the subject of a naughty trespass into other people's lives, it's the virtuous script itself. The small-talker is doing very big talk, in fact, since she isn't speaking solely for herself but for the social world she inhabits – which world, through her talk, she helps to sustain by speaking for that world's conventions, codes and values . . . *And how is the lovely Charlotte? I imagine she'll be thinking about dating soon.* Merely by being polite, the small-talker aligns herself with powerful forces. It was Helen Fielding's revisioning of Austen's marriage plotting in *Bridget Jones's Diary* that popularized the term 'smug marrieds'. A smug married person thinks nothing of meddling in the life of an unmarried person. Speaking from the lofty vantage point of someone who has met her marital expectations, the smug married proceeds to advertise her own situation as the only one anybody else could possibly want. With her small talk, she pities and punishes single life.

Might there, though, also be other things motivating her in these exchanges? The small-talker needn't always be promoting her own lifestyle, after all, but rather feeling herself in need of something dependable to say when faced with the nervous prospect of social interaction. We follow a social script because it saves us from shaming ourselves, even if using it can lead us to shame others – which same propensity for shaming we can detect lurking in the background of those ice-breaking questions that can prove so innocently injurious when you first meet someone new. There's 'What do you do?', which nails identity to the mast of occupation, obliging the person it addresses into explaining their unemployment or unloved job or whatever it is that seems unqualified to answer that question according to the values it inculcates and implies. And there's 'Are you married?' and 'Do you have children?', which are no less common, nor any less baiting with their presumption of what's expected of you and what isn't. Not that these are bad questions necessarily – it *is* interesting what people do, whether they're married or if they have children – but they can be hard to ask without drawing in a hint of social coercion.

With such baked-in value for the small-talker, then, we can see how marriage becomes, once again (even for the unmarried), a veil to hide behind when faced with the otherwise terrifying prospect of having to be an original. And yet the thing about veils is that they can always be lifted, or let slip. To wit, if marriage is a polite topic, it's also a risky one – risky because small talk of marriage always threatens to tip over into genuine talk of marriage: talk of marriage as a cover for our private lives, our love lives, our sex lives; talk of marriage as a cover for our dreams, our hopes, our fears, our wounds, our desires. By binding the social group, talk about marriage could always exceed politesse to become what's really binding.

2. Talk Within Marriage

All the talk we do *about* marriage helps to perpetuate marriage as a discourse whose official inauguration is strikingly bound to its public pronouncement. But there's also the intimate and non-public talking that people do inside their marriages. And while married couples may not necessarily talk to each other much *about* marriage, there can be little doubt that their talking plays a no less significant role in helping to conserve the institution. Indeed, a marriage, it's often said, is on the rocks when marital talking breaks down. It's why many self-help books about marriage are oriented towards improving the communication techniques of the couple. If you sample these, you quickly learn that there are arguments and flare-ups that can be avoided with a few neat rules of discursive engagement. I found all the tips in Harriet Lerner's self-help guide, *Marriage Rules* – mostly strategies for having dialogue with one's spouse in such a way that cycles of unhealthy repetition can be avoided – both enlightening and beneficial. I was a much better spouse whilst reading that book and was rewarded in turn by my spouse for my efforts. The rules worked! But like every self-help book I've ever read (or every book), I forgot what it had to say the moment I was no longer reading it. To be a really good wife I should perhaps always be in the middle of reading that manual. But if I manage my marriage so well that it becomes a successful comms operation, wouldn't I then risk losing out on whatever Shakespeare meant by a 'marriage of true minds', or on the idea of marriage as its own special form of not just communication, but conversation?

In the Nora Ephron-scripted film *When Harry Met Sally*, we watch as a couple slowly discover the inevitability of their marrying over twelve years of proving irresistible conversation partners while resisting each other sexually. This contrasts with the many other modern movies where sex is what passes for an icebreaker. In those films, only after a couple have been to bed together can they then, in more languorous mood with cigarettes held aloft, get into the deep stuff . . . so who are you, what's your name, where do you come from, etc. Sex is an intrinsic part of the conversational format – a quick and efficient way of getting down to the really risky business of *talking*. Whereas in Harry and Sally's case, their conversation begins about the sex they're not having and the impossibility of a platonic friendship not vexed by the sex they're not having. This is very much Harry's conviction when they first meet: that friendship between a man and a woman he finds attractive is impossible because he'll always have sex on his mind. But as their relationship matures over the years, it moves on to other things to the point where, when sex finally does occur between them, it's traumatic because it leaves them speechless. You can see why. If all along their conversation was really, at least one of them suspects, a cover story for their sexual interest in each other, then what, after sex, do they have left to say? Rather than a conversational icebreaker, sex is suddenly what they have to recover from in order to recover a conversation that can include the possibility of sex *and* friendship. And what's beaten them into this embarrassed silence is the discovery that they *thought* they knew what they were talking about when they were talking about sex, but having now had sex (was the sex good? bad? It isn't clear, though they both seem to agree it was fine) and yet still finding themselves curious about each other, what sex reveals is that they've never really known what they were talking about. Although Sally, arguably, summed it up pretty well after she first met Harry: 'It was interesting.' It really *was* interesting – and precisely because they didn't know what to make of each other even as they pretended to know exactly what to make of each other. Yet this posturing becomes harder to achieve post-coitally since they've effectively confirmed Harry's take – they can't have a platonic friendship – while simultaneously confirming Sally's take – the interest that lies between them isn't just about sex after all.

In fact, it's a curiosity of this much-loved movie that the obligatory words of love and the kissing we see at the end of the film – when Harry and Sally have admitted to each other that they must marry – is far less interesting than the relatively trivial conversation they return to straight after the proposal has been accepted. Their kissing and mutual exchange of 'I love you' is even a repetition of unoriginal scenes we've already seen both of them engage in with previous part-ners. What's unique to their relationship is therefore not its declaration of love, but a conversation whose subtext turns out to be its pleasure because neither of them can know for sure what the subtext is. Here is a couple, in other words, who decide to marry only at the point when they reach the understanding that neither of them understands what's going on. In this sense, it's a movie motivated less by the romantic idea of love – for love can be moved around between part-ners fairly easily – than by the slow build-up of a necessary coupling that cannot, by the end, be denied by either Harry or Sally. Put dif-ferently, Sally and Harry decide to marry when they realize that they are, for all intents and purposes, already married – reminding one of the remarriage genre identified by Cavell: 'only those can genuinely marry who are already married. It is as though you know you are married when you come to see that you cannot divorce, that is, when you find that your lives simply will not disentangle. If your love is lucky, this knowledge will be greeted with laughter.'

One of the captivations of Harry and Sally's relationship is how they always manage to pick up their conversation – sometimes six years apart – very much from where they left off, with each one remembering more of what the other said than they'll readily admit to. These are conversational breaks and continuations that take place over a long unwitting courtship. Yet the same, presumably, can be true of conversation over the course of a long marriage. For some lucky couples, conversation may pick up where it left off each day, or each week. For others, the thread gets picked up again only after months, or years. It's a peculiar anti-chronological quirk of conversation to be able to leap over history in this way. One rule of marital dialogue, says Harriet Lerner, is not to bring history into it. Never begin an argument with the words 'You always'. Believe me when I tell you I've found that to be good advice, though not advice I'm especially good at following. Yet it's equally the case that a good conversation in a marriage will depend on the conversation's history, as wrong as it would be to raise it. Conversation deepens into itself via recurrent patterns, topics and motifs and the way these can recalibrate in new or shifting contexts, sometimes colouring tragic, at other times comic. It's the historical dimension of a conversation that turns that conversation into something personal; sufficiently so for it to become its own form of private language. Although, as private language, conversation must be both historical and current, for the word that has been deepened or leavened by history also belongs to a continuous present – a present not dissimilar to the effortless presence we tend to associate with childhood itself. But how is this confusion of ages and tenses maritally achievable? Is there a couple out there who can tell us how to keep the present tense of a marital conversation going over the long haul?

Explaining the success of his marriage to the philosopher and psychoanalyst Julia Kristeva, the writer Philippe Sollers has this to say: 'faithfulness is a kind of shared childhood, a form of innocence. Here, in a nutshell: we're children. If we stop being children, we're unfaithful . . . True infidelity resides in the congealing of the couple, in heaviness, in the earnestness that turns into resentment. It's an intellectual betrayal above all.' The idea that fidelity to the word of marriage demands, in the first place, an intellectual commitment is an interesting claim, albeit one that ought to be caveated with the acknowledgement that it's intellectuals who are making it. The conversational agenda within marriage clearly can't be construed as wholly intellectual, after all, unless what's intellectual is reimagined in such a way that it includes the conversations of non-intellectuals as well – as one would assume it must do if these intellectuals are also declared children. But either way, marital conversation obviously isn't for intellectuals alone. Anecdotally, I've heard it said by many different people who've grown unhappy within their marriages that what they feel they've lost is a conversational spark – a loss that means even the good aspects of their relationship can feel like insufficient compensation. Whereas a nourishing conversation is hard to give up on no matter what other problems a couple may have to deal with. As such, I wonder if *any* marriage can afford to forfeit this aspect of the marital project entirely. When spousal communication is as void as it is for Madame Bovary, for instance, what adultery seems to promise is primarily the excitement of *talking* to somebody else. Such is the basis of the conventional wisdom about those who have affairs wanting to meet not another person necessarily, but another version of themselves; one that the other person might awaken them to the possibility of. Indeed, it's on the back of many years of clinical observations that relationship therapist Esther Perel has promoted the idea that couples can learn to make use of the other man or woman – the affair – to catalyse new conversations that might lead to new things happening between them.

The other man or woman is not, however, what Kristeva and

Sollers choose to make the basis of *their* conversations. In fact, it's their particular claim to enjoy a marital conversation between two people who take language itself as their special ability and object. In this regard, they compare themselves to that earlier pair of famous French intellectuals, Jean-Paul Sartre and Simone de Beauvoir, whose enduring partnership was said to outlast their 'contingent lovers' by virtue of keeping their conversational eros alive even after they'd lost interest in other forms of intercourse. But whereas Sartre and Beauvoir supposed what was most original in their conversation was its unerring honesty – its daring to say everything – Sollers and Kristeva allege theirs is the superior relationship because of what they don't say to each other as much as what they do. As Sollers puts it: 'I must stress that I don't believe in transparency. I'm against the kind of contract agreed between Sartre and Beauvoir. I'm all for secrecy.' He's got a point. Whatever one's policy on secrecy, it's surely reasonable to suppose that a relationship can't claim to be entirely transparent. Although Sollers does seem to imply that he and Kristeva *do* enjoy a kind of transparency in their relationship merely by giving space in their marriage to the keeping of secrets. But can that really work? Is it truly possible to quarantine one's secrets in such a way that whatever gets said is transparent, while whatever doesn't is already covered by prenuptial agreement?

I suppose why I'm slightly mistrustful of the claim is because something that does feel pretty transparent, even to outsiders and even if it remains unsaid, is the likely nature of these secrets. For it's not as if Sollers and Kristeva are the kind of writers to view words as the rudimentary instruments of a communication whose meanings can always be fully determined or divulged. Much as Maggie Nelson characterizes her marriage to Harry Dodge as 'an infinite conversation, an endless becoming', thus taking, as it were, the originally creative word of marriage *at* its word, one can assume, with Sollers and Kristeva, that here too we're talking about creative people whose conversation thrills at language's own suggestions of secrecy, and that that's the critical part of the pleasure they take in it (and that this too is what keeps their conversation present, notwithstanding its history). But if that's the case, a peculiar thought then arises: that it isn't what's said that's transparent while what remains unsaid is a secret – if anything, it's the other way around. And so that has me wondering: mightn't such strict demarcations regarding what will and won't be discussed within a marriage have the unintended consequence of overly determining the meaning or meanings *of* that marriage?

In some ways the paradoxical openness of a couple confessing what they deem best kept secret is conveyed by the very concept of 'open marriages' – as in marriages whose overarching commitment allows for the kinds of extracurricular relationships Beauvoir pursued and called her 'contingent lovers'. Albeit these contingent lovers, whom both she and Sartre at times seem to have treated quite mercilessly, so fierce was their primary commitment to each other, weren't always easily described as contingent; Beauvoir did on occasion recognize that Sartre's lovers could arouse her murderous jealousy, just as her own lovers aroused in her occasional doubts over Sartre's priority. But in the end, it does seem that their conversation's adherence to truth and honesty (rather than transparency) did preserve the ultimacy of their union. Whereas for Sollers and Kristeva, it's the silencing of all talk of these shadowy other men and women that they turn into the pact that binds them. Which is a pact that also, crucially, is supposed to have stamped out the dread bugbear of sexual jealousy too. Unless the official secret of which they may not speak is the affair, while the unofficial secret of which they dare not speak is how the affair has really made them feel.

To this impertinent suspicion, Kristeva's response is adamantly denial. Discussing female patients who feel betrayed by their husbands' wandering eyes, she confides, 'As an analyst I understand them, but not as a person. To feel betrayed implies zero self-confidence, a narcissism so battered that the slightest affirmation of the other person's individuality is felt as a crippling blow.' Yet since she does, therefore, as a practising analyst, have people she *can* talk to about the intimate details of sexual jealousy, mightn't it be that these same conversations are in some ways helping to assuage and displace her own? Which, based on no kind of evidence, is not, I admit, a fair insinuation, and it's certainly not a provable one. Although Kristeva's further attestation that 'I don't like other women enough to be jealous of them' did give me pause. Could this apathy regarding other women, proffered here as part of the formula for what makes her own marriage so successful, be based on what she's seen or heard of those distraught women talking about their marital pains and sufferings in her consulting room? And if that's the case, is it women's habits of conversation specifically that have rendered her so apathetic? If so, then that, I'd imagine, would be likely to have its own effect on the conversation she shares with Sollers – possibly increasing its subjects of exclusion not just to their mandated secrets alone.

That said, whatever my doubts or projections regarding the eclipse of sexual jealousy in an open marriage, I certainly don't doubt that Sollers and Kristeva do enjoy a marital conversation far too special for either of them to risk giving it up. When they ironically entitle their book *Marriage as a Fine Art*, it's very much a testament to this. Their specific allusion is to Thomas de Quincey's consideration of murder as one of the fine arts, i.e. marriage, like murder, as a source of conflict scandalously suited to an aesthetic no less than a moral consideration. Albeit Sollers's own marriage, he says, is no such conflict zone. It's a realm in which 'both partners equally preserve their creative personality, each stimulating the other all the time. It's the instance of a new art of love, then – something that can't easily be accepted by a broken-down society that sets great store by order.' Perhaps this 'new art of love' is why Sollers and Kristeva decided to open a window on to the private conversations that make up their marriage (their book is mostly written in conversational form), precisely in order to enlighten the broken-down society their marriage is staged to oppose. While by moving what's essentially private about their marriage into the public domain, they might also be said to link up with a longer aesthetic tradition, one that has brought marriage's present tense back into the realm of history by acting as the interface between the conversations that take place *within* marriage and the conversations that are had *about* marriage.

3. Talk at the Interface of Marriage

Sharing private conversations between married people with the populace at large, even if those people are fictional characters, is to make of private discourse a public interest. Just here, for instance, is where political significance has often been ascribed to the intimate dramas of Austen's social comedies. Although, for the marriage-curious philosopher Stanley Cavell, it's the dawn of the talkie that represents the key development in this history of exposure. For it's the talkie that, with dramatic historical symbolism, enabled the big screen's previously silent figures to speak before mass audiences who had never heard such things said aloud in public before. Moreover, the talkie came into its own with romantic comedies whose appeal was the back and forth of witty dialogue between the stars. More than just a technical feature, in other words, talking in the talkie was the pleasure principle itself.

By calling these films 'comedies of remarriage', Cavell was drawing attention to the dynamics of couples who aren't discovering each other but are rediscovering each other and so effectively renewing their vows. In the new world in particular, there were good historical grounds for this innovation. Once divorce was legitimized as a reasonable response to unhappiness in marriage, then marriage had to be re-legitimized or bought back into. As such, it's tempting to view the movies themselves as ideologically motivated to re-legitimize marriage at a time of crisis. But that isn't quite right. Cavell's subtler point, I think, is that what these romcoms were really showcasing for their audiences were the conditions of possibility required to make marriage as good as its word. And the greatest of these conditions concerned the word itself, which had to be released into a culture free enough to allow couples to learn how they might speak to each other anew.

In *The Infinite Conversation*, a series of dialogues that aren't quite dialogues, the sinuous French writer Maurice Blanchot proposes that we 'might learn to speak', only when 'the experience of strangeness may affirm itself close at hand as an irreducible relation'. It isn't marriage he's referring to, but his description could help to delineate the special form of conversation that *is* marriage. 'Marriage is so unlike anything else', observes *Middlemarch*'s Dorothea Brooke. 'There is something even awful in the nearness it brings.' Looking for a practical solution to this awful nearness, Marie Stopes's Edwardian bestseller *Married Love* identifies 'perpetual propinquity' (propinquity meaning proximity) as a fundamental dilemma for married couples; the malaise of which, she says, acutely afflicts men. Yet of this 'the wife, particularly if she be really in love, is seldom fully aware.' His 'longing to be roving is not completely extinguished. In the true lover this unspoken and unconscious longing is perhaps less a desire to set out upon a fresh journey, than a longing to experience again the exquisite joy of the return'. While in terms of bringing freshness to the couple's domestic conversation, says Stopes, it's equally important for both spouses that they resist the kind of languishing that can take hold if they don't venture out into the world alone so as to talk freely with others from time to time. The world to which Stopes refers is specifically the dinner party, where she warns that couples 'are always within the possibility of earshot of each other, which very often deadens their potentialities for being entertaining. The mere fact of being overheard repeating something one may have already said elsewhere is sufficient to prevent some people from telling their best stories.' If not managed meticulously, in other words, marriage not only hampers the chance of gathering new stories, it threatens to spoil your older ones as well. Ergo, Stopes's rule of thumb for married people is to stretch out the space and time intervals between them. That way, they might keep what risks becoming overly familiar still sufficiently strange as to be interesting.

Writing about the intimate sufferings of married people forced, during pandemic lockdown, into more than their fair share of perpetual propinquity, Zadie Smith evokes the rude awakening faced by spouses suddenly faced only with each other: 'now there is no clocking off *ever*, and no drowning of artistic anxiety in a party or conversation or frantic exercise. Married men are confronted with the infinite reality of their wives, who cannot now be exchanged, even mentally, for a strange girl walking down the street. Her face, her face, her face. Your face, your face, your face.' *The infinite reality of wives.* Awful nearness indeed. But then, as Dorothea knew, what's awful isn't only what's dreadful or dangerous. It's also, potentially, a portal to reverence, inspiration, awe. Her face – your face – the face-to-face. This last encounter is how Emmanuel Levinas was to envisage our most everyday experience of sublimity and transcendence. To *really* see the face of another, he urged, one must recognize that 'the face resists possession, resists my powers'. *You might want me*, says the face (and it says this without even having to move its lips), *but you can never really have me*. Which is why, when faced with the face of another person, I am not only forced to relinquish my own wish for mastery, but 'I always demand more of myself'. That does, you have to admit, sound wonderful – her face and your face as the gateways to mutual edification. Yet surely this is too much to ask of couples enclosed in an awful nearness. Can any spouse tasked with lockdown really have spent that time staring in dumbstruck humility at the face of their bedfellow? I'm guessing not – even if no face marks the intimate strangeness of the human relation better than the familiar visage of the person one sees, with dull predictability, every waking day. For what's equally human, and all too human, is to not really much bother looking at her face.

The face, however, turns out to be just a philosophical hoodwink for Levinas. Because what the face really makes visible, he explained, is the other's *invisibility*, which is why, in his subsequent effort to imagine the ethical significance of the face-to-face in less pictorial terms, he represented the space between faces linguistically, by drawing a distinction between the 'saying' and the 'said'. 'Saying' was a word to denote the irreducible sense of meaningfulness (meaning sans any concrete content) that swirls within the intimate realm of human relations; or the way in which another person's face, in its infinite strangeness, exposes us to their metaphysical significance – thereby rousing in us the dim recognition of our need to translate, decipher, interpret and understand, however inadequate, partial and uncertain our approximations in this direction cannot fail to be. For when we speak, or when another person's nearness arouses in us a desire to speak, while we may be striving for some form of connection, our speaking must be improvised in the apprehension of their fundamental untranslatability as well as our own. The 'said', on the other hand, refers to the intelligible content of the communication that passes between us. While language as 'saying' is an ethical openness to the other, once it becomes 'said' it closes the other down (as I sometimes try to do in my own marital conversations by quoting Levinas, which invariably does the trick). Still, no matter what gets said, if one attends carefully to what someone else is saying, one can usually just about make out within it an inchoate cry or summons – an appeal for something else, or something more than mere communication alone.

So what does marriage tell us of this? For just as one often fails to really look at the face of the person one sees every night and day, it is not especially hard, in my experience, to flip that round; to ignore the concrete content of what I'm being told by my husband whilst still perceiving the pleading of his very person. The way in which the adult you got hitched to comes to sound like just another needy and babbling infant over time – isn't that marriage's practical joke? Or could this be a joke whose punchline I've failed to fully get? Maybe the problem is that I've refused to recognize how the fundamental infancy I can always hear somewhere in the background of my husband's talking (and he in mine) is precisely that which could bring me face to face with marriage's most sublime metaphysical gift and opportunity. The gift of marriage, that is, as that which, rather than speaking for us, might instead become a means of our *learning to speak* – by responding to the logic of another person in their irreducible strangeness and their strange irreducibility. For if anyone bears the logic of that other person, it's one's spouse.

The logic of another person is not, then, a dialogic. Conversation, on this framing, isn't about winning or losing an argument, nor about arriving at the kind of transparency or agreement that flattens out and overcomes differences. While knowing what the other is going to say and finishing their sentences for them can be cute, a marriage can't survive on predictive text alone. What makes Harry and Sally's conversation so special, for instance, is the fact that it doesn't much matter what gets said because what keeps them interested is what remains unsaid, which neither of them can say, though they can hear it very well in what each other *is* saying. And obviously one hopes this will continue for them once they've set up home together too – though that's by no means guaranteed. Home, as once described by the poet Adrienne Rich, can be the 'most dangerous place' – and dangerous not only because of the domestic abuse that can thrive there unwitnessed, but dangerous because the people who profess to love you, and who feel so awfully near to you that they collapse any sense of the distance between you, are the same people who presume they can speak for you, or over you, in your best interests.

With a knowing nod to Stopes, Tessa Hadley's short story 'Married Love' tells the tale of a marriage that we can see from the start is bound to be awful. Lottie, a nineteen-year-old violinist, falls in love with one of her music teachers at university. He's a man forty-five years her senior who divorces his second wife to marry Lottie, led to do so, as he explains to her incredulous parents, because 'the erotic drive was a creative force he felt he had to submit to' – not that he expects those with a more 'ordinary perspective' to understand. 'How dare he think we're ordinary?' the family rage. Yet it's Lottie, too, who wields her romantic and, she newly insists, *religious* convictions as a stick to beat back their ordinariness with. What do they grasp of music, creativity, art? If her family think they know what's best for her, she figures, it's because they lazily presume to know who she is without perceiving her difference, her singularity, her originality. She and her lover, meanwhile, are united in their 'unworldliness', and in their rejection of the world. But of course, Lottie's parents were right to be worried. By the time their daughter, no longer playing her violin, has three children of her own, her marriage has become, as predicted, miserable. And now it's Lottie who is 'impatient if anyone tried to turn the conversation around to art or music.' While she and her husband share a weight of duties and tasks, they barely talk to each other any more. He, in fact, mostly spends his time talking with his ex-wife, a woman of his own age, whereas Lottie continues to have her best conversations with her brother Noah. It's Noah who also visits her at home, and who dares to ask if her husband's music, the music for which she has sacrificed her life, is 'actually any good?' She thinks it probably is, she tells him, and confides that he's composing something: 'He pretends this new piece is for me. But I know it's not about me.' Yet in the story's remarkable final scene, Noah observes how his sister, in earshot of the domestic noises her husband makes through their apartment's thin walls, hungrily follows 'the ordinary kitchen music – the crescendo of the kettle, the chatter of crockery, the punctuation of cupboard doors, the chiming of the spoon in the cup – as if she might hear in it something that was meant for her.'

What's awful can still sometimes burrow into itself to discover what's musical. Could this 'ordinary kitchen music' then constitute something of the special conversation that is marriage itself? For reasonably or not, Lottie *is* still listening out for something intentional in what clatters routinely through the close quarters of her domestic sphere. What she manages to make of her narrow world stands, in this sense, in marked contrast to the palace of bourgeois convenience that taught Madame Bovary to experience her own world as having nothing whatsoever to say to her, to the extent wherein she could no longer believe in the possibility of any meaning at all. Whereas the transformation of Lottie's world-defying romance into the most workaday of marriages, though it may well have come at the cost of lofty conversations, does not, for all that, require that she suffer the death of meaning. On the contrary, marriage under these conditions would seem to be where and how meaning gets fine-tuned to levels of almost unbearable intensity.

So even though there are good pragmatic reasons why Lottie chooses to stick it out in such an awful situation, could yet another reason for her sticking to her guns be because she still wants to hear the music? Or because marriage is a situation that has even somehow deepened her capacity for hearing music? The story ends by twisting the knife. Lottie is listening to dull sounds in the vain hope they'll become a version of the musical piece her husband is writing, which he's claimed is meant for her. Neither she nor we believe he has any such intention. But then, who is to say what his noises mean? What comes from us is no longer ours to determine at the interface wherein it gets shared. And if that's true even of our words, then it may be all the more so in the case of our non-words, our sounds, our intended or unintended music. Who is a piece of music meant for? For its composer the answer can only be that their music is for whoever listens to it and imagines it's meant for them.

In Joanna Hogg's film *Exhibition*, a couple of married artists who hardly engage in sexual or conversational intercourse, know, with more certainty than Lottie can, that just about everything they do – closing a cupboard, turning on a tap, running up and down the stairs – is within earshot of someone who can hear it, interpret it, and recognize in its ferocity a message intended only for them. They don't have to communicate through thin walls, however, as theirs is a stunning modernist house with sliding walls – walls made of nothing but windows and light. In the midst of such largesse, this is a couple who can stretch out the time and space intervals between their interactions, and they have no children to intrude with demands. Instead, in the little pockets of privacy which they create for themselves in this house of moving parts, these two pursue their erotic and creative lives – he's a painter, she's a performance artist – in such a way as to channel into their work all the libidinal energy they're depriving each other of. But are their lives really so private in a house made of glass? To those with a street view, their marriage could appear as an object for exhibition. And indeed, what *Exhibition* exhibits for its furtive spectators would seem to be a marriage turned inside out. For what we're purportedly watching is an exhibitionist marriage in an exhibition house, which house bestows upon this mostly silent film the fluency and eloquence of a talkie, or better still, a musical – like an opera perhaps, or, more literally, a chamber piece – since here, too, marriage appears as a sort of echo chamber; one that resonates at all times with the wide compass of its contract.

Exhibitionist is a word that freights the act of sharing, which can often be a creative act, with shame, and which implies as well that it knows the rules of what one should or shouldn't show. To call someone an exhibitionist is to make assumptions about what the public and the private are and how and where to draw a line between them. And yet marriage, which has always and for ever been both, has never been able to fit easily into that framework. To get married legally, one must share the word of one's bond and commitment to each other with the world of witnesses. So should the future of that marriage exclude the witnesses who formed such a critical part of its original contract? Or should the couple, after their wedding, limit these participant observers to witnessing them only formally, say at dinner parties?

I have my own reasons for being sensitive to the charge of exhibitionism. And it's no doubt because it strikes so close to my (more conventional) home, that I find *Exhibition* – as a film of a married couple who exhibit themselves to the world while hiding away from each other – unnerving. My own marriage, after all, is also one between two people who have produced docufictions portraying ourselves and our married lives. The films are collaborations, but that hasn't stopped them from being conflict zones. Much blood gets spilt on our cutting-room floor. So why have we been moved to expose ourselves in this way? Is this our manner of seeking some escape from the awful nearness of our own relationship? Or is it that we fear real intimacy, or real conversation – so much that we're led to triangulate our marriage with the world? Does turning our private lives outwards indicate that there's something inwards which we can't bear, or can't share, or won't dare? If I choose to confide my marital anxieties with you, for instance, rather than with my spouse, am I thereby betraying him, or our marriage?

Perhaps it's instructive that the couple in *Exhibition* are planning to move out of their showhouse. What they've decided, presumably, is that what they or their marriage needs is less transparency, more opacity. What it doesn't need, necessarily, despite their perpetual propinquity, is much more company. Although it does need the suggestion of company. Indeed, there's one moment in the film when the couple leave their self-imposed lockdown and make a foray into social life. They don't go very far – they're just visiting their neighbours for dinner: a couple with children, jobs, and the small talk to go with it. Yet faced with these adults next door, our married couple fake an emergency as a means of escaping and returning to their own vitrine of play and isolation. It's a comical moment, and one of hopefulness as well; a moment to show us how an unhappily married couple, if they can recover that spirit of two against the world, could still find their way back into complicity, conspiracy and laughter. While the scene also makes a larger point: one that pertains to how much this couple must have *needed* to exhibit themselves in order to achieve such a reconciliation. Could *any* marriage survive over the long haul otherwise? To be true to its original word, and to be true to its own continuous conversation, mustn't every marriage, on occasion, present itself as a performance and an exhibition?

In a conversation for *Granta* magazine following the release of *The New Man*, the first feature film my husband and I made together, the writer Hisham Matar asked us a difficult question: 'Why do you think that for you marriage is something to think about, talk about and make work about?' I attempted one answer: 'Josh sees me at my least made-up, my least attractive, and yet he's the one who needs to feel attracted to me. And we're both quite slovenly people. So one thing couples often do is have "date nights" when they go out into the world together. And in that outing the eye of the world acts as a third character in their relationship: a character that's intrinsic to the sexuality *of* their relationship. So yes, the element of exhibitionism can probably add a kind of interest.' But my husband's answer was subtler: 'If we make a film of ourselves, or invite people over and talk about how awful our relationship is, we make it sound like an ongoing romantic comedy . . . perhaps we make ourselves feel like characters involved in the plot of choosing each other rather than being just stuck with each other.' After all, it's clear, at least to us, that there is a gulf of difference between who we are on camera and who we are at home, even when the camera is recording us at home. What isn't so clear is *why* we're so sure that's the case. Why are we convinced that our marriage becomes at once something else and yet all the more itself at the interface wherein we sometimes share it? Increasingly, I've come round to my husband's idea. The idea that what we choose to show others, rather than rendering us static – like objects in an exhibition – is instead what stimulates us, however falteringly, to be active both inside and outside our marriage. As such, making a film is just one of many examples of our public outings together, no more revealing than anything else we happen to share. And in the end perhaps what it really means is that we're a couple of married people looking for ways to ensure that we'll always have more and more things to talk about.

6

Conversation Pieces

i

The Deed is Done

'. . . our refusal to share what was a secret to neither of us, but which was, nonetheless, becoming a secret by virtue of our not sharing it.'[1]

Javier Marías, *A Heart So White*

Straight after my wedding I felt shell-shocked. It was my big day, and now it was over. I didn't imagine I'd have any other big days ahead of me – or none that could meaningfully compare with that one. I was crestfallen. I felt as if my life was already concluded. I was uninterested in thinking about or talking about much else besides the wedding I'd just had. I was honestly worried I might never get over it, or past it. I couldn't even focus, during the first days of our honeymoon in France, on the idea of a romantic holiday and its pleasures. If anything, I felt slightly annoyed with my new husband for taking me so rapidly away from my wedding, directly into my marriage.

Then I made my next strange move, for a honeymoon. I started reading the very long, very hypnotic, and very distressing novel *2666* by the Chilean author Roberto Bolaño. Bolaño was brought up in

---

1 Reader beware: secrets of the novel will be shared in this section.

Mexico and the novel is set there, in the town of Santa Teresa, on the Mexico–US border. As in the real-life and similarly situated town of Juárez, Santa Teresa is where untold numbers of young girls and women keep going missing. What is the secret of these disappearances? The secret, it turns out, is a crime which, though known about around the town, is not much spoken of, and never properly investigated or prosecuted. The crime is perhaps too large, so large that it sometimes seems, in this large novel, to cover the whole of reality: the crime of violence, rape, murder, misogyny and unacknowledged histories.

During the time I was reading that book, on my honeymoon, I was having nightmares. I kept dreaming of protests being forcefully disbanded by police. In these dreams, I was often somewhere lost inside large crowds of angry women carrying revolutionary banners. I was perplexed. Why would I dream of such things so soon after my lovely white wedding? Indeed, why was I even *reading* of such things so soon after my lovely white wedding? Was I becoming so lost to anger that I couldn't even imagine myself into my own passions? Now that the deed of marriage was done, had I been suddenly transformed into a crusader *against* the institution? Was some sort of inchoate fury towards men my deep dark postnuptial secret?

I didn't really want to discuss the novel, or my nightmares, with my husband – because it was our honeymoon, and because these thoughts and feelings didn't seem like a good sign. Then my husband read the novel after me, and though he was likewise gripped, he didn't really discuss it with me either. So we kept at it, our honeymoon, relaxing, sightseeing, enjoying the scenery, the food, the weather, and the erotics of our being together, yet all the while I was secretly seeing the world, and sexual relations, through the fevered eyes of Bolaño. Was that how my husband was secretly seeing things too? I didn't dare ask. At some point, however, we must have broken this pact of silence. Perhaps it was when we'd both finished the book. Then, when we did start to speak of what terrible brutalities we'd been reading, my nightmares came to an end, and I also felt less arrested by the past tense of my wedding, and my honeymoon started to feel exactly like the place where I wanted to be.

Still, there are many traces of that earlier experience of something shared but apart that continue to crop up in the everyday of our marriage. Sometimes, I'm aware, my husband hesitates before discussing certain topics with me. And sometimes he avoids them altogether – because he knows how readily I get affected and upset, and because he often sees me as akin to a child unable to bear too much reality. He might be right. Maybe that's even the secret of why I *wanted* to get married – in the hope that marriage might save me from having to know all the things that I don't wish to know. But what if that means that I don't wish to know myself, or my own husband?

The very long opening sentence of Spanish author Javier Marías's novel *A Heart So White* begins with the words 'I did not want to know but have since come to know'. In what follows, we learn how marriage is the condition of this transformation: a married person is a person who winds up knowing what they don't want to know. A curious proposition. What exactly *is* this postnuptial knowledge?

Our narrator is a newly-wed husband. 'Since I contracted matrimony . . . disaster', he announces at the start of his matrimonial tale. Marriage, in this formulation, is something one contracts like a disease; a disease that, though it may show signs on the surface, really signals that something far more malignant lies beneath. The discovery of this malaise occurs soon after the change of status. Our narrator had wandered blithely into his marital contract, which seemed to him, at first, little more than a social necessity; the only honourable means into adulthood. But once married, what he feels instead of adulthood is a sense of restriction, such as he felt as a child. Earlier in his relationship, for instance, he could choose to go home with Luisa, his partner, or not. Now that decision has already been made for him. 'It was as if the future had disappeared', for by this 'act of mutual suppression or obliteration' he and his lover, now wife, seem to have nothing further to look forward to – all is decided, settled, known. Or is it? For what's equally the case is that, by virtue of being married, our narrator encounters the peculiar sense that Luisa has become not more familiar to him, but rather less so. 'The more corporeal,' he observes of her married presence, 'the more remote' she appears – not unlike a mother. Indeed, when he returns from work trips to encounter his new wife ensconced at home, he finds her stranger and stranger. Each time he re-enters something is different. His house has changed, her clothes have changed, her hair has changed. Thus, counter-intuitively, it's the life lived at home rather than the life of the traveller that sees new things keep on happening, which feels disconcerting for our narrator. It's as if, after their wedding, Luisa is married and he isn't. While she has been turning into his wife, he hasn't really started turning into her husband.

Our narrator and his wife first met when they were both working as translators for the UN. Luisa was his superior, supervising the translation of conversations between the Spanish Prime Minister and the UK Prime Minister (a woman conspicuously resembling Margaret Thatcher). In order to flirt with his boss, sitting just behind him in this small translation studio, our narrator takes a chance. When the two politicians are forced to make small talk with each other until they can resume their formal conversation, he takes advantage of their mutual incomprehension in order to compel them to say risky things to each other; things about the nature of love, and about whether love of a leader can ever really be true love, and to what extent power and manipulation might be aspects of familial loves as well as political ones. By translating the politicians' real conversation into a fraudulent one, he thus simultaneously translates a fraudulent conversation into a real one. He even at one point gets the UK Prime Minister to quote Shakespeare, specifically *Macbeth* – the play where a political power couple strengthen their own alliance by means of a misdeed; a murderous misdeed that Macbeth performs and Lady Macbeth is a party to. Just as, in this same moment, our narrator performs his misdeed of translation while the woman with whom he's flirting remains quiet, indulging in his conspiracy with her silence. And it's this silence that causes him to fall in love with Luisa, because she's game for making both politics and love something more daring, more inventive, more narrative.

It's another conspiracy of silence, however, that attends our two lovers on their honeymoon. And it's here, in a hotel in Havana, that we find our narrator fretting that his marriage could lead to disaster – a presentiment brought on by his wife's falling ill. With a high fever, she's bedridden and delirious, and he fears her dying. So as not to disturb her rest, he goes out on to the balcony and watches a woman on the street below waiting for a date who hasn't shown up. It's due to our narrator's position on that romantic precipice that a curious misrecognition takes place. The woman on the street mistakes him for her missing date and becomes furious – why won't he come down and join her? He cannot reply to her, though, without perturbing his sleeping beauty. Yet his silence unleashes, in this stranger, the Furies; the sort of Furies that often spring into dialogue between two familiar people when one of them isn't delivering the expected lines. So now our narrator finds himself, on his honeymoon, and on a hotel balcony, guilty towards two women at once – both his wife, who needs him to step inside and wipe her brow, and this woman on the street, whose amorous betrayal he's found himself implicated in. He feels paralysed. Should he go back indoors and upset the woman outside further, making her rage even shriller and more likely to cause a disturbance, or should he remain outside on the balcony and prove negligent of his wife? Who even is this other woman? She's someone's mistress, it turns out. Specifically, the mistress of the travelling businessman in the room next door to his. But that other man hasn't forgotten about his date. On the contrary, he's there in his room, deliberately keeping her waiting while secretly enjoying the spectacle of her agonies below.

I'll get back to that scene shortly, but first, for reasons I hope will become clear, a quick philosophical detour: all ideology, expounded the Marxist thinker Louis Althusser, 'hails or interpellates concrete individuals as concrete subjects', which is a bit of a mouthful, although it's simpler than it sounds. Because what Althusser really means by interpellation or hailing is a process to help us explain how helpless we are before the shaping forces of the ideologies amidst which we must live. What hails you is what implicates you, like it or not. The email that lands in your inbox, for example. Or the ad that pops up on your screen. Or the question 'Are you married?', or, as it might be posed to a young girl, 'Who will you marry when you grow up?' Or when you're called upon as a member of a certain race, or class, or sex, or religion, or ethnicity. It doesn't matter if you feel recognized or misrecognized by what or who is hailing you – it's the very recognition that you've been hailed that puts you within their relation. Once you've been called upon, something has been con-tracted between you and the other, rendering you as responsible for what you're mistaken for as for what you take yourself for. It's an experience whose inescapability can be maddening. Though perhaps especially so if the manner in which you've been called and the name by which you are called seem at odds with each other. Say, if you're called upon as a man. The man who gets hailed as such is that entity who has often been called upon to act as master – even though self-mastery is precisely what the fact of the calling gives the lie to.

Many people know, even if they've no idea of his philosophy, that Althusser, who had once been a prisoner of war, strangled his wife, the French revolutionary and sociologist Hélène Rytmann, to death. Having done so, he knocked on the door of the doctor at the École Normale Supérieure and confessed his crime. In his confusion, he also muttered something about having believed himself to have been massaging, not throttling, her neck, appearing to the doctor to be uncomprehending. The doctor, thus called upon, in turn called upon various others in their institutional capacity: the police and the hospital sanatorium. The clinic, in fact, was already known to Althusser who had spent months there previously on psychiatric grounds. In his precise and delicate dissection of this episode, the writer Peter Salmon notes that Althusser, before meeting Hélène, had been more or less phobic of women. Hélène, however, Althusser latterly explained, 'initiated me . . . into my role as a man, into my masculinity. She loved me as a woman loves a man!' What did it mean to Althusser, the great thinker of interpellation, to feel convinced that it was a woman (a specific woman whose throat, the seat of her voice, he subsequently targeted for attack) who had called him into a role he seemed glad, at least at first, to occupy – that of a man; that of masculinity?

When we experience ourselves as subject to manipulation by the forces of ideology, it can be tempting to misrecognize the other person with whom we interact as the source of our own perceived powerlessness, even though they must be no less interpellated within their subject positions than we are ourselves. So was Althusser in some sense enacting the sort of failed mastery that his own philosophy has been so critical in illuminating? I write this hesitatingly since it's seldom wise to speculate about the motive of a murderer lest one risks appearing to exonerate or excuse the act in the effort to interpret it. Yet nor is it a stretch to suggest that there's something pertinent in Althusser's thought that *could* potentially help to shed light on the long history of male violence towards women. For a philosophy like Althusser's, as Salmon observes, 'where all our subjectivity is the creation of malign powers, and there is no way out of the trap of ideology, is a strong liquor'. Clearly the person who feels he's been hailed into being by malign powers isn't absolved of the work of his own hands. Still, it's curious that, as much as Althusser represented his political struggle as one with a world that renders us complicit with histories we would prefer to disavow, he was never given the opportunity to take responsibility for the deed he did in fact commit. Althusser, says Salmon, 'claimed he felt cheated that he was never charged'. The whole terrible story reminds one of 'The Part about the Crimes' that are neither investigated, prosecuted nor brought to trial in the novel *2666*.

Returning to Marías's novel, however, we can find our narrator still on the balcony quietly resisting the coupledom the woman on the street below has erroneously ascribed to them. In so doing, he also finds himself trying to conceal from his wife the extramarital relationship he seems to have, obscurely, been hailed into. It's as if, during the time it takes for this woman to realize that he isn't her lover, he, to all intents and purposes, somehow is. Both he and her real lover, after all, are not so differently positioned: both are standing mutely upstairs, looking down on her feverish distress, not responding to her calls.

When she does finally realize her mistake and gains access to her real lover in the room next door, thus quickly forgetting our narrator, he's already back inside with his feverish wife. At this point, it's Luisa's turn to get caught up in the other woman's story. For both our newly-weds are now listening as best they can to what's happening on the other side of the wall. But unlike when they met, they are not this time conspiring to cement their own relations via the relations of another couple. Instead, our narrator perceives that his wife seemed

as if she wanted me to continue to believe that she was asleep, as if she didn't want to give rise to any conversation between us, either now or later, about what both of us – I now realised – had overheard . . . she preferred each of us to listen separately, alone, not together, and to keep to ourselves, unexpressed, the thoughts and feelings aroused by the conversation next door and the situation it implied, and to know nothing of what the other thought or felt, even though these thoughts or feelings might well be the same.

By refraining from confiding their shared act of eavesdropping through the wall, another wall is created – a wall of silence. And this has implications. When two people are silently in the dark imagining things about another couple, which may or may not be the same things as each other, what they're imagining begins to concern their own coupling as well.

What Marías's novel is interested in is the special manner in which couples communicate: what's said and what's unsaid, what's shared and what's unshared, what's shared verbally and what's shared silently, what's shared in conspiracy with the other and what's shared in isolation from the other. Secrecy, as we meet it in this novel, isn't simply a question of knowing or doing something without confiding it; it's also the atmosphere evoked by choosing not to verbalize a mutual experience – and in the case of our newly-weds, that's what they overhear on their honeymoon. Which was what exactly?

What they're listening to through the wall is the mistress demanding of her lover that he kill his wife. Either you kill her or I kill myself, she threatens. Which is why, our narrator explains, he chose not to speak to his wife of this matter, hoping (the hope of the professional translator) that what 'one doesn't say doesn't exist'. For what he certainly didn't want was to have to introduce a topic so toxic on his honeymoon. These newly-weds are in Havana to celebrate their love and commitment, after all, which talk of adultery and murder cannot possibly help. And in our narrator's case, the risk of raising these themes was also intensified because he fears for his wife, who has already fallen seriously unwell. As such, the story of another wife whose life might be in danger, possibly from her husband's own hands, strikes him as inadmissible. And yet it's precisely because they do not verbalize what they're overhearing that the secret of the couple next door becomes, in a strange but palpable way, their own secret.

Put differently, what we can glimpse in Marías's novel are the stirrings of censorship within a marriage during its honeymoon period – which censorship each spouse assumes must be necessary in order to keep the fantasy of the happiness that pertains to marriage alive. Marriage as the contraction of adulthood is thus what propels these newly minted adults to baby one another by co-creating a series of cover-ups – particularly with regard to the truth of the world as they both (secretly) see it. What they do out of their shared fidelity and commitment to their marriage, in other words, is deny what they believe about reality. Their marital happiness, each one assumes, can only be sustained if they continue to suspend their disbelief, or imagine that this is what they can enable for their spouse through their silence.

The way marriage contracts both adulthood and the recurrence of childhood is one of the great matrimonial mysteries: how wedding someone allows you to break away from your family and your past whilst simultaneously rekindling elements of your familial past – elements that you may not have been conscious of *before* getting married. Our groom, for instance, has chosen to honeymoon in Havana, where the Cuban part of his family once lived. And it's in Havana too that he not only gets assailed by ominous premonitions regarding his marital future, but finds himself haunted by a long-forgotten nursery song his grandma used to sing. Like most lullabies, the song is dark, about marriage as the bloody chamber of the bride who enters it. Can it be an accident, then, that the distant memory of this song returns to him on his Cuban honeymoon with an already ailing wife?

Given the microscopic attention this novel pays to what does and doesn't get communicated between a couple from one moment to the next, as if marriage was really a channel for accessing the unconscious life no less than the intentional one, it pans out that our protagonists are both professional translators and interpreters, i.e. people who consciously decide what to say and what to leave out when making sense of things. For it's only via marriage that our narrator discovers how some communications can elude even the ear of experts. And it's also only on account of his marrying that he slowly begins to realize that there have been messages encoded throughout his life that he has unwittingly *refused* to translate. So while the adult act of marrying leads our narrator to get to work deciding what to translate and what not to translate in order to curate for their marriage a child-like innocence, his marriage is simultaneously doing its own work – that of bringing his personal history's undivulged secrets back into the light.

It's our narrator's father who appears as both the source of his family's secrets and the counsellor of silence within marriage. On the day of his wedding, his father gives him this conjugal advice: if you have any secrets, don't tell. It's the advice of someone who knows from experience the risk to those one loves if one confides in them too much. Do not take any such risk, he advises his son. Instead, enter upon marriage as a means to an unexciting but 'bearable tedium'.

As such, the person to hint to our narrator what his father's secrets might be is not his father but a childhood friend of the narrator's; an older boy who has since gone on to befriend his father. This friend is not a man who can easily bear tedium. He's someone with a zeal for stories and secrets; someone who cannot tolerate the thought that there are things going on behind closed doors of which he can have no inkling. Once our narrator is married, in fact, this old friend gets back in touch and rudely presses him to spill the secrets of marriage. What goes on in the conjugal bed? This friend is not himself married. He's even something of a Don Juan. Is that why it's the marital bed that especially intrigues him? Because he longs to know, in all graphic detail, how the marital deed is done? For he's not a man, our narrator surmises, with much talent for invention. Indeed, our narrator ponders if marriage might not be the right institution for his old friend precisely because he wouldn't know how to convert monogamy into anecdote. The Don Juan character, in this iteration, is less the aesthete than the one who lacks aesthetic abilities. He's the kind of guy who has to *do* everything because he can imagine nothing, whereas marriage is entertained by our narrator as the more imaginative life insofar as it's a life that *depends* on the imagination. Which doesn't mean his friend has any less desire to share his life than our narrator does. In fact, it's precisely this desire to share that is assumed to animate the philanderer as someone who fears, without his exploits, he'd have nothing left to say for himself.

Meanwhile, given his tendency to hound others for their secrets, it's from this friend that our narrator begins to know what he does not want to know — namely, that his father is a man who has had three wives, all of whom, mysteriously, died young. Our narrator remains largely in the dark about this history, but still, he heads home and informs Luisa what his friend 'had told me and what I hadn't wanted him to tell me.' It's a marked development since the censored sharing of the couple's honeymoon. On this occasion, he can't resist the confidence, figuring that the conjugal bed — whose secrets his friend wished to know, though our narrator gave nothing away — demands a kind of 'pillow talk', such that, between the couple who lie in it, there can *be* no secrets: 'the bed is like a confessional'. Whether they speak or not, a couple, should they care to know what they might not wish to know, can grasp how to listen even to each other's silences: 'in the end, there's not a single tiny corner of all the events and thoughts in an individual's life that remains untransmitted, or rather translated matrimonially.' Marriage, thus framed, is a means of translating the unconscious; a way of making what's been covered up reappear. Marriage, our narrator deduces, 'is a narrative institution.'

Viewed accordingly, infidelity implies a failure to commit to narrative. It's an odd thought. A thought that implies the decision to look upon marriage as the site of a bearable tedium already constitutes marital betrayal. A narrative, to be truly narrative, must, at the very minimum, prove itself hospitable to surprise, novelty, risk. Does that then entail that each and every time a narrative moment presents itself the faithful spouse must seize upon the moment for the purposes of sharing? And would that therefore render non-narrativizing a type of deceit? As, indeed, appears to be the case when it comes to our narrator's relation with another woman, Bertha, the friend and former girlfriend with whom he stays when visiting New York. For it's our narrator who's now the one in the role of the travelling businessman. While Luisa remains, after they marry, at home in Spain, he still serves in the UN as a translator.

When our narrator and Bertha are alone together, they form a kind of couple. It's something he notices whenever the first-person plural appears. If Bertha says 'we', he thinks she's 'assimilating me into herself' and resists speaking in the same mode. But if he finds this 'we' discomfiting, maybe even disloyal, he's no less discomfited when Luisa uses 'we' in his connection as well. And indeed, while he and Bertha no longer sleep together, their coupling isn't altogether lacking in sexual content. Bertha, for instance, asks our narrator to take a video of her naked; which video she intends to send on to another man, Bill, who has requested this as evidence of her sexual appeal via an internet dating app. 'We don't have to give it to him,' our narrator, again discomfited, tells her, assimilating Bertha to his own person when a third character threatens to intrude on their arrangement.

The story of Bertha and Bill is a curious one – it's exactly the kind of anecdote that he could entertain his wife with upon returning from his travels. Yet it's precisely because of this 'we' that he's been forced to acknowledge between himself and Bertha that he doesn't share any of these things with Luisa. Even though he hasn't cheated on his wife, he *has* been interpellated into a connection with another woman, just as he was briefly with the mistress who mistook him for her lover in Havana. In both these cases, the temporary connection he feels and forms with another woman is one that leaves his wife outside. Couples, he reflects, 'tell each other everything about other people, but not about themselves, unless they think that information belongs to both of them.' What couples narrativize for their partners, in other words, is only what can be assimilated by a 'we' they each feel happy to share.

And yet our narrator is not the only one to get hailed, postnuptially, into such obscurely adulterous first-person plurals. This is something he soon discovers when he returns home early from his travels to surprise Luisa. Resting upstairs in their bedroom until she gets back, he suddenly registers noises below – the noises are those of his wife entering their house with someone else, his father. Our narrator is unsure whether he's left signs of his presence, sufficient to alert his wife that he is at home and likely to be all ears. Another triangle is thus forming, although our narrator cannot at this point tell who, between these three, are the co-conspirators – the 'we' – and who is the one left outside the couple's eternal pact.

Hence, in a scene paralleling the earlier honeymoon scene, not only does our narrator find himself, once again, eavesdropping through a wall on the private conversation of a man and a woman, but the secret being shared is, once again, a secret about the murder of a wife. For what his father confesses to Luisa is that his second wife died on account of his decision to share with her, on their honeymoon in Havana, his most deadly secret: that because of his love for her, he killed his first wife. It was his desperation as a lover that made him say something he could never take back. He'd wanted to share anything, everything, even the criminality of his own fall into love. His new wife was no Lady Macbeth, however, and refused to be a party to her husband's misdeed. His confession thus leads to her suicide. He had hoped, mistakenly, that his word would mean more to her than his dealings. And this notwithstanding that, when you've committed murder, the hazard of confessing should probably be obvious. Yet to prove one's love, the father explains to Luisa, one feels compelled to tell all. Whereas to protect one's love, the father had advised our narrator on his wedding day, one must give nothing away. So how should a son translate such contradictory messages? Unless the successful transmission of his father's love is to be found precisely in its untranslatability. For certainly we've seen our narrator deploying a no less unruly logic, alternately holding back secrets from Luisa or else compulsively confiding them in her.

In the history of the novel as marriage plot, certain conventions have shaped how we expect men and women to talk. And *A Heart So*

White, a novel that both upholds and undermines these gendered expectations, is also a novel that reflects upon *why* men may have traditionally resisted the kind of talk women are supposed to engage in. Men who swerve gossip, the novel speculates, have been given to understand what women apparently don't: that the secrets men conceal by means of their marriages are so dark as to be deadly, should they come out. To which end, the novel proffers its own proof: for the story of what killed the father's first wife is the same story that also, by virtue of his sharing it, killed his second. So why, we might ask, does he share this crime with his son's wife? Is he moved by a similar ardour to risk confiding a secret that he knows could kill whoever hears it? In which case, if he's in love with Luisa, is this act of sharing a form of infidelity to his son? But then, too, we might ask what's Luisa's motive in soliciting such sordid confidences from her father-in-law?

In the relatively calm manner of Luisa's reception of her father-in-law's secrets, our narrator senses something in the course of finding out what he has never wanted to know, which his wife – or which his marriage – has forced into his hearing. He senses that Luisa is not a co-conspirator with his father. She isn't, he registers, being unfaithful to her spouse, even as she becomes another man's secret-sharer. Because the reason she's eliciting this confession, it dawns on him, is for the sake of their marriage, that it might live free from the dangers of such histories as could wreak havoc on their union via their unconscious repetitions. As such, the newly married couple can finally, at the end of the novel, speak to each other of what they overheard together but apart on their honeymoon. They can finally narrativize together, by assimilating into the conversation that is their marriage even the darker stories, whose secrets they render less malignant by sharing them as their own. Hence 'I can now say', our narrator genially concludes, '*we're going to buy a piano* or *we're going to have a baby*'.

So, does the 'I' who can now say 'we' presume a happy-ever-after?

And does that conclusion imply that Marías's contemporary novel, notwithstanding its postnuptial topography, still belongs to the marriage plot's most idealistic traditions? Possibly, if we can expect our married couple to remain faithful to their narrative commitment. Although nor should we ignore what the novel, in its postscript, suggests haunts such happy endings in every generation. The song of the nursery: 'A song that is sung despite everything, but that is neither silenced nor diluted once it's sung, when it's followed by the silence of adult, or perhaps I should say masculine life.'

The song of the nursery is the song sung despite everything – everything, that is, that we know but don't wish to know about the world; which dreadful knowledge we hear lullingly when we hear it for the first time, before we're old enough to receive the official story. What's the official story? In this novel, it's what gets said in lieu of what doesn't get said, which the teller would prefer to keep silent: the true story of adulthood, and of masculine life. And yet this silenced, unofficial story is the story we also hear first when we hear it in the nursery before we can understand it. So it's a story we hear, or overhear, in a different register – the register of music, of infancy, and of feminine life. It's whilst we're still in our cots that these feminine sirens sing to us of what we don't wish to know, which at some point we'll *have* to know. And the song they sing is one they know must haunt us, which will one day – such is the nature of song – return to us, whenever we're ready to hear and translate the messages the song contains.

The fact that these messages are, in Marías's representation, gendered in our historical reception of them, rubs up strangely against what's also demonstrated by his novel: that we're interpellated in any number of different ways and so don't always take up the same position in every relationship, or even, very often, the same position over the course of the same relationship. What, then, could gender stand for here? Presumably its use of stereotype pertains to a style of relation, and less so to the fixed properties of particular bodies or persons.

For if the latter was the case, why can we hear the song of the nursery in the fictions of male authors? Such as in Bolaño's novel, for example, or in Marías's novel – in which the married couple spend much of their time trying to co-create a marital innocence, only to find themselves assailed by the dreadful knowledge they first overheard *in* their innocence, which knowledge comes back to them only after they get married. What's the implication of this? Is it that the novel itself, or marriage itself, or the novel as an institution bound to the institution of marriage, may be interpretable as ways and means of translating the dreadful knowledge we have of ourselves and our histories, which knowledge, because unspeakable, is carried to us initially by the song of the nursery? If so, then what could transform that dreadful knowledge, making its translation hopeful, desirable, even idealistic – in the novel or in marriage – would be to imagine that, translated appropriately, the song that haunts successive generations might have its meaning interrupted. For even unbearable knowledge, once shared and assimilated, might be made, if not safe, then less toxic, more bearable.

Why, then, has the transmission of this largely silenced knowledge, framed by Marías's novel as the knowledge of masculine life (and as a knowledge which, though it may be shared, has been shared more often apart than together), been considered the responsibility of feminine life? Is that because women have borne the brunt of these malign ideological powers' most violent histories, meaning they're the ones who've felt called upon to siren its warnings to each new generation? Or might it be, too, that their voices are also communicating other messages between their lines of dark premonition? Messages perhaps even less translated than are their words. For not everyone who feels called upon feels called upon to make a case for their own self-mastery. And some, rather than railing against their dependency on others, may have other tales to tell of interpellation too – of interpellation's pleasures as well as its pains, of its opportunities as much as its treacheries. For let's say we lived in a very different world; a world in which the ideological forces acting on us were more agreeable, even ideal. Still, in that utopia, interpellation would remain the inescapable condition of our shared reality. Who and how we are cannot *fail* to depend on the calling of others. As such, when envisioning the paths to our future happiness, we'd do better to think of our dependence less as a bug than as a feature.

ii

What Do Women Want?

'She speaks, yet she says nothing. What of that?
Her eye discourses. I will answer it. –
I am too bold. 'Tis not to me she speaks.'

Act 2, Scene ii, *Romeo and Juliet*

In 1974, the year I was born, Grace Paley published a short story called 'Wants' – you can find it freely online. The story is one of renewal and it's one that I return to often even though its characters and concerns – women and men, women who love men – might seem to some old-fashioned. It never gets old for me.

The story is two and a half pages long. Paley's stories were all short, she once explained, because she was a woman with more wishes and responsibilities than those of a writer alone. She was also a mother, a daughter, a wife, a friend, an activist, a citizen. Pressed with such demands, her time, inevitably, was limited. And 'Wants' is a story not only engaged with what a woman wants, but with a woman's time: with what her wants and her time might have to do with each other.

It begins with our narrator sitting on the steps of the 'new library' and seeing her ex-husband in the street. 'Hello, my life, I said. We had once been married for twenty-seven years, so I felt justified.' A wry, melancholic but nonetheless friendly opening is thus oddly concluded with the sort of inward justification that alerts us to what machinations may have dissolved their marriage: accusations, ripostes, words always barbed, braced, ready for the next charge. And indeed our narrator is met with an instant rebuff: 'What? What life? No life of mine', which she quickly accommodates: 'I said, OK. I don't argue where there's real disagreement.'

In my own marriage, my reluctance to argue where there's real disagreement has itself been a source of real disagreement. It's not hard to see why. When I fall silent or turn coolly compliant in the midst of a heated discussion I'm often accused of withdrawing into a cold frigidity or passive aggression. And to the extent that I am, like Paley's narrator, inwardly constructing my own unstated justifications, there's certainly such a case against me to be made. But there may still be a case to be made for refusing to make my case. Because who wants one's marriage to be a battlefield where positions must always be established and sides defended or attacked until a victor has been declared?

Introducing *What Do Women Want?* (1983), co-authors Susie Orbach and Luise Eichenbaum quote the sociolinguist Deborah Tannen: 'Boys and girls grow up in what are essentially different cultures, so talk between women and men is cross-cultural communication.' Sexual stereotypes regarding styles of discourse have tended to hinge on the idea of women chasing conversation in the hope of connection and intimacy, while men are supposedly looking to trade information, solve problems and bring unnecessary chatter to a close. (There are punning parallels to be made here, too, to stereotypical notions of what drives female vs male sexuality.) When women make it known that they want to 'talk', for example, and yet, men quickly discover, this talking is open and meandering with no obvious content, direction or end in sight, that's when men predictably turn an exasperated cartoon shrug to the camera: 'You see how impossible they are, how there's nothing I can do to mollify them . . . what on earth do women want?'

This is pretty much the run of things in my own household. What we're arguing about turns out to be how to speak to each other at all. What is conversation good for? Arguments at least appear to have a sense of direction, and yet an argument, even if won or lost, tends to preserve the disagreement in some form, which may be the inevitable outcome of any kind of intercourse that's been declared decisively 'over' – cf. the history of war. So while arguments can seem a noble quest to bring disagreements out in the open, and hence to an end, it's equally possible that arguments are provoked by the very *fear* of what's open, i.e. the sort of open-ended back and forth that hasn't bothered to determine its aims in advance. Arguing could then be viewed as an attempt to ward off the unpredictability of endings by calling time on time.

When thinking about conversation, it's worth considering a type of conversation informed by a built-in reflection on its own purposes: the psychoanalytic session. The psychoanalyst D. W. Winnicott once observed that session endings can be a way for the analyst to insinuate hostility towards their patients, even when those endings are consensual, amicable and agreed upon in advance. Discussing a case study of a female analyst who found it hard to end sessions with a particular client, a businessman, after the allotted fifty minutes, Anouchka Grose remarks that the analyst suspects herself of having haplessly colluded with her client's wish for 'her to see him for love, not money' because of 'social conditioning around women and caring. She thinks a male therapist would find it easier to end the sessions'. Love as unwaged labour is meant to be the special domain of women, after all.

But do male therapists really find endings less vexing? Perhaps. Yet the psychoanalytic situation is also one that invites us to project sexual identities that have less to do with anatomy or social conditioning than with the fluid and transferrable characteristics that make sharing possible. Gender, in other words, as a question of what position you're occupying in a particular discourse – such as who is doing the talking and who the listening. In my own case, for example, I know I've certainly tried pushing back the finishing line of sessions with my male analyst in the past. Asking myself why, it's as if I've been protesting the way in which 'time's up' forces me to reckon with the economic nature of our relations, thereby disillusioning me of the romantic notions I may secretly be harbouring (about his desire to do nothing but listen to me). So isn't it conceivable that, like that businessman, the mystery of what I want (which I usually claim not to know) is no less bound up with a fantasy of what might be signified or promised by 'free time'? Hence too, no doubt, why I'm just as likely to be the first to announce when our time's up in the manner of someone pre-emptively ending a relationship before the other gets a chance to.

No matter the instigator, efforts to tie things up are frequently marked by this wish: a wish to close down a state of openness and uncertainty about what the other really wants; a state that's experienced as threatening. As such, it's not unreasonable to suspect that the patriarchal question 'What do women want?' might be posed by someone whose purported wish to know may be disguising their wish *not* to know. A question, after all, calls for an answer, but what if what 'women' want is a chance to speak or share unhampered by the demand that they get to the point?

As so often, Freud is simultaneously both the purveyor of the problem and its best response. For though it was he who made infamous the question, he's also the curator of a way of talking and being listened to that doesn't claim to know in advance what a conversation's ends are supposed to be. It's precisely the 'point' of psychoanalysis that talking can never really get to it. 'To speak is to want', as Adam Phillips puts it, 'and to be heard to be wanting – otherwise than one intends'.

In Paley's story, whatever arguments may have once brought this marriage to an end resume the moment the former spouses see each other again. So it makes sense that the story mostly takes place at the library's Books Returned desk, where our narrator has gone to return overdue books which she's had out for eighteen years. For it's at this point that there occurs between our narrator and the librarian a conversation that mirrors the one she's having with her ex. Once again she's accused of a past misdemeanour. Once again she accommodates. 'I didn't deny anything. Because I don't understand how time passes' – an explanation we can accept, having just discovered that the so-called 'new' library is one to which she has owed books for nearly two decades. Indeed, one way of reading the story is as a sort of coming-to-consciousness on the part of a narrator who has been stuck, unable to progress or move on – a consciousness that seems connected to her understanding of 'how time passes'.

So what does it mean for someone to become conscious of time? Perhaps time-consciousness, in Frank Kermode's apt phrase, is simply the sense of an ending. A narrative sense, then, but also one that might, through its historical awakening, have the potential to ignite a sort of political sensibility; one that, at its best, would allow us to glimpse that the way things are does not require us to suppose that they correspond to any natural law that renders them inevitable, but rather to a set of relations and actors that have shaped them in the past and might shape them differently in the future. And one that, at its worst, arouses a fervid apocalypticism such that the end in sight looks a dead certainty.

In any case, given its hold over the imagination, the sense of an ending, while it may endow a sense of time passing, doesn't assume adherence to chronology. What the perils of a fateful trajectory mostly seem to inspire, in fact, is the wish to move backwards in time. But even here there are different paths to be taken. Sometimes we long to return to the past out of nostalgia: terror of the present, a horror at the way time changes things, or because the unknown in the form of the future is frightening and, of a sudden, too brief. Yet the past needn't solely be sought out for the security of what's known. One can just as well look backwards because one's history – or what one believes one *knows* about one's history – seems to be arresting one's development.

In 'Wants', his version of their story has a definite outline: their marriage ended because 'you never invited the Bertrams to dinner'. 'That's possible', our narrator concedes, 'but really, if you remember: first, my father was sick that Friday, then the children were born, then I had those Tuesday-night meetings, then the war began. Then we didn't seem to know them anymore. But you're right. I should have had them to dinner.' It's at this juncture that Paley, if not her narrator, must surely have been tempted to rest her case. For isn't this what one's really up against in a marriage? The whole of life – the way it balloons. Our narrator's version of what she was responsible for back then is thus both more all-encompassing and less plotted, in part because, as she evidences, she had no time to notice time passing. Since busyness is rarely an acceptable excuse, however – the people we let down suspect that we *do* make time for the things we want – she admits her fault. Or does she?

While her admission sounds, on the surface, pretty peaceable, as an anticlimactic wind-up of so much history it also feels like an escalation. Indeed, for her ex, the uninvited Bertrams remain a debt still owed him, as if time was unable to heal the wounds that her lack of time inflicted. Although these two warring reactions – his aggressive one, her passive aggressive one – are juxtaposed with that of the librarian, who immediately 'trusted me, put my past behind her, wiped the record clean', once her debts are paid. So it's the lending library that offers a vision of what it might be like to feel free of the past. With books, she's forgiven. And what this inspires in the story is renewal. Our narrator at once renews the same two Edith Wharton novels she'd come to return, reflecting that though she read them long ago, 'they are more apropos now than ever.' The books are *The House of Mirth* and *The Children*, both stories written fifty years before Paley's, at a time when women were beginning to organize themselves politically, by making their demands and wishes known.

At the 'liberating' Books Returned desk, therefore, we're returned to an earlier emancipatory moment, and to the period when the pace of change was accelerating for everyone, though for women, as Wharton showed, most especially. Indeed, the historical consciousness we find in Wharton's fictions suggests that women could begin representing their own desires only once they'd become conscious of those of their time. And they became time-conscious in large part by reckoning with the conditions of their *own* desirability – by noticing, for instance, how their place in the marriage market, along with that of so many other consumer objects, was tied to a sense of their built-in obsolescence.

Despite her poverty, her rumoured wantonness and her wish for not only status and money, but also love, *The House of Mirth*'s Lily Bart remains marriageable while young. All such prospects are lost to her, however, as she ages. While in *The Children*, a man in his late forties ceases to want the grown woman with whom he's been matched as he finds himself falling for a teenage girl – though it's the novel's irony that a man of means, leisure time, and scant responsibilities possesses none of this girl's maturity ('Judith's never been a child – there was no time').

In our own times, predators are making the news: elevated to the loftiest positions on one hand, hearing their time's up on the other. Yet looking back over one hundred years of the women's movement, from the first wave of feminism when Wharton was writing, to the second wave when Paley was finding her 'more apropos than ever', reminds us that these days are by no means the first in which women have sought to call time on the exploitative nature of heterosexual relations. Nor, as that history shows, does declaring something 'over' necessarily mean the future won't repeat the past. But we can still hope that the present clash in the ongoing battle of the sexes might afford its combatants a chance to pause, reflect and learn from their shared history. Not least because, if the sense of an ending calls forth an historical consciousness, it can cause us to question those things that may have passed previously unnoticed, by appearing inevitable, natural, obvious . . .

For instance: what do men want?

It looks all too obvious in the scene of the older man predating a young girl – the most indecorous version of what it's often said men *really* want. But that charge not only unfairly smears all men, it also fails to probe, as Wharton did, the confusions that abide within stories of wanting. Because what if we were to turn Freud's question on its head and suppose that what women *and* men want is *not* to know what they want; a chance to be surprised? On this account, the predatory male may desire the ingénue precisely for her fantasized ignorance. Though if he finds himself consistently chasing the new, believing that passion can only dull with familiarity, then he has mistaken his object. For in wanting the unknown but pursuing the unknowing, he encounters nothing new, but rather locates in another's sexual ignorance a means of shoring up his own narcissistic image – the image that an older woman threatens, by knowing too much.

In his essay 'The Uses of Desire', Adam Phillips reflects on two different types of wanting: perversion and desire. Rooted in early experiences of frustration, humiliation and powerlessness, a 'perverse state of mind' encounters objects of desire primarily as threats. It accordingly enacts a revenge fantasy on its objects by envisaging all pleasures as calculable, all relations instrumental and all futures predictable. By guarding against any chance of being surprised, 'the fantasy of knowing what one wants', suggests Phillips, 'is a form of despair'.

In 'Wants', after watching our narrator renew the books she'd come to return, her ex-husband seems suddenly hopeful that he too might get a second chance. We sense this when he recalls a 'nice' time together at the beginning of their marriage. But his nostalgia only has the effect of renewing their disagreement:

That was when we were poor, I said.

When were we ever rich? he asked.

*

'Oh, as time went on,' she says, they were a family that didn't want for anything. Which isn't his memory: 'I wanted a sailboat . . . you didn't want anything.' It's the kind of line that sounds like it knows what it wants: to bring things to a close. Whereas our narrator, though her irony is unmistakable now, still keeps her line open: 'Don't be bitter', she tells him, about that sailboat, it's 'never too late'. And 'with a great deal of bitterness' he for the first time agrees: 'I'm doing well this year and can look forward to better. But as for you, it's too late. You'll always want nothing.' To win an argument, as we know, you must have the final word (and you must believe there *can* be finality in words). As such, he seals his victory by following word with decisive deed: 'I sat down on the library steps and he went away.'

Time's up.

So what, between these two, was wanting? Perversion and desire, says Phillips, entail 'two ways of writing history.' By turning wanting into something predictive, as in knowing exactly what one wants – for instance, a sailboat – the perverse mind looks forward to what can only ever be a self-confirmation, sacrificing 'the future in the name of the past.' Desire, by contrast, is not restoration, 'but a making new.' Desire, seen thus, needn't imply that what one wants must be bound to one's own recovery, e.g. by filling in a pre-existing blank or lack. Yet desire may still be driven by the sense of an ending and a wish to move backwards – though here in order to undo whatever in the past threatens to foreclose the future by inhibiting the chance of the unpredictable.

Time, we find in 'Wants', can never be fully determined, no matter how decisively one tries to end things. Thus the ex-husband's judgement – 'for you, it's too late. You'll always want nothing' – only provokes where it intended to close down. 'Now, it's true, I'm short of requests and absolute requirements. But I do want *something*', our narrator reflects, continuing to converse with herself even after he leaves. She wants, she realizes, 'to be a different person', such as the type of person who returns library books on time. She wanted to be a good mother, an effective citizen, an ender of wars. She wanted and still wants love: 'I wanted to have been married forever to one person, my ex-husband or my present one. Either has enough character for a whole life, which as it turns out is really not such a long time. You couldn't exhaust either man's qualities or get under the rock of his reasons in one short life.'

While *he* might think his wants are obvious, his reasons straightforward, on that there remains between them real disagreement.

Soon after, this is how the story ends: 'Well! I decided to bring those two books back to the library. Which proves that when a person or an event comes along to jolt or appraise me I *can* take some appropriate action, although I am better known for my hospitable remarks.'

So it's a happy ending: she returns the books not only punctually, but ahead of time. Yet as endings go, it hardly sounds conclusive. There's a risk, for instance, that she could be lapsing back into the perverse logic of claiming to know too much about what has determined her own history. Because what changed her exactly? She implies it's her ex-husband's accusation of passivity that jolted her into appropriate action. But when we first encountered her on the steps at the beginning of the story she was already taking those overdue books back to the library. So even by then something had shifted.

And what of the 'hospitable remarks' our narrator claims she's 'better known for'? They sound a lot like the conversational style we've been observing throughout the story via her various acquiescences and accommodations for the sake of non-confrontation. One possible implication of the ending, then, is that this putatively feminine style has been vanquished by the classical motif of man's propensity for heroic action – action that depends on knowing exactly what one wants. But since it's those open and inviting 'hospitable remarks' that are the story's actual last words, a question, implicitly, is left hanging as to which of these behaviours – action or conversation – has been the real agent of change. Because isn't hospitality, as a form of admission, of letting others in, the more likely, in the long run, to make a lasting difference to a disagreeable situation? Viewed accordingly, refusing to argue where there's real disagreement, while it *can* be a cover for aggression, may also be a way of playing for time: the time it takes, for example, for real changes to emerge, or the free time beyond the finishing line when relations, being no longer subordinated to the laws of instrumental reason or economic exchange, seem fashioned not for money, but for love.

'There is a roof on our language that holds down our love', George Saunders has written. 'What has put that roof there? Our natural dullness, exacerbated by that grinding daily need to survive. A writer like Paley comes along and brightens language up again, takes it aside and gives it a pep talk, sends it back renewed, so it can do its job, which is to wake us up.' It's the idea of literature as a space of hospitality. Or of the book as that which welcomes you under its covers like another kind of nuptial. And in a world like ours, where disagreements are raging, stances are hardening, and where in both private and public, in both sex and politics, an atmosphere of intimidation stalks whoever fails to know in advance exactly what positions to take, it's a blessed relief to imagine there's still somewhere we can go that remains open, accommodating, ready to admit new possibilities. Every time I return to 'Wants' I read it differently. On every reading I find it timely. But it's a story that strikes me as more apropos now than ever.

iii

Best Intentions

'We were considered an ideal married couple.'
Johan in Ingmar Bergman's *Scenes from a Marriage*, Scene 1

It was at a fairly early stage of my development that I was told – by a man – what men want. As a rule, I mean. And I was grateful for the info. I saw it as a vital life lesson, on the basis of which I've since felt able to judge men, envy them, urge them on or hold them off – all because, with men being what they are, you do have to wonder about their intentions. But now that I find myself seriously wondering about intentions, it strikes me that I've very little sense of what I intend by making assumptions about them – be those intentions man's, woman's, or my own.

What's intention? Straight off, it's one of the words we have for describing purpose. As such, it's normally wielded by people who profess to know what they're doing and why. In the sexual sphere, when we query someone's intentions, we usually imply a concern that they might not be acting honestly, or honourably. *Are* they as committed to the relationship as they purport? Are they thinking seriously about the future? Are they going to propose marriage? The best intentions, after all, are those that intend towards marriage. And towards marriage's depths and responsibilities rather than merely its carnal pleasures or guarantees.

But isn't marriage also what robs us of knowing our own intentions? If marriage is the system we've tended to rely upon to conjure our future horizons, then our intention, insofar as it pertains to marriage, must be an inheritance of some kind. Someone who has the best intentions towards marriage can only be following the dictates of a teleology that preceded them. If that wasn't the case – or if intention wasn't associated with duty – then how else would we be able to judge whether intentions are good or bad? All of which puts intention in both conflict and strange sympathy with e.g. instinct or desire as the words in our vocabulary we have to describe those forces that seem to drive us *unintentionally*. To drive us, that is, towards passion, or love. For the person who has been led into marriage by their noble intentions, one can only assume, must not have dared to fall in love. For a fall to really be a fall, it cannot have been intended.

In *Best Intentions*, a novel written as a dialogue, like a film script, the Swedish writer and film-maker Ingmar Bergman reflects on his parents' marriage. Everyone in the novel is at some point forced to acknowledge the significant gap between who they are, how they behave, and what it is they think they intended. However, it's the priest, the character based on the novelist's father, who is not only particularly prone to losing the plot – especially in relation to Bergman's high-society mother – but prone, too, to taking this discovery hardest. What he believes to be his greatest sin, he tells her, is not to know what he wants. And that, we're to understand, is a truly dangerous confession for a man of the cloth. If *anyone* should know what to want and how to act, he should. What, then, should his son make of this obscure testament, which appears to him as the legacy of his own father? Can a lack of intention also be an inheritance? To lose sight of what one wants, after all, isn't only a professional hazard for a priest; it's no less a crisis for a film director.

The moment in Bergman's family novel when the father confesses his greatest sin shares a curious symmetry with the depiction of Bergman himself as a father in the Norwegian writer Linn Ullmann's novel *Unquiet*. This too is a novel in which certain sections are written as a dialogue, like a film script. And Ullmann, the youngest of Bergman's nine children, represents her father in her novel as a man of absolute purpose, precision and punctuality; a man who always knows, and takes pride in knowing, what and who he wants and how to go about getting it. Yet in her series of conversations with him not long before he died, which conversations became the basis of her novel (though the book had originally been conceived of as a collaborative, reciprocal project), every direct question she asks him seems to provoke his anxiety, resistance and doubt. It's as if, by the end, there is little if any direction left in the great director. And this faltering tone, which takes him over at the last, leads Ullmann to review what preceded this ending as well. Was he really, as he so often appeared, the ultimate figure of a man who doesn't need to ask anyone else for directions? Or might the very things that have bolstered that reputation be recruited to frame another story, even an opposing one? When someone has quite as many wives and lovers and children as did Ingmar Bergman, after all, we seem to be in the realm of compulsion rather than intention. Contemplating, at the end of her father's life, such an embarrassment of fecundity, he cannot have intended it, his daughter reflects.

Liv Ullmann, Linn Ullmann's equally famous mother, was the star of a number of her celebrated partner's films, including playing the wife in *Scenes from a Marriage*, one of cinema's most acclaimed and enduring depictions of marriage. Why depict a marriage by means of scenes? Well, 'scenes' presumably because its original incarnation was as a series of episodes for TV – episodes that were subsequently rendered by Bergman into his feature-length film (the one I'll mostly be referring to). But 'scenes' too because a certain notion of generality and even, putatively, normality (hence also the normative and the ideal) can often find itself generated by popular media and by the very process of the episodic, thus tying such scenes to the broader social scene of both the audience watching them and the individuals pictured on the screen. And yet 'scenes' as well because scenes, considered as such, can simultaneously create havoc for our more conventional expectations of genre or narrative. 'With the first scene', writes Barthes, 'language begins its long career as an agitated, useless thing.' Whereas in a scene's very insignificance – making a scene isn't an effort to solve a problem, it's what one enacts having given up that effort – it also struggles against insignificance. What's scenic can also be spectacular.

At the start of *Scenes from a Marriage*, we meet Johan, a man with good intentions, sitting on an heirloom sofa with his wife, Marianne. They're surrounded by all the accoutrements of a bourgeois home, and both show the requisite knowingness of a couple conscious enough of their privileges to be able to check them when the situation demands. They are, they tell the women's lifestyle magazine interviewing them for a series on love, 'indecently' fortunate; content with their lot 'to an almost vulgar degree'. That indecency is open to numerous interpretations. At this stage, however, what it primarily seems to suggest is that theirs is a happiness that's indecent because unearned – even, they hint, inherited. So these can't be romantic heroes; their match is far too convenient for that. Indeed, Marianne initially proposed they get together for precisely that reason; not because they were in love – they never claimed to be at first – but because they were obviously respectable as a couple, and because they were both miserable having just lost something very precious to them – he had lost his pop-star girlfriend; she had lost both her first marriage and her baby, which had died no sooner than it was born.

Both Johan and Marianne are professionals. He's a scientist; she's a divorce lawyer. But when they're asked by their interviewers to describe themselves, while he can easily boast of his accomplishments, she's lost for words – describing not who she is, only who she's related to. He is a man of intention. She is a woman of relation. Yet neither are these very convincing performances. As much as he may wish to appear as a man who knows who he is and what he wants, we've learned that he's only in this marriage because he was won over by the persuasive skills of his divorce lawyer wife. And however persuasive she may be, we can see she's a woman who knows nothing of who she is or what she wants either, but only what society is and what society wants. And that, as it happens, is what caused my first sense of discomfort when I watched the film with my husband (also a film-maker). Was this basically the truth of our own marital situation too? I wondered. For a director and a devotee of Bergman, my spouse seems to have found himself in a very square set-up thanks to *my* powers of persuasion. Indeed, the word 'bourgeois' when uttered self-consciously in the film feels altogether intentional, as if it's being directed towards an audience who, watching from a perhaps similar sofa with a similar spouse, may well find themselves recognizing aspects of *their* marriages and lifestyles within this one.

The film, in fact, is almost entirely comprised of close-ups of just this husband and this wife. It's only in the first few scenes that we see other people drift in and out of the frame. We don't meet the children with whom they constantly busy themselves. We never meet the parents who loom so large in their lives. Nor do we meet the younger woman Johan subsequently runs off with, or the husband and wife they each marry after their late second-act divorce. These occlusions are dramatized particularly at one moment in the film: when Marianne begs to see a photograph of her husband's mistress. Reluctantly, he shows it to her, but while she describes what she sees (young, thin, pretty, big breasts, betokening a rather clichéd and vaguely pornographic imagination – is that imagination hers, or his, or mine?) and he confirms it, we do not see this other woman ourselves. So it's a film whose visual storytelling constantly reminds us, regarding these intimate realms of love, sex and marriage, that what we can't see we're forced to imagine, which thus forces us to question the reliability of our imaginations as well. Is what we see always a kind of projection; an image of what we may or may not recognize as our own intentions?

Early on there's a scene of Johan at work with an attractive female colleague. Quickly we draw a straight line between them. Surely this woman must be his secret lover – because we all know what men are like, and what men want. But if we allowed our imaginations to lead us in that direction, we were wrong. She isn't his lover. Instead he invites this colleague to draw a straight line from A to B on a fluorescent projection slide in the dark. It's a scientific experiment, but one that parallels the conditions of spectatorship in a cinema – lights off, screen gleaming. And when the lights come back on, she can see, and we can see, that her line has gone all over the place. She's made a real muddle and mess. She hasn't even come close to where she intended.

Meanwhile, in another of the movie's earliest scenes, we see our couple hosting a dinner at home with another couple of married friends. However, what looks at first to be a scene of perfect bourgeois civility – fashionable clothes, fashionable cuisine, fashionable wine – soon enough gets messy when these dinner guests do something scandalous. They quarrel with each other furiously, claiming their marriage is a bitter failure, one whose horrors they're intent on displaying in order to educate their happily married hosts about what hell a marriage can be – a hell whose road, they assure our protagonists, was paved with good intentions.

But hang on. How scandalous is that scene really? Isn't this exactly the kind of hot mess we might well expect to come across in the dramatic arc of relationship cinema? Rather than adulterating the bourgeois paradise, in fact, such a scene could sweeten, for the hosts, their own marital set-up. For the absolute mainstay of bourgeois happiness is, as we know, to be happy in comparison with others. Indeed, mightn't that spirit of competition be the very thing that makes bourgeois happiness so fundamentally indecent? Unless it's the quarrelling couple who are showing us what indecent happiness looks like. Even amidst their volleys of vitriol, after all, we can hardly fail to notice which marriage looks passionate and which one staid.

Afterwards, when they're washing up, we see Marianne and Johan alone. But if we've been anticipating that our couple might prove no less fiery than the other couple behind closed doors, we've again been misled. Alone together they're a picture postcard of marital harmony. As they reflect on the evening, they happily reassure themselves that they're nothing like their miserable friends. They even embrace and tell each other they've never thought about wanting anyone or anything else. They're so adorable that it's the very decency of their happiness that begins to feel indecent. And this becomes still more unsettling when they turn their felicity into something of a mantra: *We are happy.* Or is that just what feels particularly galling to me? (It's when my husband and I are washing up after our guests have left the scene that we've often sought to reassure each other of the same.) Meanwhile, Marianne seizes on this moment to extend her campaign of conjugal persuasion. 'They don't speak the same language', she muses of their departed guests. 'They must translate into a third language they both understand in order to get each other's meaning . . . We talk everything over and we understand each other instantly. We speak the same language. That's why we have such a good relationship.'

We are happy. We understand each other. We speak the same language. We have such a good relationship. Methinks she doth attest too much. Or you don't exactly need to be a shrink to suspect that within such marital affirmations there must be some clue as to the couple's marital frustrations – frustrations that should feel familiar to pretty much anyone who has been married (when it was first aired, *Scenes* was held responsible for a spike in global divorce rates). And indeed, Marianne soon expresses her resentment at the fact that they can never seem to commute their married lives into the passion of love lives – by, for instance, spending a whole week alone in bed together. They can't do this because of their duties: to their kids, their parents, their jobs, their whole social scene. That's just the life we've chosen, he reminds her. But then, he never really felt he *did* choose this life, which wasn't his idea, or his wish, or his intention, and nor was it hers really – she just moved towards what she imagined was appropriate. So is *that* – the dawning recognition that they're in an unintentional because overly intentional marriage – why Marianne and Johan do, subsequently, break up?

With Bergman, of course, we're being both led and misled by an auteur (*the* auteur) film director. As such, we can be fairly confident that, once all hell in the protagonists' happy marriage does break lose, the somewhat narrative start to the film will be similarly cratered. But what does that imply? That one can't change the direction of art until one changes the direction of marriage? Or vice versa? And what do scenes have to tell us in this regard? For what we're left with is a series of scenes from a marriage that do not add up to anything so distinctly outlined as a precise story or portrait, such as you might find written up in, say, a women's lifestyle magazine. But these scenes are not static either. For it's during these scenes that he changes, she changes, their marriage changes, our sense of the meaning of marriage changes, our expectation of genre changes, and our idea of cinema changes. So does that mean we're being directed to change our own scene too? If so, then it isn't easy to derive from the logic of scenes how it is one might go about changing *intentionally*.

Rather like the art that claims to have been created for its own sake, to make a scene is to commit to the perverse pleasure of, for instance, arguing without aim of resolution. And yet even as they exult in themselves, scenes, as we've seen, can set the scene for the actions that follow. In *Scenes*, for example, what ensues is set up by the curdling sense of marital disappointment, the waning of eros, the accumulating resentment at the lack of time the couple have for each other. Hence: betrayal, adultery, abandonment. As a series of events, this is all, by the look of things, his doing, his wanting, his intending. Things, at this point in the movie, are heading in/at his direction. And it's a hard watch – especially when we see him treating his wife contemptibly. After telling her of his intention to leave her for another woman, for instance, Johan acts towards Marianne as if she was a child – someone who wants and needs to be directed, to be told exactly how to react and what to do. And it's true that she seems to accept his authority utterly, never questioning, only begging. But even here, in this scene of absolute mastery, Johan's capacity to direct is more limited than initially appears. For Marianne is not only like a child, she's also like a mother. Once Johan's decided what's to happen, she's the one who takes things in hand; sending him on his way with his clothes freshly washed and ironed, and even setting his alarm clock for him.

Then there's another scene, some time later (time becomes harder and harder to parse between the scenes). In this scenario, it's Johan and Marianne who are having an affair. And now that the wife has become the mistress, their sexual chemistry, barely existent previously, looms unconquerable. Over the course of his absence, we learn, Marianne has come to realize that she never really knew what she wanted because she'd always been doing what she believed everyone wanted of her. This is something she's grown conscious of, she says, because she's started writing a journal and she's formed a relationship with a therapist. It's through inhabiting these different styles of language, she intimates, that she's no longer the person she was before.

Another scene, years later. The exes reconvene for what we now realize must be a long-term affair. This time it's Marianne who has turned contemptuous, sleeping with Johan before casting him off, though not before insisting he signs their divorce papers. Things are now, we see, heading very much in/at her direction.

The final scene. Our couple are tucked away in a cottage somewhere, enjoying a week on their own in bed together. They've both since remarried, but both also concur that, for all they might be married to other people, they're still entitled to celebrate twenty years of marriage to each other – a marriage that's only been strengthened by their divorce. If, in the first scene, they claimed to marry because they were a respectable couple, their renewed commitment is assumed because their coupling is no longer respectable. They have, that is to say, finally arrived at their marriage's indecent happiness in true form. But is it only the thrill of the transgressive that's brought them to this juncture, or might it also be down to the changes that have been taking place within and between them? Changes such as her liberation from social expectations; or his liberation from what he terms his 'great expectations'. For it's in the reduction of those expectations, he confesses, and in the humiliation of being cut down to size, that he finds himself more capable of compassion and love. Still, as redemptive as that sounds, it's hardly the dreamy happy-ever-after of the traditional marriage plot we're watching. In this final tryst, in fact, there's also a nightmare. The nightmare is Marianne's: she wakes in the night and screams in horror at a vision of herself limbless, slithering in the sand like a serpent, unable to reach Johan. As to this dream's interpretation, they can't be sure what it is, but they're both inclined to agree that 'we're living in utter confusion . . . we don't know what to do.'

For Bergman the priest and for his son, Bergman the director, utter confusion as regards one's intentions opens itself up as the gateway to hell. And there's a hint that something similar might be going on amidst the confusion of this respectable married couple turned sinful adulterers who've been woken from their sleep by the hellish image of a slithering serpent. But there is too, in this final scene, a hint that new intentions towards intentions could likewise be emerging. 'Sometimes it grieves me,' admits Marianne, 'that I have never loved anyone. I don't think I've ever been loved either.' But Johan disagrees. He loves her, he says, in his own 'imperfect and rather selfish way', just as she loves him in her 'stormy, emotional way.' Yes, theirs is a messy kind of love, but at least they've been able to wrestle their ideal marriage into something resembling human form. 'I don't know what the hell my love looks like', he ventures, 'I can't describe it and I hardly ever feel it in everyday life.' Thus if we find ourselves, at the end of the film, back inside that dark scribbly morass of misdirection on the illuminated slide, it now seems that we're being invited to wonder if that muddle *was* perhaps the right direction after all. Does that then imply that Johan, who knew exactly what to expect when his female colleague didn't, and whose professional scene bore such a striking resemblance to the techniques of our own auteur, has all along been controlling the meaning of and between the various scenes we've been watching?

Even as 'the slipper changes hands', remarks Barthes, 'the victory goes to the player who captures that little creature whose possession assures omnipotence: the last word.' And in *Scenes from a Marriage*, it's Marianne who concludes the script. But what words she utters, 'Good night', are rather banal: she's merely reciprocating his own good wishes in fact, in a polite exchange of pleasantries that seemingly ignore the recent evidence of her propensity for night-mares. 'This is the meaning of what is euphemistically called *dialogue*', writes Barthes, 'not to listen to each other, but to submit in common to an egalitarian principle of the distribution of language goods. The partners know that the confrontation in which they are engaged, and which will not separate them, is as inconsequential as a perverse form of pleasure.' But what if Marianne and Johan's words are not quite so inconsequential as they once were? The same words spoken in a different context can intend something different. Perhaps now, that's to say, they really *do* intend to wish each other whatever goodness might be made out of the night. The night not as a euphemistic cover for dreams and nightmares to be politely overlooked, but as the direction they both see themselves heading in. When all are in the dark and nobody can gauge the truth of their own intentions, they might, for that reason, find they have better intentions towards each other. Indeed, just before they wish each other a good night, Marianne proffers Johan another pleasantry; another utterance she might easily have said to him in her more deferential days: 'thanks for the talk'. As last words go, these do not assume much mastery over what's come before. Yet they do not reprise her earlier obeisance either. The line may be hers, the scene seems to be saying, but the words, the talk, and the marriage, can only belong to them both. Or as Barthes puts it (I'm giving him the last word, which is now also mine), when two subjects speak to each other 'according to a set exchange of remarks and with a view to having the "last word," these two subjects are *already* married: for them the scene is an exercise of a right, the practice of a language of which they are co-owners; *each one in his turn*, says the scene, which means: *never you without me*, and reciprocally.'

Marriage as Entertainment

7

Co-watching

'What one sees with one's own eyes is mixed up with the question of what someone else sees.'

Darian Leader, *Stealing the* Mona Lisa: *What Art Stops Us From Seeing*

Published in 1993, 'E Unibus Pluram', David Foster Wallace's essay about the now pretty much bygone age of cable TV, reads today as a kind of critique *avant la lettre* of the culture that's since been spawned by the digital streaming services – services that allow us to take charge of what gets channelled into our homes such that we need hear only what we want to hear and see only what we want to see. At the time, the particular target of Wallace's essay was his own breed, American writers of fiction, whose art he thought at risk of TV's malign influence. As the ultimate window on to American normality, he warned, or what 'Americans want to regard as normal', TV looks like a godsend 'for a human subspecies that loves to watch people but hates to be watched itself'. Yet the risk for these professional oglers is that they could lose sight of reality thanks to the ease and comfort of its televisual substitution – a risk, he added, that was by no means theirs alone. If it's true that the average American watches TV for six hours a day then the screen must be a dark mirror of the democratic ideal itself. Wallace didn't, by this, intend to lambast arthouse TV such as Bergman's *Scenes from a Marriage*. Although the lower-brow TV he had in mind did in some ways resemble that sophisticated modernist bend towards formal self-consciousness. The TV you gleefully derided along with your like-minded friends had not only metabolized your own critiques of it, it was already speaking to you in the register of your own mockery. TV was practically begging you to hate-watch it in fact; and it was doing so long before social media's algorithms had figured out that it's the pleasure of hating that gets you hailed, homogenized and hooked. Bergman, after all, isn't the only one to have considered the small screen an ideal match for marriage. Amongst the family-centred sitcoms Wallace mentions are such specimens as the *Cosby Show* or *Married . . . with Children*. Marriage and TV, in other words, may have enjoyed such a binding and lasting relationship because it's those two hitched together that can provide us with the most compelling picture of normality. As such, they can also help to hitch together a TV-watching populace that knows exactly what to say and how to say it in the 'cynical, irreverent, ironic' tone that Wallace deems the method, mood and meaning of the screen age. Or the TV screen age at any rate.

That said, binding the populace with a vision of normality was much easier to do back in our analogue days when we were all forced to watch what was on at the time it was scheduled, whereas living as we do now, in the solipsistic and siloed future Wallace's essay predicted, we can all decide for ourselves what's on. Where couples used to fight, in their most eloquent of marital disputes, over the remote control, peace has since prevailed over home entertainment as every household member can reach for earphones and laptops and turn on whatever it is that turns them on. Not, though, at my address. Here we *do* still continue to vie for the remote control, our quarrels notwithstanding, because we still feel the need of shared televisual experience as pretty much the only zone of interaction we have each day that doesn't feel like a management meeting. This TV time, we tell our children whenever they get out of bed to interrupt us, is special, sacred, *adult* time. Once we've watched over them, we get to watch the next episode of our box set. We do this so religiously, in fact, that if either of us was to jump ahead and watch that next episode alone, it would reasonably be declared, within the terms of our current contract, an act of infidelity. So is this what middle age looks like, or looks like for us? We look forward to looking forward together and there are few things we look forward to quite as much. Spoken aloud, that doesn't sound great. Have we then consigned our own romance to the past, or delegated all further romancing to the actors we watch on the telly? Not necessarily, I tell myself. Wasting time after all, *pace* Cavell, is what lovers do in the belief that no time spent together could really be wasted. And there's no time wasted like TV time. Physical intimacy aside, could any time spent together *be* more intimate? Yes, that's what I tell myself. But we do, it's true, my husband probably more than me, have reservations about our TV addiction. And I sometimes wonder what we might really be looking for when we're looking forward to the box. Observing that one starts looking for things only once one thinks they're lost, the psychoanalyst Darian Leader has suggested this might tell us something about looking per se. Are we always looking for what we've lost? And if so, when we're distracted by our laptop or phone or TV could that suggest that we've even lost a sense of what we've lost, or what it is we imagine we're looking for? What *are* we seeking when we're staring at our screens? Is it something different when we watch our screens alone as opposed to together?

Tracing the ways we look at each other back to childhood and the looks first exchanged at home, Leader notes that Freud's early work on scopophilia (the pleasure in looking) is linked to a sexual curiosity aroused by the veiling of parts of the body. Viewed thus, looking becomes part of an effort to reveal what's been hidden in order to complete the object – so it's infused as well with an incipient form of distorted memory or nostalgia since its veiling is what also allows the looker to imagine the object had once been satisfyingly whole. In an earlier chapter I associated this veiling of the body, or of sex, with the wedding veil, and with the claim that marriage and clothing appeared at the moment when something – call it paradise – feels lost. I suggested that via this 'civilizing' move, the effort to socialize the sexual simultaneously sexualizes the social. Once veiled, that is, interest gets displaced on to the veil itself, whose mystery is now rendered both physical and metaphysical. For which reason, says Leader, we needn't take the sex organs in this story too literally. After the veil has been added to sex, sex seems to stand for something else – something 'that eludes visualisation.' But what is it that, when we're looking, we can't seem to see? One answer, says Leader, is that we can't see our own act of seeing. Which is true, I'm finding, even intellectually. Few things are more slippery than endeavouring to look at looking. You really feel yourself going round the houses as every look sends you off looking somewhere else. Although it's true in the mirror too, of course, that we can't focus both our eyes on both our eyes, 'we can only imagine the way someone else is looking at us' – as if someone else possessed the power to complete us.

If it's 'someone else looking at us' who we fantasize has such power, then this someone else must also, presumably, possess the power to dismantle us by the same means. Face to face may well be a portal to the ethical relation, as in Levinas's philosophy, but it can equally awaken the anxiety that a more hostile or even aggressive confrontation could be taking shape. Albeit how we feel about being looked at is also likely to have its own specific history; a history that probably relates to the looks we exchanged with the caregiver who first watched over us. While being watched might be viewed by some as an essentially benevolent, beholding act, therefore, it might, by the same token, also recall in us a sense of our underlying powerlessness and utter dependency. There are those for whom it is only ever persecutory to feel oneself the object of another's gaze.

Leader makes a subtle distinction between the act of looking (e.g. at art) and the act of watching (e.g. TV). Specifically, he notes that when we're watching rather than looking, we often correlate our watching with compulsive snacking. We might watch a movie in the cinema while stuffing our mouths with popcorn, for instance. And this, he intimates, could be a sign of what, when we're watching rather than looking, we're unconsciously looking *for*, e.g. a psychical return to the fantasy of the bountiful breast; to that time when we were being fed and looked at simultaneously in what seemed to promise a continuous source of care, pleasure and gratification. To want to watch rather than look thus takes us back to that moment when we had her exactly where we wanted her; or when we perceived in the other's gaze the look that looked after us.

Such a memory, however, were we really to have it, would likely, for Freud, be considered a 'screen memory', as in the kind of memory we invoke to calm ourselves about who we are and what our histories contain in order to block the experiences we cannot bear to recall, and which we cannot visualize either. With screen memories, Freud explained, 'the essential elements of an experience are represented in memory by the inessential elements of the same experience.' So if it's infantile pleasures and gratifications we're seeking when we're watching our TV screens – during our 'adult' time – then what we may simultaneously be seeking to evade with our *watching* could be that which gets more readily aroused by our *looking*. For it's with looking that we can better sense how the object of our gaze has her own appetites, demands and desires; as if she's not merely looking *after* us, but also looking *at* us. As such, it's looking that we may wish to avoid, since 'nothing prepares us for when the object looks back'. If we turn out to be the sort of incurable oglers who prefer to observe others unobserved, therefore, that may be because we've been driven by our desire to regain mastery over what first disturbed or dispossessed us in our earliest experiences of looking.

As a bid for mastery, however, ogling is a pretty limiting one. This is what Wallace intuited when he warned that watching people on TV as a way of resolving anxieties about *being* watched is liable to damage both artists and the art they're capable of producing. For you view a screen, on this reading, precisely in order to be screened from view – and lest negative consequences ensue should your gaze be caught in flagrante. It's not for nothing, for instance, that the most widely recycled internet meme, which gets enlisted to comment on just about anything that hooks the passing attention of a fickle world, is the one where a guy walking along a high street with his girlfriend has just turned his head, his face all wide-eyed and wowed, at the sight of another woman's ass. Meanwhile, his girlfriend is left tugging on his sleeve, reminding him whose ass he's *supposed* to be thinking about. Clearly she's offended. And not only, one assumes, because he forgets her the moment another woman catches his eye, but equally because he doesn't even bother to pretend otherwise – he doesn't keep up the public performance of two people looking forward in the same direction. Spotting that other woman's backside, it's as if he's decided he *can't not see that*. Seeing him spot the other woman, it's as if she's discovered she *can't unsee that*. But while what *he* saw will likely vanish from his mind just as quickly as it flashed into view, what she saw might never leave her. Such is the impact, very often, of glimpsing even a flicker of amorous betrayal. Although the irony, of course, is that a meme inviting us to identify, internet Puritans that we are, with the outraged girlfriend, reveals, by our use of it, who it is we perhaps really are – her faithless and easily distracted lover.

The critical question, however, is what that meme couple will do now that the different directions of their gaze have been witnessed. Are they off to make good on that other woman's ass by seeing it as, for instance, the opportunity for an open-minded and exploratory conversation about what they each want from or feel frustrated about in their own relationship? Or by going home and, say, watching porn together. Though if even TV is becoming an increasingly solitary affair, then porn, I'd guess, is still mostly what people, in or out of couples, watch alone. Might that be what adult entertainment even implies? That the adult is someone looking to escape from the shared world of relationships and responsibilities – the world in which they feel, no less than children feel, that their every move is watched – so as to enter the zone of their special, sacred *me*-time.

Writing in the *New York Times* in the post #metoo heat of public and private arguments about sex, gender, power and abuse, the film critic Wesley Morris reflected on the watching habits of the on-demand populace. He was struck, he said, by 'the two cultural planets these people seemed to be coming from . . . romantic comedy and porn'. Yet despite plenty of research into the warping effects of misogynistic pornography on the development of young boys and girls, there's been little interest in exploring the impact of the romcom as 'an entire genre about people coming together, as opposed to one that prefers your coming alone.' As a jumping-off point into adulthood, therefore, didn't that suggest a more socially binding erotics of entertainment? Albeit the romcom's real value could easily be missed by those tempted to treat the genre derisively as merely chick flicks, thus failing to acknowledge how romantic comedies have historically encouraged diverse audiences to watch them together, 'everybody absorbing images of what it looked like to engage with each other'.

Not that watching things together always means engaging with each other. In lockdown, as Zadie Smith put it in a passage quoted before, married men, confronted with the infinite reality of wives they can no longer even exchange mentally 'for a strange girl walking down the street', are accosted by the awful nearness of having to see each other's faces exclusively. 'The only relief', she continues, 'is two faces facing forward, towards the screen.' Imagine lockdown, in other words, but without Netflix. Problem is, in my household, my husband has very strong views about Netflix. For all we may be a couple of TV addicts, I'm the real addict, which has led to some occasional strife between us. As a film-maker, my husband has very strong views in *general* about what we watch, and where we watch it, and when, and how. His views are so strong on these matters that he even once wrote an opinion piece about them for the *Guardian*. 'If you're anything like me,' it began, 'what shared emotional life you might still have is mostly achieved by mainlining shows on a streaming service with your loved one perched on the sofa nearby. When I say loved one, I mean co-watcher.' Since that loved one/co-watcher is me, I can vouch for the fact that he's not knocking the streaming platforms – because it's true that we depend on them, much as all internetted beings depend on such shows to, in his words, 'dramatize the bits of our relationships we're too exhausted to undergo the drama of ourselves.' But when he then comes out against bingeing such series the way cinemagoers binge popcorn, I can vouch for that too. For my husband – and this has been a point of contention between us – wants us not only to watch things together, he also wants us to *look* at things together. And he wants this, he sometimes tells me, for the sake of our marriage. Although to save our marriage by such a method, he acknowledges, we must also risk it. Contrasting episodic TV, whose pleasure is 'precisely because it confirms our sense of ourselves,' to the languishing art of cinema, aka 'the part of enjoyment that's closer to pain', as a general indicator, he explains, the latter 'is more likely to lead to you and your partner sleeping in separate rooms.' Which, naturally, I can also vouch for.

Although I'm generally conscious of the splitting of our collective vision during the screening itself, normally we only row once it's over. This is seldom an issue when we're making our way through a box set. Then I don't bother much to look at my spouse because I don't doubt what he's thinking. It's when we watch art films that I'm less sure. I notice myself stealing glances in his direction. Why do those glances feel stolen? Why does the dignified practice of watching art cinema draw my attention to what's furtive, transgressive, even guilty in the art of looking? Is it because, as Leader intimates, there's 'a dimension of theft always present in art'? The object accorded the status of 'artwork' appears as if it's been highjacked from common sense reality and resituated – 'the key is that it finds itself in a new place' – such that we not only see the object differently, but recognize too how its removal from where we normally picture it could precipitate the tumbling of all the norms by which we live.

My husband's piece also cites examples of cinema that's like TV and TV that's like cinema and those that are a bit of both. So less than the medium, what's more determining of these classifications is whether what we're watching turns our two into one or turns our one into two. Regarding the latter, for example, I can even think of instances when co-watching films did seem, for a while, to separate us – particularly after watching films that featured or *made* a feature of married couples. Once, for instance, after we watched the Kenneth Lonergan-directed feature *Manchester by the Sea*, I found I'd associated my husband with the figure of the husband in the film; a husband whose party-animal antics mean he winds up burning down the couple's house with their children still inside. When it was over, I was furious. This was precisely the kind of thing that I was always warning my husband could happen when he didn't stress out about everything as much as I did. And while I hadn't on the whole been proven right – I always appeared as the highly strung mum to his fun dad – look where his failure to fuss had led to! You could see it clear as day on the screen! Even if what also appears on the screen, after the couple, in the wake of their tragedy, cannot stay together, is the sense that their loss is so profoundly shared that there really isn't anyone or anything that could now or ever come again between them.

Which is quite the opposite of the plot of another film that caused my husband and I to sleep in separate beds: the Ruben Östlund-directed Swedish feature *Force Majeure*. In this film, a perfect bourgeois family are enjoying a skiing holiday in the Alps when they witness, during a terrace lunch, what looks to be a major avalanche heading their way. Its approach creates chaos as guests everywhere flee for their lives. The mother, Ebba, does all she can to protect her children and calls on her husband, Tomas, for help. But Tomas, acting as if he hasn't heard her, elects instead to save himself, and also, in a split-second decision, his phone, abandoning his family to their fate. In this case, then, the tragedy turns on what doesn't happen. It wasn't a real avalanche. The kids are still alive. The family stay together. But something akin to an avalanche has now come between the married couple. Tomas wants to gaslight Ebba into disbelieving the evidence of her own eyes, but they both know she can never unsee what she saw. And nor, for a while after we watched it, could I stop myself from seeing, whenever I spotted my husband gazing at his phone, what I now perceived as a kind of existential threat to the life of our family.

That said, it's sometimes my husband who gets to identify with the long-suffering wife, as he did after we watched *Revolutionary Road* together – Sam Mendes's exacting adaptation of Richard Yates's novel, in which April's husband Frank has led her to believe he's not your average American Joe on the block. He's different: a bohemian, a romantic, a revolutionary. She's married him accordingly, dreaming they'll leave the suburbs and head out on a grand adventure together. But Frank's vows, it turns out, were hollow ones. He was all talk. And he always cared what the neighbours, aka the normal people, thought. He's Netflix. She's cinema. They each have visions of what could save their marriage, but their visions are diametrically opposed.

Having witnessed the effects of co-watching couple-centred movies before the pandemic laid down the conditions of the new normal, we knew the risks these things could precipitate at home. But during the torpor and dishevelment of the first UK lockdown, when we rarely bothered to get ourselves fully dressed, we still co-watched another novel's adaptation, this time for TV: the adaptation of Sally Rooney's *Normal People*, which also centres on a couple. They are Marianne and Connell, two school then university friends whose maturing sexual bond and intellectual kinship begins in shameful secrecy before slowly winding its way into a social scene where affection demands public display – which is the kind of exposure that Connell in particular can't stand. And which, watching their affections' considerable exposure from our sofa, we weren't sure quite how to take either. Talk about an intimate drama! *Should* we be watching this? It's a question that the adaptation even seems itself to invite. For the profound erotics of this young couple's relationship is what they develop in secrecy, as if, by means of sex and seclusion, they've invented a paradise all their own; an escape route from the social pressures and prying eyes that inhibit them both. As such, the resituating of their intercourse from the relative shelter of the text on to the public panorama of the small screen has an uncanny effect on the viewer. Uncanny because the intercourse we watch Marianne and Connell having a lot of, for all that it may be (clearly is) gorgeous, seems unusually intimate and personal in the context of what normally passes for 'screen sex'. Indeed, its exceptionality from the world of screens might even be construed as the real significance of what's going on between characters whose identities have otherwise been fully interpellated by screens in all aspects of their lives.

Rooney, in fact, has often been held up as the voice of her generation – putatively the first generation to be wholly raised under conditions of the internet. As has, in a more comic mode, the US writer, director and actor Lena Dunham. In the first episode of her groundbreaking HBO series *Girls*, Dunham half-jokingly ventures the claim that she ought to be viewed as the/a voice of her/a generation – a claim seemingly validated by the same episode's depiction of her generation's sexuality as a sexuality unmistakably informed by internet pornography. For unlike Marianne and Connell, the young couple we're viewing in this case are figuring out how to come together with, we can take it as read, reference to the highly performative sadomasochistic exchanges they must have watched others enact on their laptops. Many of the series' first viewers were thus stunned by what was – on a TV show! – being exposed. Much of the initial commentary alighted on Dunham's unclothed body, which wasn't typical of a screen star, and looked more like the body of, well, a normal person – yet the real scandal likely pertained much more to what the show was showing its audiences about contemporary sexual relations. For it's in the depiction of these that the mediation of screens feels, however indirectly, to be directing a couple whose sexual intercourse is otherwise hardly what you'd call cinematic. But hey, at least it's consensual, and at least they both seem to be equally into it; which is why, after some initial discomfort, I found *Girls'* sadomasochistic 'scenes of a sexual nature' quite curious and funny to watch.

That wasn't what I felt when watching the version of sadomasochism that plays out in *Normal People*, however. The latter occurs in the second part of the miniseries when Marianne displays masochistic tendencies in relation to Lukas, the Swedish boyfriend she sees during a break from her on-off relationship with Connell. That these scenes are set in Sweden reminds us too that this is a vision of feminine sexuality which has a longer screen history. For while Rooney's Marianne doesn't immediately call to mind Bergman's Marianne, she does, in subtle ways, and particularly with regard to her submissiveness and her ability to enter the social logic of scenes, recall her small-screen precursor. Normal people, this screen history seems to be telling us, are sadomasochistic people. Which only serves to underscore what a remarkably different sexual scene and dynamic Marianne is getting into with Connell. For with these two, it's as if they've been able to find in sex a means of escaping sexual history. Admittedly, the two actors playing their parts on TV *do* possess screen-star bodies – the sort of bodies so uniformly beautiful that their nakedness may as well *be* a uniform. But laying that to one side, their on-screen sexual intercourse sees them feeling their way towards each other as if they had no inkling of what constituted normal power relations. As such, despite the fact that the sex we see in *Normal People* is more explicit, more sustained, and more intimate than the sex we see in *Girls*, it's also far less aligned with the pornographic. The sex they're making is what you'd call love, in fact, and oh look, they can even come together too (not strictly necessary, but it makes its point). So it isn't hard to understand why that might make for an uncomfortable co-watch. Because the sex looks personal, not social. Because it looks felt, not performed. And because they're often enough looking each other in the eye in a way their hidden co-watchers, gazing upon such intimate scenes from the intimate scene of their own sofas, most likely aren't, and very probably, during such scenes, can't.

What is it that's so discomfiting, not to mention exciting, about watching sex alongside someone else? As a kid, I found few things more shameful than watching TV with my parents of an evening only to be confronted with a sex scene. Was that just the incest taboo making its awkward way into our living room? Perhaps. But why then am I no different now? Even as a grown-up watching TV alongside other grown-ups – or my spouse – I still get embarrassed at the sight of the primary scene on the screen. It's as if, within my adult experience, I remain somehow haunted by an echo of that earlier childhood experience. Unless it's something else that bothers me – such as the sense that the sex that doesn't bring you together can come between you, even if it doesn't force you apart. Seeing sex alongside one's parents might be such a rude awakening, after all, because sex can be a turn-on in more ways than one. Indeed, it's the very thing that's liable to lead the child one day out of their childhood home in search of new objects to love. So sex on-screen can be a jolting intrusion into the official unity of the family home; a reminder that everyone inside it has their own bodies, their own histories, their own feelings, their own desires, their own dreams and fantasies and lives to live. But whereas, for the child confronted with sex on the screen, there might be the arousal of the secret desires that will lead them out and onwards towards their future, for a middle-aged married couple watching young people discovering passion and sexuality for the first time, the desire aroused is more likely to be tinged by nostalgia – a desire that doesn't look forwards, but looks backwards, to the past, and not necessarily to a shared past.

What is this past? It's tempting to envisage it as a time of stolen glances, of first loves unable to take their eyes off each other. Although what that kind of nostalgia invariably forgets is how quickly habits can form. It doesn't take Marianne and Connell too long, for instance, to relieve themselves of the heady drama of so much furtive looking and settle into their own accommodations with each other. In the TV adaptation, this is best symbolized by a scene in which we see them lying in bed together watching something on the laptop. We don't know what they're watching. At this cosier stage of their relationship, you'd have to guess it's the standard TV fare of their milieu of normal people. And it does look nice, this adult scene of domestication, particularly after their earlier struggles in coming together. But for all that a shared screen might symbolize their more comfortable companionship, and for all that co-watching may render them people of the same kind, thus helping to cover over whatever markers have led them, in the past, to feel isolated, abnormal or different, a screen, as we who co-watch their co-watching are well placed to understand, is also a window on to a world whose projections, even in the intimacy of the bedroom, could yet one day come between them.

Still, watching Marianne and Connell thankfully didn't lead my husband and I to sleep in different beds. I think that's because what we were seeing on the screen was a relationship maturing as the characters themselves come of age; a relationship whose oneiric depiction of sexuality and what it takes to come together made its TV adaptation, at least for us, an achingly nostalgic co-watch, but one which was ultimately about love entering history, and so which seemed in some strange way to be in sympathy with our own intimate lives. But then, during three consecutive nights of the second UK lockdown, we decided to co-watch a more radical reflection of a couple ageing: Richard Linklater's romantic trilogy of movies filmed over a twenty-year period – *Before Sunrise, Before Sunset, Before Midnight*. This was a daredevil move on our part. We knew beforehand that these movies would take us on a nostalgia trip since we'd be watching actors – Julie Delpy and Ethan Hawke – who are roughly our own age, and who we'd already watched in those films when each one was first released. So to re-watch them, this time as co-watchers, was to watch a speeded-up ageing process that was no less true of the actors' bodies than our own.

Before Sunrise. Two early twenty-somethings spot each other on a train traversing Europe. They're both good-looking and they're both good *at* looking. Stealing glances her way, he can't quite believe his eyes – she's like a work of art; like Botticelli's *Venus*, only clothed. And she's stealing her own glances back his way too. How to break the ice though? As luck would have it, a middle-aged married couple on the train begin furiously rowing with each other, which public display of non-affection gives him his chance to strike up a conversation. Their conversation is great. He suggests she spends twenty-four hours in Vienna with him before he flies back to America the next morning. The conditions are thus set for the perfect romance. Having stolen glances, they now seem to inhabit a stolen time, a time-limited time during which they've temporarily gotten off the tracks of their normal lives. Together they become sightseers and Vienna becomes their grove: the alternate reality where magic can happen and rules can be broken. And where they can speak of many meandering things as they themselves meander through the streets of an unfamiliar but welcoming city that seems to have been erected as the backdrop of their fall into love. Although their repertoire of falling in love does also include declarations about their scepticism regarding love and romance over the long term. With regard to love they're cynics, they both imply, all the better to challenge each other: make me fall for you in such a way that my view of reality is completely rearranged and I myself am reincarnated. And that's what happens over those twenty-four hours. The film doesn't conclude with marriage, but it does end with vows: they promise to meet each other on the same platform in six months' time.

Before Sunset. Nine years later we meet them in their early thirties. He's a successful writer whose debut novel tells the story of the events we saw during the first film. He's come to Paris with that book, where their lives collide again. They never met as they'd vowed to on that platform because her grandmother's funeral fell on the same day. More's the pity. He's now married and has a child. Yet once again they wander the streets together, his presence turning her into a sightseer in her own city. They still profess cynicism about love and the waning of sexual desire in long-term relationships, and their cynicism feels a little more earned this time round. But nor have they stopped stealing glances, and their conversation still flows, even if they speak around their subjects so as not to risk talk of what they really want to say to each other.

After co-watching the second film, my husband and I felt harrowed. And we were harrowed, I think, by the undeniable fact that you can't get any of that back. Plus, this was lockdown, remember, when things had never looked less pretty at home. When the film concluded, it really seemed as though it might be an actual issue between us that I'm not Julie Delpy circa 2003. And it also felt faintly embarrassing to have to turn to each other's faces and not be graced with *their* faces, or even our own faces from earlier years. We tried to make polite conversation, but the movie was browbeating us. My husband didn't want to watch the final film the following night. He couldn't take much more of this, he said. I just about managed to persuade him. I figured it would do us some good to see them heading off into midlife.

Before Midnight. Now they're married to each other and in their early forties and therefore not *that* much younger than we are. And like us, they also have two young children together. And oh look – they've become that rowing middle-aged couple making a spectacle of themselves in public. Many of their rows are to do with gender roles and expectations: who does the lion's share of the emotional labour, the housework and the childcare, and who gets to be a creator and a dreamer. He, for instance, has now written a bestselling second novel based on the events we saw in the second film. It's hinted that they both may have had affairs. They're on a family holiday with friends in a beautiful villa in Italy, so in an enviable situation, but they don't seem quite so enviable now. They're at their most convincing as a scintillating sexy couple when they appear to be performing their relationship for their friends, as if they've turned their love life into a matter not for amateurs but professionals. Yet soon we see them wandering off alone, doing their habitual walking and talking, although a kind of quickstep seems to have entered into their earlier more leisurely meandering, and their conversation too seems to have grown more effortful. And what they're holding off saying to each other isn't the compliments that are bursting to get out. On the contrary, they're left fishing for those while fighting back their bristling words of criticism. It's quite a depressing picture. Especially because the chief theme of their conversation is still the question of whether or not they believe in love over the long-term. Earlier, when inflamed by their passions, they both denied its possibility. This time, however, they both have to say something to demonstrate that they do believe in love's endurance, but we're not sure whether to believe them, just as they don't seem too sure whether they can believe each other. So does that mean the young lovers were right to profess such cynicism? Is the romantic trilogy ultimately an anti-romantic cycle of films?

What I found most confronting in the film's third reincarnation (the belief or not in reincarnation being one of the recurring topics of the couple's conversations between the films), is the fact that there *is* a reality to be seen on the screen. By which I mean that not everything comes down to performance. These, after all, are the real bodies of actors we've now watched growing together over a twenty-year period. And even though they're film stars and so not exactly normal looking, they still, like normal people, have to deal with the consequences of ageing. Indeed, the ageing process is something she in particular refers to a lot. Would you pick me up on the train if you met me now? she challenges him.

Reminiscent of the scopophilia that begins by being excited by the spectacle of a seductive (adult) body with some parts hidden, works of art, suggests Leader, are as evocative as they are because they seem to be alluding to something beyond their own image. So, what art stops us from seeing is also what art provokes us to want to see. The word 'screen' is therefore a useful one because it sends us in these two opposite directions at once – a screen being both what shows and what conceals. Artworks have such a screening function. An artwork like Botticelli's *Venus*, notes Leader, is sufficiently dazzling 'that one is tempted to forget where she came from: after Saturn castrates Uranus, his mutilated genitals are thrown into the sea, and from this horrific act the goddess of beauty is born.' Our vision of beauty is what we *will* ourselves to see in the very place where we've concealed the history of what we refuse to see.

In Linklater's trilogy, it's only in the third film that the viewer/voyeur gets to see Venus unveiled. Here, finally, twenty years later, is the female form unadorned in the hotel bedroom where the couple have gone to spend one stolen night away from their normal duties as their friends, spotting their need of a break, have offered to look after their children. What's the implication of this unveiling? Is the film suggesting that marriage is the state that denudes you? Although even now, she's not completely undressed. Yet what's left on of her clothing doesn't feel like an erotic choice exactly, but more of a practical one – because time is short, and because their sexual relating has become rather routine, predictable and perfunctory. Indeed, they're halfway into their act of intercourse – an intercourse that gets broken off by the resumption of their quarrelling – when she complains to her husband about just that fact. In this sense, her body, though not yet a complete object for the eye, appears even more naked for its being partly veiled. For it's in her state of semi-undress no less than via her flesh that we can glimpse something of the reality of her life, her responsibilities, her relationships, and her feelings. But what, then, are *we* being invited to see via this spectacle of the real body of a real woman? Or rather, what are we being shown that we can't see here? Is *Before Midnight* disclosing the naked truth about love, marriage, and the course of desire over long-term relationships? Or are we being asked to cast away our ideas about what we'd always assumed we wanted to see and challenged to perceive the hidden history animating our looks and desires all the better to see something else – something that might, like love, cause us to rearrange our view of reality and reinvent ourselves?

For the trilogy's now married couple, too much is riding on a single night alone without their kids in a hotel room. Any married couple could have seen that coming. The love they're about to make has to be destroyed before they can recover it. Old habits – including the old habits of already knowing what turns each other on – must be deposed and recalibrated. It's a dynamic that I can relate to, although I still prefer the erotic disturbance of the first two films (romance, longing, nostalgia) to the final film's disturbing of the erotic with its implicit claims to realism. Not least since what particularly shook me was seeing on the screen the insecurity of a woman getting older – insecurity being the nakedness she tries to hide but can't, as when she claims to be angry about his male entitlement. There's no doubt that hers is a righteous anger and that she has good grounds for feeling it. But what it really looks and sounds like is that she's hurt; and that she's hurt because she suspects her spouse of not loving and desiring her in the way she used to feel loved and desired. She suspects him, that is, of still only wanting Julie Delpy circa 2003. So seeing that, I felt hurt too. My husband, though, appeared relieved after we watched it together. He said the third movie had cured him of the second one and that its realism had helped because he quite liked the marriage it depicted, which reminded him of his own, and reminded him that our relationship's miseries and resentments are just those of normal people, not damning verdicts specifically on our lives. And I was reassured by his reaction, even though it's possible, of course, that he just fed me that line in the way Ethan Hawke, at this stage of their marriage, has to feed similar lines to Julie Delpy.

Revisiting our conversation, however, I now reckon we shouldn't have resigned ourselves so readily to the film's portrait of a realistic marriage. Because why *shouldn't* marriage be entertaining for adults? The idea that the pleasure principle gets hitched, via marriage, to a reality principle that then, increasingly, takes over, and the supposition that this compromise is the best you can expect to get out of a relationship over the long-term, suggests, to me, a rather impoverished and, yes, cynical view of adult life. Might it then be possible to view the trilogy differently, and not as such a completed picture? If, indeed, what sets off the spark of the trilogy's enduring romance is a young couple seeing a middle-aged couple fighting, could we be, as a couple of married co-watchers watching that young couple turned into a version of that middle-aged couple, thereby reincarnated as the young couple on the train ourselves? Albeit a couple informed by the mature experience that tells you the things you can see in other people's relationships are also evidence of the things you can't see, but who, even still, could use the spectacle of another couple's relationship as the stimulus for their own new and inventive conversations about how to imagine love, desire and the future of marriage.

After all, a married couple do not necessarily get old together. A couple's bodies get older, sure, and their looks do too, at least in the eyes of strangers, but the person you see every day doesn't really age as other people do. And even if, from the vantage point of those strangers, your looks *are* getting old, your ways of seeing, to borrow John Berger's term, may yet grow younger, especially if you're in the fortunate position of having more than one pair of eyes through which to see the world. Long-term couple experience doesn't have to make you more cynical. It could equally be the experience that cures you of your youthful cynicism and returns you to your youthful exuberance. Although that will depend on how you look at things, and on what you look at too.

After writing *The Return*, his memoir reaching into the depths of the most painful and unresolved parts of a history marked by profound losses, novelist Hisham Matar felt the need to get away somewhere for a while to try and take his mind off what he'd been writing about and the anxiety that would likely attend the exposure he'd face upon its publication. He chose to go to Siena. He'd long since wanted to visit in person artworks from the Sienese School which he'd loved since his youth, believing these works to be amongst the earliest examples of the kind of art 'whereby the subjective life of the observer is required in order to complete the picture.' The kind of art that welcomes your own perspective. He spent the first days in the city with his wife, the photographer Diana Matar. No sooner had they arrived and begun to wander Siena's meandering streets than they fell into 'one of those rare conversations, one whose beginning and end were not definite.' It was an intimate conversation about art, direction and freedom, which they conducted against the backdrop of a city that seemed to offer itself to them as if it was a realm all their own. But then, when they came upon Siena's central square, the Piazza del Campo, the city's cloistered lanes gave way to something else: 'No matter where we were in the square, we were able to see the entire place. Not one person was hidden . . . It was a space of mutual exposure.' It was a space where one could be looked at, and a space where one could look back. A space where everything was on show, but where one's private tête-à-tête felt all the more protected for that reason. It was the very space, in other words, Matar had come to Siena looking for: the space of art.

As someone whose transition from childhood into adulthood combined with the transition from his homeland of Libya into exile, art has been for Matar a 'mental as well as physical location in my life.' A home away from home. So it is that, sightseeing in Siena with his wife, he was brought back to memories of other sights in other cities they'd visited together. Cities such as Rome, a couple of years earlier, when they'd lain on some grass under high pine absorbing the scenery. At that moment, he recalls, Diana had declared herself in possession of 'such a beautiful perspective' and he'd wished not to be distracted from his view in order to imagine her different one. 'Besides, it was impossible to know hers, to see exactly what she was seeing.' Although just this refusal to shift perspective is also what led him to a chain of association involving other memories, friends, conversations, and sightseeing trips with Diana, including the one they'd recently made to Tripoli together after he'd been away more than three decades. He recalled a conversation he'd had with a friend there about desire and how this had caused him to meditate on his own insatiable desire to see life 'through Diana's eyes'. Hence, at the very moment when he chooses not to see the world through the eyes of his beloved, he discovers that the world through the eyes of his beloved is what he most wants to see. Such is the contrarian logic of desiring, of looking. But was this desire, he wonders, symptomatic of his hunger to achieve a complete conquest over the 'mystery of her consciousness'? Or was it, conversely, 'my desire to be inked by her and therefore momentarily escape the confines of my own existence. Only love and art can do this: only inside a book or in front of a painting can one truly be let into another's perspective. It has always struck me as a paradox how in the solitary arts there is something intimately communal. And it suddenly seemed doubtful to me . . . whether I would have written anything or could ever write anything if I had never loved.'

In the solitary arts there is something intimately communal. This paradoxical thought – that sometimes we come much closer together when we allow our visions to separate, whether physically or mentally – precedes the moment when Diana then leaves him alone for a month in Siena to look at the pictures. In his book about that month, we're invited to look at these pictures through his eyes too. And what we can see is that his beautiful perspective on art and the art of looking is one that doesn't fail to acknowledge what so often underlies the efforts of artists to show us what they do – including the most brutal scenes of history, violence, persecution, grief and loss, but including as well what remains unrepresentable, ungraspable and even unvisualizable within scenes of beauty and love. To which end, the final picture from the Sienese School which he describes in his book isn't actually one he encounters in Siena. He sees it instead on a visit to New York following his return. The evening after he'd arrived in the city, he'd gone to dinner with a couple of successful married friends whose conversation took an unexpected turn when they began to express bitter disappointments in ways suggestive of 'veiled sentiments that seemed to conceal powerful criticisms of one another. Each listed, with the hint of blame and quiet violence that some couples are capable of, all the missed opportunities, the roads not taken, the now uncorrectable regrets.' The next morning he'd visited the Metropolitan Museum of Art to look at *Paradise* by the Sienese painter Giovanni di Paolo. It's a painting imagining a reunion in the hereafter: 'According to Paolo, such a reunion would take place in twos, with each person facing the other, holding hands.' Musing on this vision of paradise as the place where one can look directly and without shame into the eyes of a partner or one's beloved for a long time, or for eternity, he surmises that 'what lies behind our longing and nostalgia' is the need to really be seen by the other. And seen, I think he means, particularly in those secretive, shameful and isolating ways wherein one feels that one's own life and vision do not quite correspond with the prevailing mood or idea of what's normal in people. 'The painting understands this', writes Matar. 'It knows that what we wish for most, even more than paradise, is to be recognized; that regardless of how transformed and transfigured we might be by the passage, something of us might sustain and remain perceptible to those we have spent so long loving.' Yet this recognition, insofar as it takes account of how we're constantly changing, would have to be one whose beginning

and end are indefinite, ergo its need for sharing in a continuous relation. Since such a gift of recognition cannot properly be bestowed
upon us by a pair of eyes we have not spent much time loving, however, and since it cannot properly come to us from an earlier year,
such as, say, the year 2003, then what we desire, even midst the frantic
confusion of our longing and nostalgia, is something that must, necessarily, be situated and resituated before us as that which we have, and
which we always *have* had, to look further and further and further
forwards to.

8

Romantic Comedy

'History repeats itself, first as tragedy, second as farce.'
Karl Marx, *The Eighteenth Brumaire of Louis Bonaparte*

'I wondered why I was so hopelessly bourgeois that I couldn't even have a fantasy about a man without moving on to marriage,' muses Rachel Samstat, the heroine of Nora Ephron's novel *Heartburn*, after she briefly interacts with a policeman who 'wasn't exactly my type', but who she still fancies. And this, in the wake of her own unsuccessful second marriage, is a question she ponders when she's pretty sure that marriage isn't the means to a happy-ever-after, but is more likely a conspiracy *against* her happiness; even if, somewhat masochistically, it turns out that she's both the plotter and the victim of this bourgeois conspiracy. Which sounds mad, but you can see why she might have suffered such self-delusions given that happiness has traditionally been and remains, as the critic Sara Ahmed observes, the most popular cultural conception of 'the best of all possible worlds'. So if you're unhappily married, you might be tempted to imagine that your lack of marital fulfilment is a symptom of your own moral failure. Marriage hasn't let you down; you've let marriage down.

'The demand for happiness,' Ahmed writes also, 'is increasingly articulated as a demand to return to social ideals, as if what explains the crisis of happiness is not the failure of these ideals but our failure to follow them.' Viewed accordingly, we might suppose that Rachel Samstat's instant conversion of her sexual desire into the desire for marriage is a means of diverting her wish for pleasure into the wish instead to signal her virtue – with virtue-signalling here implying someone's acceptance of reality as opposed to any dream of changing it. To desire marriage, in other words, is to prop up the status quo by consenting to one's own subjection. To desire marriage is even to desire the relinquishment of desire altogether. And by the same logic, to desire sex outside of marriage puts sex on the side of radical politics and liberation. That, at any rate, is what Rachel seems to suspect when she lambasts herself for still hankering after the ultimate bourgeois fantasy. Although even *that* criticism was first planted in her head by her cheating husband, who'd been 'haranguing me about my total lack of interest in politics'. Yet when she finally got interested enough to take their son with her to a protest in Atlanta, he used the opportunity to take another woman to bed. 'That would teach me to be political', she concludes with a bitter irony that makes for a very funny line, but a line that also represents what Rachel takes to be a real political lesson: that if she pursues marriage, she gives up on politics, and if she pursues politics, she gives up on marriage. So is there really no way for her to marry the two?

When love first conquered marriage, it was a subversive force, one that defied special interests and entitlements for the sake of its own liberty. Whereas few people are inclined to get dewy-eyed over romance's services to the right side of history these days. It may well have initially rattled the authorities, but the love match soon enough got repossessed by those same authorities who exploited the romantic imagination to suppress the women, in particular, who repeatedly fell for it. Women including this one, I should confess, who still finds herself looking hopefully towards the latest romcom even though I already know what cheap tricks it'll turn on me. For I am not, let's face it, living through a golden age of the genre. The early Hollywood 'remarriage comedies' celebrated by Cavell had at their heart a radical provocation: could marriage make itself viable in the 'new world' and for the 'new woman'? Which was a big ask of a genre committed to a happy-ever-after, and not least because that happiness had to be credible. If comedy was going to appeal to audiences, after all, it needed to make them believe in a world that *could* be altered sufficiently to accommodate the utopia it advertised. And that's not something tragedy has ever had to properly contend with. The lovers in a tragedy say yes to love, but the world in which they figure says no – allowing, in that genre, for a divorce between romance and reality. The yes in a comedy, on the other hand, ultimately conjoins not only the lovers to each other, but love to the world in which that love must then go forth and prosper. Which is precisely what the effective romcom writer understands: that audiences will never fall in love with a love they don't believe could work in reality. So, even though romantic comedy can be fantastical, it also has to be realistic. Indeed, it's comedy's claim to know reality well enough to be able to work with it. If you want your marriage to function in the real world, its genre implies, then you're going to have to conduct yourself as if you were in a comedy. The marriage that works *is* a comedy. But what sort of comedy is romantic comedy?

It isn't, after all, every comedy that says yes to love. For many a comedy, in fact, there's nothing funnier or more absurd than love's proposition. Not that it's always easy to distinguish between varieties of comical experience. The lovers in a romcom or, say, a satire, won't necessarily appear all that different to each other. They might be equally egotistical, foolish, even cruel. Where they do turn out to be different, however, is in the manner of their subsequent framing. For the lovers who wed at the end of a romcom will have first had to confront their own true features in the mirror. And that, claims the satirist, just isn't realistic. Because nobody can really look themselves in the face. Because people can't change. Although in a romcom, the belief is that some people *can*. Or better to say, they can within limits. For however revolutionary the romcom's premise, the genre's bowing to realism requires that it's equally attentive to just how far the world is or isn't liable to bend the rules. The fact that, over the course of its history, cinema's (particularly Hollywood cinema's) wealthy white romantic leads have so often wound up together could even be viewed as symptomatic of what we might call romance's lesser discussed propensity for pragmatism. Which may well, for certain viewers, be reason enough to feel cynical towards the whole business. Because what sort of art compromises with the world on the question of values? Tragedy? No. Satire? No. Romantic comedy? Apparently. Yet that happens to be the one genre I completely refuse to relinquish.

Nor, it seems, am I alone in this attachment. In a wonderfully elegiac essay on the dying art of the romcom, the critic Wesley Morris wonders why he – a black, gay man – should have become increasingly wistful about these 'corny and retrograde' fairy tales for grown-ups. Why would he miss watching predominantly wealthy, overwhelmingly white and unremittingly straight Americans moving mountains for each other? In asking the question, he resembles, in some ways, the protagonist of many a romcom: the hard-nosed and cynical protagonist who's been hurt too many times before to take another risk on romance. For just like that protagonist, what Morris not so secretly wants is to be surprised again by romance's ability to win you over. He wants to fall back in love with love. Albeit not, this time, with the exact same characters. The romcom, should it ever make a comeback, will need to include a more diverse and less heteronormative cast. And it needs this not just to prove itself adept at surfing current tides, but because that was always part of the genre's most radical provocation – to interrogate the world of witnesses and ask if anyone present knows of any reason that this couple should not be joined together?

There *are* theories as to why it is that romance and comedy, who always seemed so perfect for each other, shouldn't be joined together any more. And at least one of these theories is optimistic. Romcoms, it supposes, no longer work precisely because they *have* worked. Reality, on this view, has only gotten better, and that's thanks in part to the genre's own historical success in creating the very culture and future to which it aspired. If lovers were once tasked with overcoming the various obstacles standing in their way, today's attitudes and values (especially in Hollywood) are so liberal that love has no further obstacles left to negotiate. This theory, however, sits rather uncomfortably alongside another theory of the romcom's rise and fall. According to the latter theory, the romcom, for all that it may have encouraged the triumph of liberal values, has cynically failed to represent the true nature of reality and the true cost of those values. Whereas, faced with the conflicts and crises assailing us today, we can't continue to put our faith in a genre that promises us a better future. Can anyone watching history as it's unfolding right now sincerely subscribe to the view that romance has the capacity to be transformational, or that love can overcome the many things that divide us?

The objection here isn't simply that romcoms can't help us out of our historical crisis. What genre of art could convincingly claim to be able to do that? Rather, the objection is a severer one accusing the romcom not only of failing to improve reality, but of actively distorting and concealing reality in order to cynically profit from the hopes and fantasies it's installed in us *about* reality. However much they may have deteriorated, after all, romcoms are still being made and they're still making money. So is it making money that's the real system of appreciation underwriting the romcom's purportedly liberal values?

If the crisis we're currently witnessing in the genre is really the crisis of liberal values, then the romcom is by no means the only liberal institution to find itself thus afflicted. And that, perhaps, isn't so surprising given the shared history, which one can trace back at least as far as the Puritan Revolution as the juncture when, by emphasizing the individual conscience, a supreme value was placed on the idea of consenting adults; as in adults whose consent was not only solicited in marital relations but also with regard to the idea of government by consent. In this cradle of liberal culture, what was officially intended was the collective empowerment of citizens. What it's led to, however, has seemed to many critics to tend in the opposite direction towards the depoliticization of citizens and, as a consequence, their privatization as subjects. And it's as subjects too that they – I should say we – also appear to have become so resigned to what passes for reality that we're even liable to consent to what we don't like or believe in. I don't much like the romcoms I find myself watching, for instance, but that hasn't stopped me paying for them. So, for all that the genre may be broken, if it ain't going for broke then no one who is profiting is going to race to fix it. So it is that each new romcom I turn on delivers me roughly the same plots and the same lines as everyone jumps in and out of roughly the same beds and heads out through roughly the same revolving doors. Taken together as a whole, in fact, romcoms look like they might be a cover story for what I'm really watching – a long-form bedroom farce.

What kind of comedy is farce? In its high-octane recycling of situations and characters, farce is that genre of the comic whose infinite jesting alludes to a world in which nothing really changes. New faces may appear and claim to be different, but it soon enough becomes clear that they're just more of the same – an impression that becomes ever more dizzyingly hysterical as that manic play of substitutions accelerates. In such a world, the sincerest-sounding protestations are the ones that also sound the most apish as nobody is who they say they are, particularly if they're unaware of that fact. Indeed, watching it all happen at breakneck speed and as cycle follows cycle, what you experience with a farce is the sense of a reality in which you can no longer quite credit the idea that there are *any* good faith actors at all.

Published before she wrote the screenplays of some of Hollywood's best-loved romcoms, Ephron's *Heartburn* was a novel based on her own divorce. What was it that induced this shift from divorce plot to marriage plot (and from book to screen)? Was it a cynical move on her part; a move propelled by the commercial instinct that no one likes an unhappy ending? Or was it, rather, a means of resigning herself to the reality that she must be some sort of incurable romantic? Explaining what caused her to marry her second (unfaithful) husband, Rachel Samstat remarks that 'for a long time, I didn't believe him. And then I believed him. I believed in change. I believed in metamorphosis. I believed in redemption. I believed in Mark. My marriage to him was as wilful an act as I have ever committed; I married him against all the evidence. I married him believing that marriage doesn't work, that love dies, that passion fades, and in so doing I became the kind of romantic only a cynic is truly capable of being.' A cynic is a romantic trying not to be. And this, in Rachel's case, is an attempt that fails as she still gets suckered into a cycle of erotic repetition no less compulsive that that of the Don Juans she seems to fall for: 'I go right on. I think to myself: I was wrong about the last one, but I'll try harder to be right about the next one.'

Meanwhile, just as one can keep making the same mistakes in one's choice of lovers, so one can keep making the same mistakes in one's choice of romcoms. This, notwithstanding the evidence that suggests romance has the sort of well-oiled profit principle with which no farce could even dream of competing. And if the book and film industry seem like cynical manipulators of (predominantly women's) love and marriage fantasies, they're hardly the only industries to racketeer. You could probably even *produce* something like a movie at the cost of what it takes to create an average Westerner's dream wedding. Which is just one of the reasons, a more contemporary American writer, Jia Tolentino, claims, that she's decided to reject the whole marital enterprise altogether.

To save love, therefore, you'd be forgiven for assuming that your best bet would be to divorce marriage from the profit principle. Once untied from property, after all, every romance is surely a romance we can allow ourselves the liberty to believe in. To wit, the liberal ethos that sought to free love through the efforts of romantic comedy would now presumably find its own values correlating well with that of an unregulated free market. A market such as we have today, where upward economic mobility has been increasingly attached to the idea of the autonomous individual who no longer feels the same need to maintain links with marriage or the family in order to secure his social status. From the perspective of romance, isn't that a welcome historical development? Well, I suppose that depends on how autonomous this autonomous individual really is. For the transformation of the Puritan Revolution's individual conscience into a market-based consumer – a consumer whose presence across multiple platforms allows for the collection of data on this consumer's preferences, not in order to know them (or their individual conscience) better, but in order to sell to them better – hasn't seemed such great shakes for love, or equality, or personal autonomy.

Moreover, if it's true that *his* social status has been relatively liberated from the package deal that was once called marriage, *her* social status has not shifted quite so dramatically. And even if it had, the fact remains that many people still *do* want love and marriage and children and the comforts of the family, whereas modern dating does not paint a particularly promising picture for those seeking such outcomes. If, for instance, you're a straight woman looking for love online, you may find yourself rather adrift in a free market that affords men very little incentive to settle down. As such, you may find yourself adopting increasingly extreme methods of self-promotion – such as those we can see represented in the dating culture portrayed in Taffy Brodesser-Akner's contemporary comic novel, *Fleishman is in Trouble*.

Surrounded by his fellow well-heeled New Yorkers, Fleishman, the novel's protagonist, is suffering, when we meet him, from the twin torments of narcissistic injury and marital disappointment. His 'trouble' is that his higher-earning wife has just left him alone with the kids. So what's he going to do about it? Men, Marie Stopes explained at the start of the last century, begin their love lives more romantic and more possessed of spiritual hopes for their marriage than most women, which is why 'the man is more quickly blunted, more swiftly rendered cynical, and is readier to look upon happiness as a utopian dream than his mate.' Although in Fleishman's case, the cynic he's quickly become does at least have another utopia on offer, one that he's found online where he's been blowing off steam by addicting himself to dating apps on which his prospective dates are women whose sales pitches include graphic pictures of the most intimate parts of their bodies. In a market that functions on the distinctly unromantic premise that everybody already knows exactly what it is that everybody wants, with nothing left to the imagination, what's left out of these pictures of their personal parts is, invariably, the part that's their person. (It's only at the very end of the novel that we discover what a partial picture we've been given by Fleishman of his wife too.)

It was in America that I discovered – after once taking a cab ride and getting initially perplexed by the proposition I was greeted with at my journey's end – that the phrase 'show me some love' can sometimes be a euphemism for the culture of tipping that's supposed to compensate people for jobs that aren't properly paid. And there's certainly a hint of this convergence of values in a novel like Brodesser-Akner's, in whose depiction of online spaces one can perceive how the free market, rather than separating love and money, may have bound the two up even more tightly together. Indeed, what's brought most readily to mind as one navigates that novel's social reality is Wilde's oft-quoted characterization of the cynic's world view as one wherein you know the cost of everything and the value of nothing. The cynic being the sort of character who's got it all figured out.

There *is*, however, a second part to that famous aphorism – which part, though less well known and less often quoted, is the part that completes the picture. In this latter part, Wilde addresses the sentimentalist, 'who sees an absurd value in everything and doesn't know the market price of any single thing'. The sentimentalist is the sort of character who refuses to get mired in reality. Facts? Figures? What matter these to matters of the heart? One wonders why that bit of the Wildeanism has been so frequently forgotten. Are we perhaps seeking to protect the sentimentalist? And if we are, would that suggest we're less cynical than we believe – or possibly more so? For the sentimentalist, Wilde wrote also, 'is always a cynic at heart'. And it does look that way if you're the type of person prone to knocking yourself out with the kind of romcom that's no less certain than is pornography of exactly what people want. I mean, the script and direction of these movies leave nothing – nothing! – to the imagination. So why do I keep going back for more and more guaranteed disappointments? Have I just failed to acknowledge the reality – that there's no such thing as a romantic comedy?

When Rachel Samstat grieves over her repeated romantic failures and bemoans her inability to give up the quest for love, 'That's not the worst lesson to take through life,' her shrink Vera tells her. Vera's take, as I understand it, is that there might be another way to think about the compulsion to repeat in the expectation of different results than simply as a concession to madness. Although it's not so much Vera's words as her own happily married example that renders Rachel's attempted conversion into cynicism more or less hopeless: ' "Sometimes I wish you and Niccolo would get a divorce," I said to Vera. "Your marriage is very hard on the rest of us." ' The cynic would have to work tirelessly after all, to discredit *everyone* who says they're happy:

' "I actually believed it was possible to have a good marriage," I said.

' "It is possible," said Vera.'

Vera offers no relief! Which is the problem for the one who has it all figured out: other descriptions of reality always *are* possible, and you can only fail to recognize that by wilfully cutting out parts of the picture.

Hence, on the back of Vera's counsel, and notwithstanding my numberless disappointments, I choose not to give up on the romcom either. For why *shouldn't* there be a revival of the only genre whose premise remains the radical one that, by bringing opposites together, something or someone new could eventually emerge? If our view of love is increasingly sentimental, and our version of comedy is increasingly farcical, and if the sentimentalist is deep down a cynic and the cynic is deep down a sentimentalist, then don't we still require an art form whose aim it would be to marry such polarities in the hope of modifying and transforming them both?

It was Karl Marx who claimed that history repeats first as tragedy and a second time as farce. He was musing on the French Republic, which had got itself some pretty poor returns on its substitute Napoleon – the second one looking like a parody of the first. And it was this sign of dissipation of the revolutionary struggle that also saw Marx noticing the pattern whereby those ostensibly fighting on opposing sides of a battle aren't necessarily all that different. Regarding the split within the French bourgeoisie, it was their manner of repeating traits while assuming opposition to each other that could be considered farcical. History, in other words, was turning into the sort of joke that begins by asking what the difference is between things that appear contradictory, only to show, by slip-sliding to its own punchline, that such putative opposites are versions of the same.

For a farce to really be a farce, however, it needs to repeat variations on the same theme not just once but multiple times. Writing in the America of the 1950s, for example, the critic Theodor Adorno, in an essay reflecting on current tensions and trends, noted how two such seemingly opposed ideologies as authoritarianism and liberalism could occasionally appear to collapse into each other and lose all distinction. Adorno was looking back to Marx and Freud to better understand his own age. Today there are just as many historical pundits looking back to Adorno to better understand ours. Thus, threaded throughout the history of repetition, we can see how there's also been a critical history made up of such writers and thinkers who've been wondering how to interrupt these cycles of repetition in the hope of creating another history: history not as farce, but history still tied to comedy – to the kind that promises a happier-ever-after.

Not that that's what it looks as though comedy is up to these days. No less than democracy and romance, comedy is another once liberal institution currently suffering an almighty backlash. Yet not that long ago, liberals still assumed joking was an instrument of justice to be wielded against conservatives, evangelicals, rednecks and other such humourless company. But then dawned the new era – an era perhaps best heralded by the Trump agitator Milo Yiannopoulos, who, on the run-up to the 2016 US elections, appeared across the media to disparage the cosy assumption that 'with right-wing politics, everything must be really sincere. It's not sincere.' It was this, says critic Emily Nussbaum, that put liberals in a state of crisis. A crisis she found best illustrated by the different types of joking that characterized the Obama versus Trump presidencies. For Trump essentially took the presidency by overturning the urbane witticisms that marked Obama's 'sophisticated small-club act' and supplanting his own 'stadium act', full of insults, shouting and rallies comprised largely of rage and laughter. He may not himself have a great sense of humour, but Trump understands perfectly well how to energize large crowds with well-aimed put-downs. Indeed, it's the frenzy and laughter surging through those rallying crowds that can feel so unsettling for the people who, not rallying with them, sense that some sort of powerful pent-up force is being released from its historical repression. If this is politics, in other words, then it's a politics that feels acutely personal, as if it's dragging what isn't supposed to be seen into the light to create a political movement that's libidinal, hysterical, even orgiastic. As a phenomenon, therefore, it recalls Freud's remarkable point about how joking can afford the subject the verbal equivalent of a sexual release. As such, we might guess that the difference between Obama and Trump's styles of politics, as exhibited in the difference between their styles of joking, would be expected to show itself in their different approaches to sex, love and marriage as well.

Obama's marriage, oh my. When he and Michelle first emerged on to the world stage, it was like watching a romcom. Standing on that platform together with their two daughters in hand, they really did seem like the liberal American dream made flesh. And the fact that their family wasn't your standard success story, aka a WASP family, only sold the dream more convincingly. Here was a professional couple who looked good together, who danced good together, who talked good together, and who laughed good together. They even had the good grace to poke gentle fun at each other. But if this vision of the marital ideal tempted the viewer to mistake their personal with the political, then that, it turns out, really *was* a dream. For this wouldn't be the sort of romantic comedy to end with a happily-ever-after. It ended instead with Trump, whose series of spouses, girlfriends, models, escorts and porn stars comes to us from that other American utopia; the one that doesn't feel such a great need to marry pleasure to the spectacle of virtue. Multiple wives do not, needless to say, a romantic comedy make. Trumpian comedy is more in the way of a sex comedy – which some might consider comedy at its rawest. What's comedy, after all, if not that which promises to liberate us from the oppressive norms, values and virtues that comprise civilization and its discontents? And Trump, who is nothing if not a taboo breaker – he's even an incest taboo breaker – works his wonders in precisely this sphere. Funny or not, the resemblance between his method and that of a stand-up comedian isn't hard to spot. Both indulge in obscenity. Both run roughshod over sacred cows. Both excite their fans by saying what you're not supposed to say.

Most sex-based comedy, Freud suggested, belongs to a variety of joking he termed tendentious – i.e. the sort of joking that has to have a victim. And that victim is more often than not a woman, whose humiliation at the point of the punchline affords the joke's teller and the teller's audience their sexually sadistic pleasure. Whatever its claims to liberty, in other words, comedy has also always been the illiberal method of figures seeking to demonstrate who exactly has the power, the pleasure and the freedom to screw with you, and who doesn't. You need only check out, say, Trump's infamous *Access Hollywood* tape, where we see him laugh with another man about how he acts around beautiful women, grabbing 'em by the pussy and so on. And we also hear these two men anatomize the woman about to meet them off the coach, such that the pleasure of the scene is clear – *she* is the humiliated object (the part object) and implicit target of their banter whose pussy has already been metaphorically grabbed. Which was precisely what Trump's opponents *failed* to grab, at first – that his obscene words didn't put people off, they turned people on.

Back in 1951, however, Adorno already *had* grasped this dynamic. Explaining the emergence of populist trends in the US, he noted, via Freud, how the wounded narcissist was someone who would seek, at a time of crisis, to substitute their own ego ideal for that of the group as embodied in the figure of an authoritarian leader – a leader who saves the wounded narcissist by being even more of a narcissist. Such leaders, he observed, 'are generally oral character types, with a com-pulsion to speak incessantly', and their language functions 'in a magical way' to inspire regressions in their listeners. Their popularity, in other words, rests in returning adoring crowds to an infantile experience *of* words by returning them to the sense of a time when terms weren't yet fully fixed, allowing for that playfulness, hilarity and exuberant sense of freedom – except now this freedom has been identified *with* the authoritarian leader as the word-magician with the power to create new definitions according to the free play of his own desires.

So couldn't this insight into the authoritarian's appeal help to shed light on what's happened to the formerly fun-luvin' liberal who now suddenly finds herself positioned as the *real* authoritarian, aka the one who zealously polices jokes, feelings, thoughts and words? If we wish to understand how yesterday's jester became today's Puritan and vice versa, it might serve us well, therefore, to consider whether these sworn foes are more alike than we'd previously assumed. Indeed, if the jester treats all things as a joke and their unsmiling opponent treats all things as serious, don't they *both* thereby demonstrate how everything you say, no matter what you intended by it, can be taken down and used against you?

When does history grasp its own state of emergency? Perhaps when popular consent to the common-sense picture of reality gets withdrawn. And it's at that moment too, perhaps, that a comic sensibility emerges as a way of responding to the sense of crisis aroused by the impression that words are slippery and that nobody is who they say they are. When times grow hysterical, we can guess that people may be finding it hard to keep faith with whatever the prevailing ideology has promised them. So, as their laughter erupts, we can perceive as well how something has appeared to fracture the narrative of history's smooth progress, by signalling, for instance, how unpersuasive is the idea of the individual as someone guided only by their own conscience or conscious intentions. The crisis revealed by comedy is thus a crisis of both epoch *and* ego – which is the point at which the jester can make their grab for power. For whoever abandons the pretence of virtue is surely in a better position to expose others' hypocrisies by revealing how those of us who profess to believe in our own words may really be playing games with words – even if, or especially if, we imagine ourselves sincere.

When history repeats as farce, all appear as jokers. Although what's *really* farcical is that not everyone grasps this fact. The farcical comical experience might therefore be contrasted to the romantic comical experience as the sort of comedy by the end of which nobody can delude themselves that they're the straight guy any more. And if that sounds dispiriting for the couple who are about to utter vows of lifelong commitment, it behoves the marrying couple to recognize that it's this very renunciation of their own straightness that allows them to *make* such big-time promises. Because it's only by virtue of being slippery that the marrying word can work in and with reality. Nobody knows like a spouse, after all, how easily what you say can be taken down and used against you, or how ludicrously ineffectual it is to lay claim to standing on the right side of a shared history.

Could it be, then, that marriage's historical success in proving itself the most reliable delivery system of social reproduction is rooted in the fact that it's also our most untrammelled and intimate site of social *deconstruction*? Is marriage, that's to say, actually a bit of a joke? A joke such as the old joke with the familiar punchline that most newly-weds will have heard told many times before they marry, yet still they begin their marriage with the notion of putting the past behind them, only to find themselves becoming their own mother, their own father, their own child. Hahaha! They thought they were different. They're not as different as they thought. Which joke, in my own home – a home with two actual children in it – does at times resemble a bedroom farce, for there's barely a bed I don't have to visit at some point each night; and nor, in those sleepy small hours, do I always correctly remember the name of whoever it is I'm in bed with. Thus, rather than enacting the social ideal that stabilizes relations by telling everyone who they are and whose bed is theirs to lie in, what the family living under the covers of matrimonial virtue more often finds is that they've entered a much messier, more rivalrous, and taboo-breaking reality.

If that comes as a surprise to the newly-wed, well, surprise is what you can expect to get out of a comedy. The punchline that can still raise a laugh, no matter how many times you've heard the joke before, is the sign that you don't altogether know what you think you do. Besides, given that laughter's a part of ourselves we're unable to fully anticipate or control, we shouldn't assume we've ever entirely grasped what provoked our outburst. When we're in fits it's likely because we don't quite 'get' it. Hence, notwithstanding the baiting cruelty of so much comedy, surprised laughter may be no less related to the unknowing, uncynical or even innocent side to the joke. And it may be too that all jokes, including the more tendentious or sadistic ones, are tied to this wish to recover our innocence – as, indeed, Freud would conclude his book on jokes, somewhat nostalgically, by noting that the infant laughs and delights in the world because they find it fun, and funny, without any need for jokes. But what sort of joke can help us to recapture that mirthfulness of infancy? What form of comical experience might grant us not only the passing pleasure of the present moment, but the hope of future pleasure? And what sort of comedy makes of pleasure not a scarcity or a commodity, but a long-term promise?

The farce concludes that there's no real difference between people who say they're opposed. Farce functions like the romcom, in that sense, by bringing opposites together. Yet bringing opposites together in the case of the romcom doesn't imply, as the farce does, that all are the same. The resolution of the romantic comedy, suggests Cavell, isn't the acknowledgement of identity (whose thudding finality is also the conclusion of tragedy), it's the acknowledgement of desire. So it's desire that's been denied and desire that's been set free; which vision of a 'happy ending' bestows upon even the crassest of romcoms a lingering connection to the genre's more subversive possibilities. Yet as the grounds for a happy-ever-after, desire is hardly the easiest candidate to enter into an alliance with. You can get into bed with desire, sure, but can you really *marry* desire? And can it really be true that the emancipation of desire is how we recover our innocence? Isn't it more often *guilt* that we ascribe to an experience that tends to assert itself compulsively, and not by opposition but by repetition?

In *Heartburn*, Rachel Samstat goes into labour with her second child, a labour seemingly triggered by the discovery of her husband's infidelity. When she's rushed into hospital, her obstetrician, Marvin, performs an emergency Caesarean that leaves both infant and mother in a critical state. 'One of the things I'm proudest of', Ephron writes in her novel's preface, 'is that I managed to convert an event that seemed to me hideously tragic at the time to a comedy.' Later on, however, it's her heroine Samstat's claim that it 'worries me' how, via comedy, she's 'hidden the anger, covered the pain, pretended it wasn't there for the sake of the story'. Her story could only really cover its pain, though, if it had converted itself into the sort of cynical defence that says no to love in the hope of warding off further injury. Whereas Ephron's novel, though it borders on satire, remains committed to something romantic within its comedy. As indeed we perceive when Marvin feels at liberty, in the course of stitching up Rachel's most personal part, to quiz her about something even more personal. 'Do you believe in love?' he asks. Good Lord! What kind of professional entitlement is this? Is her obstetrician some sort of sentimentalist? Or some sort of joker? Comedy, after all, is all about timing, and given the timing of his question, Rachel might well be expected to denounce him for his impertinence and intrusions. But after some soul-searching, she opts instead to answer him positively: "Yes," I said. "I do."

So it is that Rachel Samstat, lying open and torn on the operating table, trusts in the good faith and intentions of her doctor, sufficiently so to repeat in his ears the language of the wedding vow. As reaffirmations of that vow go, hers could hardly be more parodic. Yet it's Ephron's exquisite comic timing to situate romantic comedy's 'yes' to love in just such a moment of obscenity. For it's precisely when she's being interrogated much too personally by a man stationed at the business end of her reproductive labours that Rachel chooses to reclaim the part of herself that's her person by refusing to give up on her own desires. Whether or not romance and marriage are a patriarchal stitch-up, in other words, she still wants to hold them to their words. For the fact remains that Rachel Samstat *does* still desire what she feels has been promised her by these things. And in admitting so she has, if you like, grabbed back her own pussy and reminded us that it's out of the most vulnerable parts of herself that something or someone new might yet get born.

Which isn't to say, as I hope is obvious, that romantic reaffirmation can lift us out of our present state of emergency and lead us towards a happy ending. And I'm certainly making no claim here that we can sidestep the scale or reality of our historical crisis. It *is* to say, however, that a wholesale rejection of that genre and the happiness it promises might be deemed more symptomatic of our crisis than responsive to it – which proposition I find nowhere better encapsulated than via the curious comic addition that has lately extended Marx's line on historical repetitions. It's a line I first encountered in a column about Trump by the *Guardian* journalist Marina Hyde and it goes: 'History repeats itself first as tragedy, then as farce, and finally as porn.' If that's our timeline, it's pretty devastating. The pornographic image, the American Marxist critic Fredric Jameson warns, is what could signal the obliteration of our sense of historical consciousness – not because we've reached the promised land's happy-ever-after, but because we've been reduced to the present tense and cannot think beyond it. This is something pornography shares with a lot of comedy – a reliance on the sort of instantaneous, real-time reactions that do not allow much room for reflection. By alighting on the pornographic image, Jameson recognizes that there's a risk he could sound moralizing, though he has no wish to be. Rather, he writes, 'It is the system that generates a specific temporality and that then expresses that temporality through the cultural forms and symptoms in question. Moralizing is not a very effective way of dealing with those symptoms, nor indeed with the end of temporality itself.' So whether we're consumers of pornography or opposed to it or both isn't his point. The problem with moralizing, he's implying, is that it assumes sides can be taken about something so much larger than issues of what we believe or like or consent to. Indeed, it's the fantasy of what's achieved by side-taking that bolsters the structures and values of a system, culture and historical moment in which we're all implicated no matter which side we've elected to take.

This isn't of course to argue against opposing what ought to be opposed. But it *is* to argue there may be reasons for us to hope something different could yet emerge from our repetitions. And that's something the talented comedian and the talented spouse, as practitioners of the sort of semantics that can expose the weakness lurking within authoritative structures of power, may grasp better than most. For it's by such means that these native wits also reveal how one's own positioning, political or otherwise, always stands to be surprised by the way in which history can turn on a dime to place us at the opposite end of the spectrum to the one where we may have imagined ourselves. Indeed, if a comic's *real* talent is for timing, that's likely because the most talented comedians are always alive to the ways in which times and contexts change things. Hence too why poorly timed jokes not only fall flat, but seem to lack what jokes should surely have: a sense of humour – which sense one might regard as the more civilizing influence of comedy. For however much a stand-up resembles a despot, one could equally observe that a sense of humour resembles a sense of justice. It's this we can sense, for instance, in the pleasure of repartee whose drive for equilibrium comes from the balancing and rebalancing of the scales – a pleasure never better depicted than in the back and forth of witty dialogue between the lovers in Shakespeare's plays or Hollywood's golden age of romantic comedies. For what those couples learn from each other, and what we learn from those couples, as they seek to tame each other into obedience, is that mastery isn't what they're looking for, after all. They're enjoying their quarrelling too much. Or they're enjoying the pleasure of a relationship that, though it might look like a battle for mastery, is really thrilling to the dynamics of equality. Without that equality, each sparring partner comes to realize, their own words would never really feel responded to. Nor could they expect to enjoy the sort of mirthfulness that comes from being open to surprise. As in the sort of mirthfulness which, rather than seeking from the other the assurance that one is right, finds in the other a failsafe way of being proven continuously and enjoyably wrong. Indeed, it's this very inevitability – that your opposite and equal number will always find a way to prove you wrong – that not only renders the present something scintillating, but carries itself over into the promise of the future as well. So if marriage, viewed accordingly, *does* provide a certain vision of social justice, that's not because justice is perceived as a virtue, whether in politics or morality. It's because justice is experienced as a pleasure. And not just any pleasure: pleasure at its purest.

'The best way to get most husbands to do something is to suggest that perhaps they're too old to do it', Anne Bancroft once quipped regarding the long-term success of her marriage to her comedian husband, Mel Brooks. It's a classical sort of punchline – the kind that reverses narrative expectations to induce the laughter that hinges on surprise as words come to mean their own opposites. So in Bancroft's case, a loss is turned into a gain as a wife games her husband by creating out of deterioration an occasion for the kind of pragmatic laugh that sounds cynical but isn't hopeless. For what we hear in this marital jibe isn't only the realism that has set into the romance, it's also the romance that has found its way into realism, i.e. their happiness is that of a couple who have been able to keep each other on their toes by moving, adapting and changing with the times. In crisis, they've found their opportunities.

But what of our own crisis? It hardly looks as though we have such opportunities these days. The unhinged hysteria of our present moment seems to have not mirthfulness but a deep cynicism at its heart – one that attests above all to the hollowness of our contemporary Puritanisms, whether in politics or morality. Still, even if we're no angels when we're laughing, comedy's attention to timing could nevertheless force us back *into* history. For if it's the trick of the despot to turn the slipperiness of comic words against the presumed sincerity of our own, then it's a trick that we can learn. What the slipperiness of words as they function in comedy also means, after all, is that, regardless of how sincerely we may intend our words, if we really *are* sincere, it isn't whether we mean our words, but what we can learn to do with them, that matters. And that, I would hazard, is what the comedian knows, and it's what the spouse knows best of all.

Marriage as Religion

9

My Heart Belongs to Daddy

'Because of our traditions . . . every one of us knows who he is and what God expects him to do.'

Tevye the Dairyman in *Fiddler on the Roof*

The second time someone asked me to marry them was the second time I said yes. And that yes is what led to my becoming a 'One Day Solemnizer'. One Day because my solemnizing had an official date ascribed to it, after which I no longer had the power vested in me to marry two people in my capacity as a wedding officiant. This was in the State of Massachusetts where such things are possible. And since it's true that I'm not otherwise ordained, being granted that temporary licence was a rare and thrilling honour, one that allowed me to enter the marriage ceremony neither as the bride nor the groom, but as the binding power of marriage itself. Still, notwithstanding its awesome responsibility, this was not a proposal I found hard to accept. I saw no reason why these two – a heavenly match – should not be joined in holy matrimony. And I quite relished the idea of standing as a woman in the shoes of such a quintessentially patri-archal form of authority. Finally, I was to be the daddy! Well, sorta. The power to marry this particular couple was vested in *me* rather than, say, a priest, only because as one came from an Episcopalian background and one from a Jewish background, theirs was an inter-faith wedding. Or more accurately, they're a couple who lead primarily secular lives and who are both politically progressive with serious misgivings about the institution's more orthodox traditions. Though I think they might still have chosen some version of a religious ceremony had they been born into the same faith. Not because they'd subscribe to that faith's dogma necessarily. Rather because, in choosing to marry themselves into marriage, what was required, alongside a mood that was celebratory, was a sense no less of the occasion's solemnity – as indeed the nomenclature of 'One Day Solemnizer' likewise recognizes. And on that one day, solemnizing did seem the appropriate word. What the three of us were doing as we stood before the wedding guests certainly felt religious, even without officially being religious.

The Bind

In *The New Science* (1725) Giambattista Vico posits that the origin of the word 'religion' comes from the Latin *religare*, to bind. Therefore, as part of his broader effort to renew the fortunes of faith against certain trends in modern philosophy, Vico turned to the bonds of marriage as the cornerstone of a civilization founded upon religion. Marriage served this purpose, he said, because the religion that binds man to God finds in marriage a means of binding humans to each other in the name of God. As such, marriage also becomes the manifestation of an ethical relation (one that Vico called 'piety') because it teaches virtues such as modesty and humility, and because it imparts the all-important lesson that humans depend on each other and require an institution such as marriage to establish and help support the vital links between them.

Binds, however, also have other, less benevolent connotations. Hence for various feminist thinkers as well as thinkers of liberty such as John Stuart Mill, binds are precisely the problem with marriage as the foremost institution of woman's historical subjugation. And it remains the case even today, particularly amongst orthodox religious communities, that marriage has proven very hard indeed to unbind from. In ultra-Orthodox Judaism, for example, where the issue's become a hot potato in recent years, the wife who won't be freed from her vows by a husband she wishes to divorce is described as an *agunah* – a chained woman.

It's likely that Vico made his claim that religion is what bestows upon marriage its binding power at a time when he was hoping marriage might in fact do the reverse by helping to shore up a religion that was becoming increasingly embattled. In the bourgeois society emerging in Europe from that period, suggests Tony Tanner, 'one might almost say that marriage sanctioned religion'. Though it was during the late-eighteenth and early-nineteenth centuries that the marital relationship became the dominant paradigm in the European imagination for an understanding of what the good life is, as one finds copiously represented in the literature it inspired. Yet it was in the narrative arts too that the marriage plot appeared a somewhat vexed one. In the novel of adultery, for instance, marriage is an institution under strain – and not necessarily from divorce. Divorce signals that not marriage as such, but this particular marriage, has been found wanting. Adultery, on the other hand, doesn't end a marriage only to begin another. The adulteress is someone who seeks signs of life on the other side of the wedlocked world in which she's forced to live. Although in the case of literature's most famously faithless wife, Madame Bovary, marriage would also find a rather bleak means of reinforcement. It's Emma Bovary's experience of adultery that, once the initial thrill of transgression has passed, her lover proves to be just as banal as her husband, offering her little more than a repetition of the suffocating dullness she's encountered in marriage. What the modern history of the novel thus seemed to show was that, to coin a phrase, *there is nothing outside marriage*. Perhaps that's what marriage as the institution that binds ultimately means.

Marriage's binding power is nonetheless easier to discern in a religiously ordained society. A recent co-authored sociological study of contemporary marriages amongst Haredi Jews, for example, was undertaken in part because the post-war renaissance of ultra-Orthodox Judaism defies popular assumptions by occurring 'against the trend of secularization, against the trend towards small families, against the trend towards a culture in which social status is determined over-whelmingly by economic means, against racial mixing, against the permissive society, against, against, against . . .' Not far off Vico's ideas about what marriage could be co-opted for, the Haredi marriage system in its contemporary form, David Lehmann and Batia Siebzeh-ner suggest, has been the cornerstone of religious revival and cultural renewal. Indeed, *all* the institutional structures of ultra-Orthodoxy, including economic, educational, family, workplace and charitable structures, are dependent on the social capital built up by means of marriage alone.

If this, a shared world view, is what's usually taken to be the basis of a good match in religious culture, romantic ideals of matchmaking have often been inspired by the contrary world view: that of opposites attracting. Although, to be fair, as an explicitly conjugating institution this more radical possibility is something that even the traditional concept of marriage might be said to insinuate. To marry can always mean to marry those who contradict. And the contradictions wedded in marriage can include not only two people with different outlooks, but different outlooks about what marriage stands for as well. Mar-riage could even be the place where we've *stored* our cultural impasses, anachronisms and contradictions. Secular marriage, for instance, is where modern people with modern ideas have tended to sublimate beliefs and impulses that were once called religious. That, certainly, is what Jacques Derrida was implying when he noted how, despite the professed *laïcité* of the French Republic, its laws regarding mar-riage are altogether rooted in the religious ideology which the State publicly disavows. Marriage is where monotheism gets transformed into monogamy, where faith becomes fidelity, where oaths become vows, and where the afterlife becomes the happy-ever-after. All of which places on marriage an awful lot of pressure when it comes to reconciling humanity to the mystery and meaning of its own existence.

It's perhaps for this reason that marriage is a somewhat ambivalent object to situate historically. For though marriage undoubtedly belongs to a history whose changing currents it has always been required to adapt to in order to stay in fashion, it lends itself no less to a counter-history – or to the type of history that Vico identified as not linear but cyclical, such that ideas and beliefs you've been tempted to assume past or surpassed are more liable, using marriage as their cover, to simply be biding their time whilst awaiting the right moment to make their comeback. Does that sound far-fetched? If so, it's worth bearing in mind that it's this more cyclical time signature that tends to operate *inside* marriage as well. While many a married couple can happily tell you how they have coffee each morning or pancakes on the weekend *religiously*, for instance, they're usually much harder pushed to think of what things they do together *progressively*.

Tradition!

In 'Matchmaker', one of the many memorable songs to be heard in the mythical shtetl Anatevka, the setting of the musical movie adaptation *Fiddler on the Roof*. We find three young sisters mockingly imagining themselves beseeching their family's matchmaker to strike them the kind of matches they would choose for themselves. Indeed, Tzeitel, Hodel and Chava are all girls with romance in their hearts and modernity in their minds. But they are not unrealistic either. They understand only too well that what their busybody matchmaker has to offer may be grim but undeniable.

Meanwhile, offset against the memorable chorus of that song, is the chorus from 'Do you love me?' In this case, the song is the duet of the girls' bewildered parents who, finding themselves confronted with the younger generation's romantic aspirations, begin to ponder whether love has any part to play in their own relations. Theirs is thus a song of love as an unexpected flower that blossoms over the long-term as something all but unnoticed within an arranged marriage. And it's also the song that relationship therapist Esther Perel cites as a source of forgotten wisdom about the practical rather than spiritual reality of love (the wife's lyrics include mention of the twenty-five years she's spent doing the laundry, the cooking, the milking, the cleaning, etc.) in a modern era where unreasonable emphasis has been placed on the shoulders of lovers to expect from each other what an entire community once used to provide.

But even as it recalls the practice and virtue of traditional marriage, *Fiddler on the Roof* is very much a romantic film; a film that's nostalgic and misty-eyed about the intimate ties that once bound the people who people its depiction of a lost world. Indeed, notwithstanding that its world was replete with misery, poverty, conflicts and pogroms, these harsh realities are by no means immune from the movie's romanticizing, no more than is the equally harsh patriarchal and religious law whose values the film criticizes, but also remembers fondly. For *Fiddler*, let's face it, is out-and-out sentimental. And it's a film that leads us, singing and weeping as we go, into that realm of art that some would call kitsch – i.e. the sort of art whose images console us to the extent that we resist any invitation to reinterpret or reimagine them. In our nostalgia for a lost world, we invent a world we refuse to lose. It's one of the reasons why our fantasies, of the past especially, can often render us fanatics.

And it's true, of course, that those who romanticize religion, or marriage as a related institution, *do* sometimes give the impression that these things – religion and marriage – are sources of illiberalism and intolerance. Even though what we're more likely encountering when we come across fanatical attachments is the intolerance that arises when the sense we have of ourselves or our histories seems to hang in the balance, as if they've been marked for obliteration. That, at least, has been my experience. I know I can get increasingly stringent and stressful when I can't figure out how to pass on to my children what my parents passed on to me. Particularly with regard to religion, which, in the context of my mostly secular lifestyle, takes on an increasingly alien or unassimilated character that doesn't blend in too easily with my regular timetable. So even though religion is something I value, I can never quite seem to communicate its value to my children in the spirit I'd like. Perhaps because I don't myself entirely understand what it means to me, or why it means so much. Though it must, I'd guess, contain some residue of what love must mean to me. Religion is something that links me to my parents, and so to my past via theirs. Although this past isn't straightforwardly the historical past. It comes closer to the cyclical time of repetition and regeneration. And so it's with recourse to that cyclical time that I try to squeeze into my family's busy schedule some basic recognition of the religious calendar of rituals and festivals. But I do notice – we *all* notice – how as I light my candles and utter my blessings of peace, I can get pretty pursed-lipped, humourless and bordering on belligerent, as if I'm saying to my children, with my body if not my words: just do this, don't question it, it isn't open to argument.

So I know from the inside something of the anxiety and confusion that can pervade traditional structures, particularly if you feel you've been tasked with upholding and passing on the sacred traditions. And I know too how easy it is to appear a hypocrite by insisting on the goodness of what has rendered one suddenly monstrous. As such, I'm not surprised that some pretty wild acting out has often occurred within families, communities and nations when it comes to reckoning with marriage's cultural responsibility for passing down the generations those things we always fear losing – life, history, love.

We begin our love lives in our infancy by attaching ourselves to those who appear crucial to our survival. And if you're unlucky with your primary caregivers, that can mean you learn early on to love your own abusers – from which source some quite damaging attachments and patterns of behaviour might also, in the name of love, subsequently result. But even if you're fortunate to have the ideal carers, the fact remains that every life begins in an unequal relation when it comes to power and autonomy, meaning existential questions are always liable to be freighted with the feeling that we must cling on to whatever or whomever we can. So when survival – or the survival of what may appear necessary to one's survival – seems at stake, people often do behave quite badly, or madly. Which, I'd suggest, is the context in which to watch a musical set in a shtetl on the verge of dissolution. A musical that stages a lost world and the historical forces that destroyed it – forces that come most decisively from the outside, but which are also a consequence of modernity's internal contradictions; contradictions that the film portrays in its intergenerational conflicts over matchmaking. The idea of tradition as the inherited vessel for the survival of life forms is indeed both song and refrain in *Fiddler*. 'Tradition!' Tevye the Dairyman thunders at his daughters, his neighbours, and even God. Although it's a film in which we're also invited to detect the weakness animating his assertion of tradition's absolute authority, which is a proclamation he only ever makes when his own authority has already been undermined.

One unusual aspect of *Fiddler*, in fact, is that its traditional marriage plot structure is told as much from the father's perspective as from his daughters'. So alongside its depiction of young women on the precipice of modernity, it also offers a vision of patriarchy personified in the charismatic father facing these distinctly modern challenges. Via the figure of Tevye we see how historical crisis, religious crisis and social crisis can all be enfolded into the theme of marriage in crisis; a crisis signified by his free-thinking daughters following their own desires by coming up with their own love matches in defiance of their elders' wishes and instructions. Which may help to explain why, despite its seemingly narrow concern with an old-world Jewish shtetl, the musical's relatable staging of how old ideas got toppled by new ones has been extremely popular with a wide range of audiences.

When I first encountered Tevye on screen in my childhood, he was my archetype of the Jewish patriarch – bearded, biblical, old (very), and the source of law, wisdom, good humour and fatherliness. But above all what he stood for was 'Tradition!' A refrain I've never forgotten. Yet it was only relatively recently that I watched the movie again and discovered that the bearded patriarch is, at the point when Chaim Topol starred as Tevye in the film, a good few years younger than I am now. (Topol is, anyway. I'm not sure whether Tevye is meant to be younger than me – it would be nice to imagine he isn't.) And since time has moved on not just personally but historically, I can also see today, as I must have seen less clearly as a kid, that there are a great many problems with Tevye's 'authority'. Interestingly, though, I find him no less lovable – it's possible I find him more so. Could I even be, like the ever-ready adulteress, now slightly in love with the milkman? If so, then what business has the erotic showing up here? Is *this* how I hold fast to my primary attachments, by eroticizing whenever I've gathered some critical reasons to *unbind* myself from them? Am I, that is, always *bound* to forgive the patriarch, as if I'm no more capable than are Tevye's daughters of forging my own path without seeking some sign of the father's love, approval and freely bestowed blessing?

If that's the case, I'm hardly alone. *Fiddler* is as popular as it is thanks in large part to the seductive power of Tevye, who appeals to us precisely because he *literally* appeals to us: he's the film's narrator and guide who charismatically breaks the fourth wall to address his audience personally, eye to eye. By turning to the camera and trusting us as his confidants, he brings us directly into the soul of patriarchy under strain. But who then does Tevye the Dairyman imagine *we* are? In *Fiddler* we're watching what purports to be the old world – the past – addressing the future. Indeed, Tevye's direct emotional appeal is asking us to remember the old world, the old religion and traditions, with a memory that thinks back, as the Jewish patriarchs do, through the fathers – through the God of Abraham, Isaac and Jacob.

Implicitly, therefore, as citizens of that future, we're here to provide this old-world patriarch with the assurance that there *has* been such a memory and so there *will* be such a survival, no matter what threatens him in his present. What we represent, in other words, is the realm of the happy-ever-after.

And yet ours is a strange kind of assurance. Because it's true that we know far better than Tevye how cataclysmic the historical dangers he faces will turn out to be – and not only those signified by his wayward daughters caught up in such modern enthusiasms as romantic love, incipient capitalism, revolutionary politics, and exogamy (marrying outside the tribe), but with regard to the nationalistic fascism sweeping across Russia and destroying the Ukrainian shtetl of Anatevka by the end. So who are we really seeking to convince with our implicit promise of survival and happy endings – Tevye's old world or our newer one? Given which of us is the fictional character, you'd think that a question hardly in need of asking. But the real question, I guess, is whether we are ourselves more fictional than we might have imagined. When reflecting on Tzeitel, his eldest, for example, who has rejected his choice of the rich widowed butcher Lazar Wolf and chosen instead her own husband in the person of her childhood friend, the poor tailor Motel, Tevye says of the young couple that they're 'too happy to know how miserable they are'. It's precisely the sort of nostalgic line that informs more on our reality than it does on Tzeitel's. But still, we'd need to reverse its terms to identify a modern, and probably secular and upwardly mobile, audience who must be too miserable to know how happy they are. *So* miserable, in fact, that they dream of a past that's all simplicity: as in the simple faith of a traditional religious community that yet somehow upholds the kind of liberal values such as romantic love that can, in our dreams, make even extreme poverty a charm to live through. And indeed since, in Hollywood, a happy ending is one in which romantic love also happens to yield abundant riches, by turning Cinderellas into princesses, so it is with *Fiddler* – a film that *formally* ends with uprooting and dispersion, but once we learn that Tevye's family are destined for America, we can breathe a sigh of relief, for what's implicitly endorsed by this move is Tzeitel's own decision to choose her husband for love and friendship rather than wealth and security. After all, not only do the ill winds blowing through the shtetl show no more compassion for the rich butcher than they do for the poor tailor, but the poor tailor turns out to be something of an entrepreneur. He's actually a modern man who gets to *own* the means of production in the form of the shtetl's first sewing machine, and so presumably, within a generation or two, he may get to own the means of movie production as well.

Unsurprisingly, then, the values promoted by the film are implicitly modern ones: Romantic love. Women's liberation. Personal autonomy. Youth revolution. Political rebellion. Innovation. America as the land of the free. And yet these values are all confusingly wrapped up in an immersive nostalgia for everything that seems to contradict them: Patriarchal authority. Religious orthodoxy. Arranged marriage. Defined gender roles. Communitarianism. Tradition! As if the real conceit of this Hollywood fairy tale is to suggest that such outrageously contradictory impulses and world views *could* find a way of being happily married together – which, if you find yourself crying, may well be the happy ending you're inclined to want as well.

As a child, of course, I couldn't have grasped any of this. I couldn't have guessed that when I indulge in sentiment and watch the sort of screen memories we see in a film like *Fiddler*, it has as much to do with cultural wishes about who we are on the basis of who we think we were as it does with any approximation of reality. Nor could I have appreciated how the musical genre works to lay down one's future memory and nostalgia – because the stirring strains of melodies we first hear in our childhoods can feel so familiar in later life that it's as if they exist to accompany the beat of one's own heart. But now I'm older and more minded of these things, I'm not sure that my efforts at critical distancing have done much to help with this either. If you're already singing along, and if you're already weeping, your critique is hardly cutting the mustard. Which must be how our emotional lives sometimes operate, by transforming the character of the things that we can't bear to look squarely in the eye – especially if we think we're having an eye-to-eye conversation with history itself – through such processes as sentimentalization, or eroticization. Is *this*, then, how we convince ourselves that we know who we are and what to do? And is this how we tell ourselves that we've received our history as it was bequeathed us . . . by imagining there's been no disjuncture, that the past *has* been passed on via a watertight tradition without any breaks or losses – at least none that can't be repaired with a little love?

To give *Fiddler* its due, love, in this most sentimental of movies, doesn't quite manage to repair everything. There *are* certain lines that Tevye isn't prepared to move with the times to cross. While he can ultimately reconcile himself to his first daughter's choice of a poor tailor, and his second daughter's choice of a Bolshevik revolutionary, because they're both kind-hearted Jewish boys, when his third daughter Chava defies his wishes by marrying a Christian, who is no less kind-hearted but not a Jewish boy, this is a match Tevye says he won't and can't accept, and Chava is the only daughter he fails to readmit into the family circle. Which is why the American feminist writer Elaine Showalter, a self-declared *Fiddler* aficionado, believes Chava should be the real protagonist. Nor is it surprising that she should feel so strongly on the matter, since Showalter herself never saw her father again after she married someone outside the Jewish faith. However, unlike Chava, Showalter didn't come from a religious family. Her family was a liberal and secular one; and yet here was a measure of extraordinary intolerance arising in their midst in the name of marriage and religion.

Casting out members of the family in order to 'save' the family, even when it's done by non-believers, is, particularly amongst groups who've been existentially threatened, a lot less unusual than one might assume. It's frequently the situation that the reaction of the liberal patriarch can be even more fundamentalist than that of his orthodox counterpart. We've seen the same thing happen in the outer reaches of my own family, for instance, where in at least one case I can think of it's been the non-practising Jews who've shown less tolerance of 'marrying out' than have the traditionalists. Perhaps because the liberal father, if he practises no religion, has nothing but marriage to cling to in order to retain his connection to the old world, and thus to the sense of his own historical survival. Hence although, in the liberal mythos of the movie version, we do at the end hear the orthodox Tevye muttering a blessing under his breath upon Chava and her Christian husband, before he died Showalter heard nothing of the sort from her real-life secular and liberal dad.

Kneel!

In Phoebe Waller-Bridge's contemporary small-screen creation *Fleabag*, the eponymous protagonist is a young woman played by Waller-Bridge who, like Tevye, seductively breaks the fourth wall to share her struggles with us, the programme's viewers. By thus usurping the position of the patriarch, it may well appear, therefore, that the future to which Tevye appealed and out of which Fleabag speaks, does, from the perspective of women's liberation, look as if it's turned out pretty well. Certainly there's no man around with the authority to deny Fleabag her rightful pursuit of her own life, liberty and happiness. Nor does she have any issue pursuing sex. One ostensible sign of her liberation, in fact, is that she feels as free as any man to do or say sexual things, even obscene things. Although, if her freedom *does* evoke the gleaming future envisaged by Tevye's daughters, Fleabag's example suggests that the happy-ever-after of woman's emancipation might be more elusive and more illusory than it looks. For unbound from patriarchal authority she may be, but she's also suffering from her own profoundly contemporary form of bondage: addiction, and particularly sex addiction. Yes, Fleabag, being no prude, chases sex compulsively. Yet one rarely gets the impression that Fleabag enjoys the sex she pursues all that much. Moreover, why does she allow herself to be called Fleabag? If hers is a story of sex unshackled from religion, from chivalry, from morality, and from sentimentalism – could her real issue be not so much with sex as with love? Indeed, could all the sex that Fleabag's constantly having even be an arena of self-hatred?

You could say Fleabag resembles the subject Barthes had in mind when he delineated a new logic of obscenity: 'Discredited by modern opinion, love's sentimentality must be assumed by the amorous subject as a powerful transgression which leaves him alone and exposed; by a reversal of values, then, it is this sentimentality which today constitutes love's obscenity.' In this context, Fleabag *can* still be considered something of a prude – for she simply will not *go there*. Until the second series, that is, when her possible redemption by love enters the picture. And it's an old-fashioned redemption on offer, of a kind much appreciated by those of us who are addicted not to sex comedy but to romantic comedy. For finally we can see that Fleabag *is* capable of falling in love – though with a Catholic priest. The fact that it's a man of the cloth gives the theme of redemption an antiquated but contemporary twist. On the one hand, if anyone can save Fleabag from herself, surely *he* can. But on the other hand, this isn't your average pastor. His language, for instance, is as strewn with expletive and obscenity as Fleabag's own, and that's what initially seems to capture her attention – his scurrilous indecency making him the perfect match. Furthermore, since he's already married to God, and so he's sworn an oath of celibacy, what we have before us is the type of romantic lead who is all the more intoxicating for insinuating a love that's illicit – and illicit in a way that Fleabag's multiple sexual partners seem, in her purview, not to be. However, it isn't just that the priest, qua priest, is unavailable and therefore the ideal love object for a genre which always needs an obstacle to work with. There's also another slight disturbance regarding this choice of lover. And that's because what seems to really be animating Fleabag's attraction to her priest isn't so much his indulgence of verbal obscenity, it's the more unnerving fact that she gets to call him, excitedly because it's a turn-on, 'Father'. Yikes. What she's fallen for is very explicitly a patriarchal figure – a figure prohibited to her not just by religion, and not just by the incest taboo, but by feminism too.

Finally, towards the end of the second series, we get the scene we've been waiting for. Fleabag falls into the arms of her priest in an act rendered all the more sacrilegious because she tumbles into those arms from her position in a church confession booth. Yet as captivating as it is to watch a sexy couple getting it together, this moment of their inevitable clinch is also a moment of profound misrecognition. Indeed, just beforehand, we see Fleabag addressing the priest from inside the confession booth, a wall of darkness still dividing them; however, when she calls him 'Father', he encourages her instead to use his personal name, Neil. Fleabag, though, mistakes his meaning and interprets his invitation as a command: 'Kneel!' And with that, she gets down willingly upon her knees. Well, it was an easy mistake to make when you consider that what she has just been confessing is that she cannot bear her freedom; and that she wants to be told, as the wife in the traditional wedding ceremony was told, to 'obey'. So 'Kneel' sounds like an answer to her prayers – perhaps even more than the relationship-altering 'Neil' she'd thought, until this point, she *had* been praying for. Is this then what, for the emancipated woman, turns out to be her greatest sin? That she despises her freedom and misses her bondage and would like someone – a man, a father – to tell her exactly what she can and can't do; all so that she doesn't have to be the one tying herself up in knots. Tevye tells us that tradition is a way of knowing who one is and what's expected. And Fleabag, from her perch in the far-flung future, seems to get what's so appealing about that, possibly even more than his own daughters. So while we've come a long way, with *Fleabag*, from the traditional heroine of the marriage plot, her heart, it would seem, belongs no less to Daddy.

As such, *Fleabag*'s a TV series that presents us with an uncomfortable image of where woman is envisaged to still be at her most comfortable: abjectly on her knees, begging to be dominated. A perspective rendered all the more uncomfortable on account of the series's popularity. For Father/Neil no sooner appeared as Fleabag's love interest than he was quickly identified by the show's legions of online fans as the 'hot priest', a phrase that seems to take perverse pleasure in the maddening contradictions that can so often put one's desires at odds with one's professed morality, or taste, or politics. *There's what I think, and there's what I feel. There's who I like, and there's who I love.* And in the case of this particular object of desire – a sworn celibate who exudes maximal sexual appeal; a man who represents divine love but who inflames ardour of the worldliest kind – one is of course returned as well to the psychoanalytic conception of the sort of desire that involves a structure of fantasy that's essentially nostalgic; the object evoking the dream of a past that was all fulfilment and thus seeming to promise as well a future that could recover such bliss. On which basis we might well ask if there's *any* desire that could reasonably lay claim to being wholly progressive?

You can't marry your own father and you can't marry a Catholic priest. More's the pity. But a romcom must end with a wedding, and in the case of Fleabag it's the wedding of her real father, who marries her rivalrous and self-centred stepmother. The hot priest is the wedding officiant, which is the capacity in which he renews his own vows of fidelity to God, while Fleabag, better able now to correctly interpret his meaning, can understand the coded message of her own rejection. Indeed, what his figure seems finally to represent isn't his own marriageability, but marriage's ability itself – marriage, that is, as the obscure object of a desire whose best representative would be a hot priest (I've been there). So, if marriage is a hot priest of an institution, maybe that's why even those people who don't approve of it so often find themselves doing it. It's as if there lies abroad some vague inkling that it's marriage's singular ability to conjugate those things within us that cannot otherwise abide in a world with no patience for contradictions, such as love and hate, morality and obscenity, the orthodox and the liberal, the secular and the religious. Indeed, insofar as it can even wed the tradition that tells us who we are with the desire that unravels who we are, marriage, one could go so far as to say, makes the wedding of our conflicts and contradictions its most vital and pressing point.

Meanwhile, marriage has likewise functioned to conjugate the disparate social elements that could risk fragmentation into fractiousness and atomism without the use of its social glue. At the priest-ordained wedding at the end of *Fleabag*, for instance, the coupling that transpires for Fleabag is the one that, after a long quarrel, reunites her with her sister. And it's in this scene of sisterly solidarity that we can also glimpse how her other internalized fantasy structures, including her patriarchal fantasy, might finally begin to unbind her. Though that's made clearest when it's Fleabag herself, the wayward daughter, who props up her own father, a weak doddering patriarch, as he heads down the aisle to marry a dominatrix.

But who does Fleabag imagine *we* are when she breaks the fourth wall to look us in the eye? With Tevye, we're envisaged in the future. With Fleabag, we belong to her past. When she addresses us, we stand in lieu of her dead mother and her dead best girlfriend. What we're standing in for, then, is lost women, and thus the chain of *women*'s knowledge, experience and traditions that time and history will erase from memory if she doesn't keep them strongly in mind; which erasure would certainly, it's implied, threaten Fleabag's ability to make sense of her present or forge her own tomorrow. For we must think back through our mothers if we are women, said

Virginia Woolf – and that's no easy feat because our mothers mostly didn't write the history books.

Inextricable

After her father died, Showalter did eventually get back in touch with her mother and sister. It was the poet Adrienne Rich who told her it was her feminist duty to do so. Tevye's third daughter, affirms Showalter, is the one who, once the patriarch has deserted the scene, must take on the future by reconstructing what family means and who can be included within it. Which is something Showalter was finally able to do in confidence, from within a happy marriage of her own choosing and making.

Yet for Rich herself, the need for reconciliation also extended to her own bullying and intolerant father, even after he'd died. This is what we find at stake in Rich's long poem 'Sources', in which she returns to the sources of her own past by returning to the scenes of her early childhood, with all its primary attachments and ill-fitting identities:

> There is a *whom*, a *where*
> that is not chosen   that is given   and sometimes falsely given
>
> in the beginning we grasp whatever we can
> to survive

And it's a poem that also addresses her father directly:

> For years I struggled with you: your categories, your theories, your
> will, the cruelty which came inextricable from your love.   For years
> all arguments I carried on in my head were with you.   I saw myself . . .
> the eldest daughter in a house with no son, she who must overthrow
> the father, take what he taught her and use it against him.

And then:

> After your death I met you again as the face of patriarchy, could
> name at last precisely the principle you embodied, there was an
> ideology at last which let me dispose of you, identify the suffering
> you caused, hate you righteously as part of a system, the kingdom
> of the fathers.   I saw the power and arrogance of the male as your
> true watermark; I did not see beneath it the suffering of the Jew, the
> alien stamp you bore, because you had deliberately arranged that it
> should be invisible to me.   It is only now, under a powerful, womanly
> lens, that I can decipher your suffering and deny no part of my own.

What returning to the sources of herself in the past taught Rich
was that the ways she had been led to deny herself were the result of
a patriarchal mindset that had led her secular father to deny himself
too. Contra the feminist ideology 'that let me dispose of you', therefore, she refuses to dispose of him, realizing that it's only by
reassimilating her father and the history he had disavowed that she
can finally free herself from her own brutalizing history – which history could otherwise prove fatal. Indeed, whose fatality, she further
reflects, she witnessed tragically with her own eyes after her early
marriage – when she was still grasping what she could to survive – to
a man, a Jewish man like her father, but a man whom her father
despised though he shared with her father the same wish to dissociate
himself from his own sources, traditions and roots; a man who eventually 'drove to Vermont in a rented car at dawn and shot himself'.
Acknowledging Woolf's demand for women to think back through
their mothers, Rich knows that her reclamation of her father may be
placing her outside the bounds of not only the dominant religious
tradition (Orthodox Judaism being matrilineal – whereas Rich's
mother was Episcopalian, which is how she was nominally raised),
but of feminist and lesbian models of heritage and belonging as well.
Yet to properly think back through the mothers, she surmises, she

must think back through the fathers as well. This, therefore, is what she requires of herself so that she doesn't distort her own memory, and because without finding a way to happily marry all the parts of herself together, including those that seem to contradict, she will be left with only one legacy – that of 'self-hatred'. Her heart, that's to say, will continue to belong to Daddy insofar as she refuses to acknowledge that it's Daddy, too, who belongs to her heart. As such, to love women the way she wishes to love women – undamagingly – she must also go back and love the men she's fought with and left behind, which she does by refusing their disavowals as well as her own, and by rebinding herself instead to a shared past precisely in order to renew her own self-chosen vows towards the future:

> *Because you have chosen*
> *something else: to know other things*
> *even the cities which*
> *create of this a myth*
>
> *Because you grew up in a castle of air*
> *disjunctured*
>
> *Because without a faith*
> > *you are faithful*

Holy Matrimony

'The success or failure of a marriage is mainly the wife's responsibility.'

Edmund Bergler, *Divorce Won't Help*

Holy Matrimony. What a lot there is to live up to in that phrase. For Milton, 'we find here no expression so necessarily implying carnal knowledge as this prevention of loneliness to the mind and spirit of man.' What's holy about matrimony, he reckoned, is the meet and happy conversation that preserves in a couple the plenitude and innocence of God's paradise before the fall. So it's very much *not* a carnal thing. Although implicit in the phrase's expression there still seems to be the Vico-ish notion that marriage transforms what's bestial about us – our sexuality – into something polite. Something manageable and decorous. Or in that other formulation we considered before, marriage makes of our sexuality something less physical and more metaphysical – which *does* sound like it might pertain to what's holy, although when put like that, it also sounds, well, virginal. As if sexuality was as foreign to the spousal couple as it is to the couple featured in a related holy iconography, that of the virgin mother with her very special child.

Most mothers aren't virgins, needless to say. Nevertheless, that image of the Madonna in blissful unity with her baby boy has certainly left its mark on the reputations of other mothers. Hence the curious situation whereby two couples, the spousal and the maternal, that are pretty much unthinkable *without* sexuality, are idealized in such a way that what brings them together in the first place is that which has been more or less erased from their histories and identities. For just as we tend *not* to think very much about matrimony, so we tend *not* to think too much about the maternity from which matrimony takes its name. But then, what did we expect? Home, nation, maternity, matrimony, family . . . these are the institutions that seem to possess, for most of us, the secret of our own origins. And given that what precedes us must be fundamentally inaccessible, it's also, for that reason, unapproachable. Ineffable. Sacred.

Having little truck with the sacred, Freud committed some of the gravest acts of modern sacrilege against holy images. With all his talk of infantile sexuality, for instance, he blemished the innocence of the child by putting the baby in conflict with a father who now had to deal with some stiff competition over the mother's affections. Although curiously, Freud may still have been reluctant to compromise the holiness of the mother, who seems, in his picture, to have no real desires besides the desire to care for a child whom she strokes, kisses and cuddles in ways that might remind one of the spousal couple, but which bears no real relation to it. It was left to later analysts, such as Donald Winnicott, to blemish her reputation as well. Indeed, Winnicott even listed eighteen reasons why a mother might hate her child, including, scandalously, this one: 'He excites her (sexually too) and frustrates her – she must not eat him or trade in sex with him.' By sexualizing the figure of the mother, Winnicott wasn't simply recalling that mothers also have their non-parenting drives, which would be bad enough; he was placing sexuality at the heart of maternity itself.

In *The New Man*, a film I made with my spouse about our own fraught journey into parenthood, my husband can be found fretting about being replaced by a younger, cuter model. At the time, this limbering up to feel jealous of an infant – an infant! – struck me as ridiculous. What a way to make an already very difficult pregnancy unnecessarily stressful. And when you added that stress to his even more stressful determination that we capture the whole process on camera – well, the mood between us wasn't exactly aglow with our great expectations. Creating things with another person can be wonderful, but it's just as often hard. The collaborative can be the divisive. And just as our baby-making nearly tore our marriage apart, so did our film-making. We fought a lot during that period. The things we were going through together we experienced as if we were going through them alone. But as it turned out, my husband had been right to fret. After our baby was born, it shocked me more than it did him to discover that this tiny child was indeed my new man. For I fell madly – and I do mean madly – in love. So much so that Oedipus struck me as anything but complex. In our household we started doing it by numbers. Or not quite, because I wasn't entirely without my own desires either. I was more akin to the woman whom Esther Perel says she sometimes comes across in her consulting room: the postnatal woman who claims she's too used up for marital relations because the demands of mothering have physically exhausted her. Which while true – mothering, particularly at the start, is absolutely shattering in a way that renders one unavailable for any other demanding relationship – doesn't fully admit of how, for some lucky mothers, such exertions at mothering may have physically *satisfied* them as well. And since I was one of those lucky mothers, my husband had a real mountain to climb to win back my interest. This, inevitably, caused frictions between us too.

What that doesn't mean, of course, is that what bound me to my child was a version of the same felt attachment as that which bound me to my husband. But what *was* similar was the feeling that my desire for my child was no less frantic and disorderly of my person. So, as the analyst and writer Josh Cohen points out, it's not that 'parental tenderness is really disguised debauchery'. Heaven forbid! Rather, it's that what feels unsettling when one draws these two very different forms of relation into relation with each other is the sense that 'Somewhere in you, the distinctions between sex and affection, between one and another mode of loving – distinctions on which your sanity, perhaps the very sanity of the world itself, depends – have yet to be learned.' Good Lord. Maybe that explains why one finds relatively few authors reflecting on the curious mix of passions that can circulate so confusingly within even the most polite and decorous of family homes. With some exceptions, such as the author Maggie Nelson, who *does* read matrimony and maternity together, regarding them both as the sort of hazily intimate experiences that can merge and converge in ways that challenge the conventions their holier-than-Thou reputations outwardly uphold.

It was Julia Kristeva who brought the problem of motherhood and its representation to the attention of philosophy. Reflecting on how maternity, in order to generate society, must be in some sense radically *other* to that society, she noted that if the social world is aligned to the name of the father, and bound by the authority of his word, then the maternal experience must be of a type that not only labours to reproduce that world, but simultaneously threatens to undo its construction. Childbirth, after all, suggests a truth about the human condition that patriarchal codes and taxonomies can never entirely master, or entirely appropriate: namely that it's from the mother that another being – wordless and infant – comes forth. Hence why, says Kristeva, maternity gives priority to a mobile, freely associative, pre-Oedipal language that makes of the maternal body 'a place of permanent scission' that will never cease to interrupt and lay waste to the 'symbolic law organizing social relations'.

In her more recent work, in collaboration with Philippe Sollers, Kristeva moves from characterizing the language of maternity (and its associated infancy) to characterizing the language of matrimony (and *its* associated infancy). And as we saw before, both Kristeva and Sollers claim their marriage possesses a playfulness that allows them to be together as adults as if they were still children. Not that that makes them so unusual. We've already noted how often marriages get portrayed as a sort of cover story of grown-upness to conceal the absence of the very same. Perhaps I shouldn't be surprised, therefore, that most of the marriage writing I've encountered, whether fiction or memoir, proffers a vision of matrimony at its best as less an institution for *making* children than as an institution for *becoming* children. Again. Which, if true of the married in general, is likely even more so of the married-with-kids. Once you have children with someone else you quickly realize how you're only ever playing at being mummies or daddies, the real mummies and daddies being always and for ever your own.

What I find still more surprising in most of the accounts I've read of marriage, though, is the somewhat skimpy representation one finds of child-rearing at all. In accounts of marriage as lived, that is, rather than as a social ideal. It seems odd to me because having children has felt such a critical aspect of my own marital situation. My husband and I think of ourselves very much as two people who came together and made two other people. We talk about that fact with each other constantly, its miracle never ceasing to amaze us. And when the children are well and happy, we delight in them and, on that basis, we can also feel pretty good about each other. But when they're unwell and unhappy, parenting can often become a source of strife, frustration and blame between us, thus reliably triggering, as all our arguments tend to, the ever-ready diatribes nestling within our other domestic resentments, not only in the nursery, but in the kitchen, the laundry and the bedroom too.

Though really there's nothing that undoes us in the way that parenting undoes us. It's as if our parenting, particularly in its less impressive moments, has shown up in order to sit like a judge upon our marriage. And not least because a good-enough marriage made up of not-good-enough parents probably *isn't* a good-enough marriage after all. Besides, being children of parents ourselves, we know it's the child who will anyway wind up judging their parents – which is exactly the kind of thought that can make those parents no less rivalrous over their child's love than are siblings over their parents' love. Even if, as most good-enough parents strive to do, they manage to conceal their rivalry from their children, from each other, and from themselves.

For the really unfortunate child, however, marital conflict can often move beyond the psychological into the real world of law and prosecution, to the point where the child may even be solicited to *literally* judge their parents, or judge between them. Such is the story one finds searingly represented in the Iranian director Asghar Farhadi's beautifully scripted and acted *A Separation*. In this film, the daughter of a couple who are separating is finally asked by the legally appointed judge to pick which parent she prefers to go home with. We don't hear her answer, but we feel acutely the pain of the decision she has to make. It's a tremendously affecting portrait of how the fracturing of a marriage can threaten to fracture the children *of* that marriage. Although the real sadness is that this can happen not necessarily for any lack of love. In the case of *A Separation*, the parents do love each other; they never really wanted to separate. Moreover, they're religious people in a religious society whose consciences are directing them to do only what they each believe is the right, decent and dutiful thing. What has separated them matrimonially, in fact, has everything to do with how they feel not about each other, but about their role as parents, or as the children of parents. The mother, wanting a better life for their daughter, wishes to move away. The father, wanting to be a good son, wishes to stay behind to look after his own ailing father. So it's their focus on the parent–child relation and its obligations that has got in the way of their spousal relation. And that, tragically, is what's also rendered them both unmarried and less good parents in the process.

Still, if it's hard on a child to find themselves fought over by their parents, at least that child may be able to infer that they're someone worth fighting for. What might go even harder on a child is to find themself not so much fought over as fought *through* – as happens to the daughter of the divorcing, then divorced, couple in Henry James's *What Maisie Knew*, in which Maisie finds herself ill-used by a mother and father who send her back and forth between them like 'a little feathered shuttlecock.' These parents are emphatically not good enough. They're careless of Maisie, of what she sees and hears, treating her merely as a means of getting back at each other and very little else. But this is just what renders Maisie's situation paradoxical. Parents who are derelict in their duties by overexposing their small child to their own adult world of sexuality turn out to be the ones who behave like children, whilst it's Maisie who is forced by her immature elders to prematurely mature. Since Maisie *is* still a child, however, this mature knowledge remains for the most part indecipherable to her. So the fact that it's via her young girlhood that these marital conflicts and intrigues are being transmitted makes for an even more disturbing image of sexuality's purportedly infantile nature.

As a parent, of course, one hopes never to use one's own children so badly. But in the unconscious soup of the family, it's only reasonable to suppose that even good-enough parents do sometimes, if unintentionally, divert to their children to indirectly communicate or fight with each other. Or else find other means of making their child feel in some obscure way responsible for their parents' relationship, whether that relationship be good or bad. This could well be why so many representations of marriage give such short shrift to parenting. For though it's often to be seen, in both life and literature, that children can break a marriage, there's very little to suggest that children can make one – and nor should any child ever have to. Still, given the sacred mission of a matrimonial tradition that's been consistently led by the command to couples to go forth, multiply and reproduce the world, one might well regard any effort to unbind spousing from parenting as a somewhat frivolous or faddish idea. Not, though, according to Milton, who assures us that it was never 'God's intention' when ordaining the hallowed institution 'against the evil of solitary life, not mentioning the purpose of generation till afterwards', to turn innocent babes into conniving Cupids.

So even if it *seems* obvious, it hasn't necessarily always *been* obvious that the best marriages tend to be between couples whose marital interest lies primarily in each other. As Cavell observes of the remarriage comedy, it's a film genre in which the principal pair recover each other only by recovering their own childlike innocence, while their actual children 'if they appear, must appear as intruders. The one obligation would be to make them welcome, to make room for them, to make them be at home, hence to transform one's idea of home, showing them that they are not responsible for their parents' happiness, nor for their parents' unhappiness.' As a genre, in other words, the remarriage comedy resists the traditional conception of a matrimony that depends on maternity for its own justification. Not because it's a genre that doesn't care for children. Because it's a genre that does. And because what probably works best for all parties is if married people, before they attempt to solve family conflicts by separating from each other, try instead to separate the meaning of their own relationship from that of their child-rearing such that the one doesn't lean too heavily on the other for its own strength or commitment.

Viewed from the outside, some of the most appealing-looking marriages I know are certainly those where the spouses' ability to recover with each other their sense of youthful playfulness has been partly enabled by the absence of any children, or else the chance of leaving those children they do have in the care of others from time to time. Likewise, I've seen married couples recover a carefree spirit with each other only once their children have grown up and taken leave of their own. Which isn't of course to deny that there are families who know how to engage brilliantly as a single unit all together, and in such a spirit that everyone gets to be playful and everyone childlike – although I do often wonder if someone within that constellation is perhaps concealing the sort of adult anxiety that makes this playfulness possible; which someone, I tend to assume, is likely to be the one in the maternal role who enables the play but who frequently finds it hard to feel playful herself. Actually, I'm telling on myself now.

And in thus telling on myself, I'm also reproducing a pretty standard picture of what's been commonly represented as normal or realistic in marriage and the family since at least the decade at the end of which my own parents got married, the 1950s. This too was around the time when the popular American psychoanalyst Edmund Bergler, addressing the problem of how to make a marriage work, very explicitly conflated the wife with the mother and the husband with the child. 'I am of the opinion', he wrote, 'that the fate of every normal marriage is decided mainly by the wife. I believe that the typical woman intuitively does not take the man too seriously. Inwardly she knows only too well that he is at best a grown-up baby with big words, gestures and aspirations, but little beyond them.' Damn. That thinking sounds familiar. Man, Bergler continues, 'never outgrows the nursery', and so it behoves the wife, if she wishes to be realistic about love and marriage, to recognize that her husband is a creature unable to mature. Generously, he even then goes on to list 'The Minimum Requirements for a Good Wife', i.e. 'facts' the wife must learn 'an inner acceptance of' if her marriage is to prosper. A good wife needs to recognize, for instance, 'That the money which her husband earns is a reality factor and not a weapon to be used against him.' Which, he explains, is because the husband has to reckon constantly with his unconscious feeling that his wife is a parasite for whom he works himself to death (a fact not dissimilar, incidentally, to one of the reasons Winnicott lists as to why a mother might hate her child).

Or for another example of a 'fact' a wife is required to accept, there's this one: 'That her husband is inwardly a little boy, who must not be taken too seriously, though seriously admired.' Which fact, as simple as it sounds, is actually rather subtle, because the helpless baby that man is inwardly is inclined to babytalk to a wife he unconsciously identifies with his own childishness – so when he babies her, it's really because he wants to do the babytalk himself. Her job, therefore, is to play along, as indeed she's required to do in the bedroom too, on the basis of this fact: 'That sex is "fun" and not a marital weapon.' Well, yes, ideally. Yet one can still discern in its instruction, I think, how even in these strictly adult sexual matters the wife must learn to play with her husband in the same spirit as she would with her child in the nursery.

In the 1950s, not long after Bergler's book came out, no one captured this version of femininity better than Marilyn Monroe. Still today the ultimate screen icon of what's unbearably exciting about her sex, she simultaneously presented the perfect figure of the wide-eyed, babytalking ingénue with the undeniable *fact* that she was ALL woman. As we can see especially in Billy Wilder's *The Seven Year Itch*, a film in which a Manhattan husband (Tom Ewell) sends his wife and kid away for the summer, determined, during their absence, to work hard and not succumb to the vices his wife has reminded him, as a mother would, he needs to avoid: cigarettes, red meat, drink, and implicitly girls. A publisher, he starts reading a copy of a shrink's new manuscript about repression in the middle-aged man. It's the sort of book Bergler might easily have written. And it's a book whose reflections on civilization's discontents our left-alone husband finds particularly stimulating. Indeed, this is a guy with access to a rich fantasy life who, as luck would have it, suddenly finds that none other than Marilyn enters his apartment, attracted at first by his air con. Soon enough, he's drinking, smoking and, rather gauchely, making a grab for her. Which, even though she's completely uninterested in him, she seems unbothered by. She's used to it, she tells him. But she's relieved he's married at least, meaning he'll proposition her but won't propose to her. In a bid to seduce her, therefore, he figures that a daring conversation about psychoanalysis is what's called for. She desires him, he explains, but cannot handle her own desire so disguises it from herself. Beneath the veneer of civilization, we're all savages, he warns. Thinking only of his air con, she asks to stay the night. He's floored; an instant neurotic, putting her off as best he can. She says she just wishes to sleep on his chair, not in his bed. Relieved, 'Why not?' he reasons. 'We're not savages.' The joke of the movie, in other words, is that a middle-aged man is really a 'grown-up baby' with a tremendous propensity for fantasy but very little capacity for reality, which could hardly be more marked than by the unreality of this woman in his apartment, who never mentions her name, though at one point he does tell another man that he's got Marilyn Monroe in his kitchen. Marilyn in the kitchen? Everyone knows that's impossible. Left alone, this guy's fantasies must have got the better of him. He evidently needs some grown-up to step in and take charge. And indeed, by the end of the movie it's Marilyn's job to send him packing like another mother to rejoin his wife, a child's paddle in his hand.

What all of this, for Bergler, comes down to in the end is one conclusive fact: 'That the balance of marital power automatically favours the wife.' Due, that is, to man's greater dependence and immaturity. Meanwhile, this is what the wife risks by failing to play her part: 'If a woman, because of her own neurosis, stresses too obviously the fact that she manages her husband, she resuscitates all his old unconscious trouble, with sorry results.' If she plays her cards right, on the other hand, she gets 'a loving and devoted husband and the repetition of a great deal of infantile pleasure.' To which we can only respond, thank heavens. At least, for the Oedipally positioned wife/mother, there's the potential for *some* pre-Oedipal returns.

Still, for a wife to fully enjoy her infantile sexuality within the adult life she alone is held responsible for cultivating does seem a tough gig, to put it mildly. The fact one arrives at, having registered all these facts, is that Bergler's marital realism allows that men are babies at home so that they can then behave as adults in the world outside the home. Whereas for women it's the other way around. Which doesn't kindle much enthusiasm for the normally functioning marriage. Although I'm fairly sure that this is a picture that does in many ways correlate with some of the tendencies to be glimpsed inside my own marriage; a marriage where we often do very little to fracture the paradigm of, in the words of psychoanalyst Jessica Benjamin, 'a holding mother and an exciting father.' Hence, even though it's tempting to see woman-as-adult and man-as-baby as a breakdown that flatters the woman, it's not exactly, I can affirm from experience, in her interests to keep things that way. Not least since woman wants, no less than man wants, the type of matrimony that can repeat the playfulness of infancy under the cover of respectable adulthood. Albeit since women and men *are* adults, and so not really children, that generational distinction must surely bear some weight when it comes to enacting these infantile repetitions. I mean, what *is* infantile sexuality anyway?

A great deal of the marital misery Marie Stopes identified behind closed doors at the beginning of the twentieth century she attributed to the fact that so many of the couples who married then were essentially children themselves, lacking any real knowledge of love or sexuality before they tied their knots. This was even true of Stopes, who counselled that 'in my own marriage I paid such a terrible price for sex-ignorance that I feel that knowledge gained at such a price should be placed at the service of humanity.' In our own times, of course, people *do* tend to be more sexually knowledgeable prior to marriage. Yet Stopes's characterization of matrimonial disappointment doesn't seem such a far cry from the wounds and resentments that bespeak unhappy marriages today. What *is* different is the tone in which one usually refers to these things. When Stopes relays the misery of marriages that have failed to deliver on their promise of happiness, she's full of pathos. Now it's the already-knowingness of cynicism or critique that's the more conventional mode.

It's fitting, then, that Stopes's *Married Love*, notwithstanding its realism, remained more romantic than cynical. It even proposes a solution to the problem her book describes by appending a kind of Miltonic conclusion: 'When knowledge and love go together to the making of each marriage, the joy of that new unit, the Pair, will reach from the physical foundation of its united body to the heavens where its head is crowned with stars.' A happy ending is thus an ending that envisages marriage as ideally the marriage of love and knowledge. Love *sans* such knowledge, meanwhile, is condemned as a sure-fire way into marital hell. But what kind of knowledge are we talking about here? If love's knowledge is simply a euphemism for sexual knowledge (as Stopes's complaints about men and women's sexual ignorance of each other's bodies as well as their own suggests) we might well suppose that marriages today ought to have fixed the unhappiness problem. But if rising divorce rates are anything to go by, sounding knowing about sex and sexuality may turn out to be no better at securing happiness than sexual ignorance. Indeed, the sheer volume of sexual authority we're now all supposed to profess in the most intimate bodily matters could even be deemed an *entrenchment* of the sort of patriarchal mindset that runs scared of what it can't claim to already know.

'Sex is private,' writes Josh Cohen in *The Private Life*, 'not only in the well-worn sense that its proper place is on the other side of a closed door, but in the rarer sense of being essentially unshareable. Sex, for all that it requires the real or fantasized presence of another, abandons you to yourself, to the untameable forces of pleasure and pain, to a region where common language, and its accompanying faith that your experience can be understood by someone else, run aground.' So it's in this sense – sex's imperviousness to common language – that we may be able to better grasp what might be meant by the still disturbing notion that there's such a thing as infantile sexuality. Indeed, to my question, what is infantile sexuality?, Cohen's illuminating response is that this rather strange-sounding formulation 'should be understood as the sexuality not so much of the child as of the child you continue to be.'

Well, the child *I* continue to be is very much the child of my parents, and indeed of their mid-twentieth-century marriage. My mother and father got married in 1959 and they stayed married until my father died in 2021. Over those sixty-two years, they hardly ever spent a night apart from each other and they rarely ever socialized apart from each other. This isn't something Stopes would have approved of very much, though their marriage did conform for the most part to Bergler's theory of what's matrimonially realistic. Once they were engaged, it was understood from the outset that my father (a GP for the NHS, which was itself fledgling when he first worked there) would be the primary breadwinner, while my mother would always prioritize her wifely duties over her professional ones. So theirs was a very traditional arrangement, but it's one she was happy with, my mother says, and not least because marriage is what she credits with giving her the self-confidence to develop in such a way that she could still go on to *have* a career. Indeed, one of the first things my mother became involved with following her nuptials was the Family Planning Association, after which, in the tradition of Stopes, she moved into marriage guidance counselling. From 1966 to 1996 she worked for a non-profit organization then called the National Marriage Guidance Council, but since, in tandem with social changes, renamed Relate and still going strong. Although the Marriage Guidance Council was a charity originally set up in 1938, it was expanded after the war to deal with the ways in which the global conflict had impacted on the more intimate conflicts between couples who had been separated during the intervening years, and who were then returning to each other, sometimes with traumatic experiences they couldn't find a way to share. The women were also finding it hard to resume life as it had been before the war because they'd had a taste of freedom bestowed on them and now that freedom seemed liable to be withdrawn again.

Over time, my mother also began to practise her counselling service privately, from home. During my childhood there were thus rooms in our house whose doors I knew not to trespass when closed;

one to the conjugal bedroom, the other to the study where my mother saw her clients. There were a few shelves of books in that room, and they all seemed to be about sex, shockingly. Recently I sat across from my mother in the same chair where her clients would sit. Between us was her 'only equipment' – a box of tissues. I was there to ask her about what she remembers and what she's learned from her long practice. She begins by telling me that if she had to sum up the main issues people were having in their marriages, it nearly always came down to problems of communication. Sexual problems too were generally communication problems and vice versa, she says. 'People don't know how to talk to each other.'

In the earlier years, my mother saw hardly any couples together, and barely any men at all. Men back then, she explains, felt it wasn't right to share their secrets with a stranger. So it was for the most part unhappy women my mother saw. Women with very little liberty or financial independence, and a bunch of children to look after more or less single-handedly. Later, when couples did start to show up together, her job was often to 'hold the anger' for the couple in front of her and promote better listening between them. Although sometimes she'd see the couple separately and that was when someone – usually the man – would admit to having an affair. 'It was much easier for a man to have an affair, especially in those days. Most of the men were going out in the world and working, and not too many women were.'

I ask my mother if she felt the women were 'oppressed'. 'I think depressed,' she prefers. 'I think lots of men were depressed too, but they didn't allow themselves to express it.' She was dealing with a very particular set of issues, some of which were historically specific and tied to limited rights and sexist legislation that has since been improved on. 'When divorce settlements changed and women had the ability to seek a viable divorce, they didn't have to put up with drunken, bullying, non-paying husbands, but when they couldn't divorce, and were married to these abusive husbands, well, then I saw my job as trying to help them to learn to value themselves, because if you're living with somebody like that, it leaves you feeling that you're not worth anything.' The couples she remembers strike me as fairly typical of the stereotypes of marriage one can read in much of the literature from the post-war years. 'One of the biggest problems, it always seemed, was that mostly, with the couples I saw, the men were older than the women, but as the women matured, they matured at a much faster rate than the men. And so suddenly the men would find themselves not married to the woman they thought they were in love with – and they often couldn't cope with that.' I wonder what she means when she claims that women mature much faster than men? 'Well, I think a lot of women got married at a very young age. It doesn't happen so much now. But women in their late teens and early twenties haven't really matured. And then suddenly they find themselves with a family, and maybe they've got a job as well. And they suddenly become very capable and the men are threatened. If the man can't accept change, then it breaks the relationship. Marriage is about accepting change in each other.' It's another critical lesson in marital realism, though not one I've read in Bergler.

Later in our conversation, my mother tells me something terrible: 'The work was traumatic sometimes. I had a client who was murdered. It was in the early days of being a counsellor, and I was seeing the wife. The husband was obviously mentally very sick and being seen by a psychiatrist, and the psychiatrist and I had to liaise after each and every session. The psychiatrist said, "He'll murder her." I tried to help protect her but it wasn't easy. I told the psychiatrist, "This needs a more professional person than me," and I still think that was right. They were very wrong to expect me to go on with it. But after each session I would ring the psychiatrist up and report on the session and express my fears. I sort of felt that she was waiting for him to kill her, and sure enough he did.' It's a shocking episode in which my mother was sirening her fears whilst still expected to function as the holding environment for an extremely vulnerable client whom she knew to be at risk. I think, in a way, she also experienced abandonment by the care systems that failed to save this woman's life.

Most married people know that love has its darker sides. Maybe all married people do. It's what Raymond Carver shows so unsettlingly via the boozy dinner party conversation between two married couples in his 'What We Talk About When We Talk About Love', a story that, while expressing the perversions of the passions, also implies that such perversions may be viewed as, relatively speaking, 'normal' – on the basis that normal people are sadomasochistic people. Or on the basis that sadomasochism is what the normal effectively is. Hence it's a story too that invites its readers to further consider whether our more idealized views about love and holy matrimony ought perhaps to be subject to a reality check. Though not necessarily via the kind of reality principle that Bergler invokes in listing the 'minimum requirements for a good wife', as realistic as that list may have been, or still be. I mean instead the realism Winnicott appeals to in his listed reasons as to why a mother might hate her own child, which was simultaneously his warning against the sentimentalization of the mother–child relation as something he deemed damaging to them both. For a mother can only really be useful as a mother, he counselled, to the degree that she doesn't imagine her only emotion is love and her only method self-sacrifice. She thus needs to show awareness of her occasional hatred of her children precisely in order to avert the risk of acting out on her sadomasochistic impulses. So if it's the invocation of the ideal that produces its own shadow, as it were, could it be the norms inscribed within our conception of what's normal that have made a norm of sadomasochism too?

One norm that's certainly characterized a great deal of psychoanalytic thinking is the assumption that a failure to pass normally through the Oedipal phase is a sign of arrested development that puts a major stumbling block between the developing subject and reality. And this even though, as we've seen with the example of Bergler, the

Oedipal route to maturity already acknowledges, as necessary, a certain block in the male subject's development. Indeed, it's this fact, submits Bergler, that places the lion's share of the responsibility for any marriage on the shoulders of the wife. Which obviously isn't fair, but is it even accurate? In marriages both past and present, after all, gender roles and identities are fluid and very often the reverse of their cultural stereotypes; a fact that would seem to challenge overly confident claims about what's normal – although insufficiently, perhaps, to puncture what appears to be underlying such norms: the common-sense view of reality.

What *is* the common-sense view of reality? To discern its outline, it may be useful to firstly consider the space of fantasy it gives on to – and particularly the space of *permitted* fantasy that, as Winnicott appreciated, can sometimes be experienced as an extension of the holding environment that recalls the child's state of dependence on a grown-up world devoted to its safety and care. For it's in this space that one might expect to find couples engaged in role play, for example, or S&M as practised between consenting adults who know how to respect each other's limits. And yet as inventive as adults at play may well be, what such a space of fantasy also insinuates is that the larger problem, when it comes down to it, is how we imagine relationships at all – for if there's still a master–slave dialectic adrenalizing a couple's dualism, code-switching isn't going to change the fundamentally unequal nature of their dynamic. As such, the matrimonial relationship is likely to be a particularly useful one for reflecting on relationships of all kinds. If marriage, that's to say, is where we go to recreate the pleasures of the nursery, then it's an arrangement that *does* imply it may be possible for adults to enact some sort of creative (rather than merely conservative or regressive) return to the openness of the prelinguistic and pre-Oedipal phase of their development. Marriage would thus be an experimental chamber wherein to playfully consider such vital questions as, for instance, if anything can be done about Oedipus? Or whether we've assumed some things are irrevocably real that aren't? Or assumed that some people are definitively one way when they could just as well be another?

'It's often the case,' Adam Phillips remarked when I once interviewed him about politics in the consulting room, 'that people come to me with, say, a sexual perversion and they want to persuade, in this case me, that really I just haven't got the guts, that *they're* the ones in touch with reality, that this is what sex is *really* like. Sex is really exciting, but you've got to be up to it. And that isn't true.' As 'a way of organizing your world', sadomasochism is 'actually intrinsically enraging. But what we're being offered culturally, broadly speaking, is a sadomasochistic solution: the idea that I'll feel awfully strong if I can make you feel weak, or vice versa.'

This widespread culture of realpolitik, suggests Jessica Benjamin, is one we've bolstered by a number of influential theories regarding normal states of human intercourse. In the tradition of political philosophy we inherit from Hegel, for example, the struggle for recognition between any couple leads to conflict, tension and finally domination, while the idea of allowing that tension to continue between the struggling duo is never properly entertained. Someone always has to win and lose. Which chimes too with the sort of psychoanalytic ideas that, in a family context, share the assumption that tension regarding one's position or identity cannot be tolerated for long. Soon enough a son or daughter needs to understand which parent they'll be required to align with.

That isn't to deny that some things *are* real. The reality principle that a baby must slowly learn to accept, for instance, is that their mastery over the world is limited, and thus that omnipotence, especially over their primary caregiver, is only a fantasy. Indeed, it's at this beginning stage of their fantasy life that the growing baby may fantasize that they can act, like the King in *One Thousand and One Nights*, as the sort of tyrant who possesses the sovereign power to dominate all others – with those others tending to be mothers (or women) especially. Yet the problem with fantasy, Phillips observes, is that 'when it doesn't lead you to a better relationship with reality, it's enervating. It's like a black hole: it draws your energy away.' Whereas there is, on the side of reality, the potential for real pleasures to be had on the part of the developing child who can accept their mother's independence (and vice versa). What recognizing one's own limits opens up, after all, is the space for not less but rather more enjoyment of the other – which, arguably, is what Shahrazad was teaching her husband over the long course of his bedtime stories too. A failure to grant this recognition of independence, on the other hand, can be fatal for the mother, for the development of the child, and for the distorted culture that their uneasy separation from each other evokes.

So if the Oedipal fantasy we've culturally rendered as a series of hard-nosed facts one must accept about reality is what ultimately enervates us, what can be done about it? To recap: within the standard social arrangements of the Oedipal schema, it's once the blissful paradise of unity with the mother has been breached and the necessity of separation is evident that the male child moves to identify with the father as possessor of phallic freedom, power, desire and individuality; while the daughter, forced back into an identification with a mother who lacks such powers of self-assertion, gives up on her own desire and grows instead to idealize the man who has what she can't herself possess. To which it's tempting to retort that we no longer live in a world of fixed sexual identities or assumed gender roles – so for all intents and purposes, the Oedipal machine for engineering normal people has *already* sunk into obsolescence. But not so fast, counters Benjamin. For when it comes to understanding how this narrative of early development has organized our reality, the greater mobility of sexual signifiers today barely scratches the surface. Better, rather, to understand sex and gender here as metaphors, since what's being culturally represented as masculine is actually self-sufficiency, while what's feminine is dependency, or in its more misogynist rendition, insufficiency. (Even if these roles switch around and between different bodies or between different parties to a couple depending on whether they're out or at home.) The key point being that the patriarchal ideal of mastery doesn't even need to be coded in terms of sex or gender any more – and indeed these days it may attach more easily to concepts such as reason, authority and autonomy instead. So if we're tempted to imagine that it's in the mystical and religious past that we nurtured all our most backward illusions, the future of this particular illusion seems to be represented by the self-sufficient individual who, in the guise of rationality, stands at the epicentre of secular modernity itself.

The continuing business of (male) hegemony, in other words, may have less to do with sexual differentiation than with the processes by which particular people strive to individuate their identities by distinguishing themselves, in the first place, from those who purportedly can't. Hence for those hugging close to the Oedipal framework, not so dramatically perhaps as the child is required to do when choosing who to go home with in *A Separation*, but painfully nonetheless, every boy and girl must learn who they are by aligning their own identities with a particular parent (or in the case of non-traditional families, with one of the two poles of the dyadic couple that the nuclear family structure has been recruited to represent). It's this process, therefore, that could stir up a sense of alienation liable to cause problems for the child as they mature into more adult relationships. And that, says Benjamin, is because what both boys and girls going through these early developmental phases appear to really want, *even* in the terms of this Oedipal schema, isn't power, it's recognition. Toddlers, that's to say, do not like to have their hands forced by picking or being picked by a particular team. They would much rather maintain their identification with *both* parents. Whereas if only the one in the paternal role is articulated as a subject of desire while the one in the maternal role has been devalued in her own right, the couple possessing the secret of the child's own origins will appear to that child as hierarchical and opposed.

Still, there's no getting away from the fact that power as the organizing principle of group life *does* remain a fairly common-sense picture of reality. When people tell you to get real, for instance, it's usually the role played by power that they're alluding to. But since few of us would claim to *want* domination to be the governing logic of all human relations, mightn't it be worth questioning this picture of reality? As, indeed, Benjamin does by focusing not so much on the characteristics of each individual as on what takes place in the intersubjective space between them. For it's in this space that one finds two seemingly contradictory things married together. On the one hand, one finds personal identities whose borders are rendered blurrier through their intercourse with others. But on the other hand, one finds individuals entering the intersubjective relation precisely in order to assert themselves and demand recognition from each other. As Benjamin summarizes: 'In getting pleasure *with* the other and taking pleasure *in* the other, we engage in mutual recognition.' So rather than entailing a loss of self, mutual recognition is the very reverse of the cult of mastery that assumes someone has to win or lose. It's a lovely thought. Still, isn't this precisely the type of thinking that the hard-nosed realists are bound to consider naive or utopian? That seems likely. But who is the real fantasist here? For mutual recognition also has a reality principle – and it's one that more accurately reflects the reality of a world in which, it's true, we never *can* presume to finally resolve the tensions that exist between us.

So it's by returning to the fantasies about reality that take shape during pre-Oedipal life that we might begin to dismantle the assumption that the sadomasochistic relation is the most realistic. Benjamin's alternative conception of an intersubjectivity based in mutual recognition, for example, envisages our states of relation as constantly shifting and as answerable only to our moments of interaction, not to anyone's objective standards or norms. And she also claims that we need to popularize such theories of mutuality in order to endow these with the credibility that the master–slave paradigms of what reality is made up of more typically enjoy. So it's striking that the marital relation remains her locus for where this social revolution might be expected to foment. Is that simply because, as a social unit, the spousal one is so fundamental as to appear vital for any future shifts and developments? Or could it rather be because just this is what marriage had promised all along: to wed the individual to the communal by showing how the independence of the one has always been entirely *dependent* on the other.

None of which is to deny, of course, that marriage can conjure the unconscious because infantile landscape in which spouses first learned the rules of a game that seeks to master 'she' who shows signs of independence, but who the child fantasizes they may still be able to possess and control – which is the sort of scenario whose repetition in later life can mean the love that binds could get dark and get dangerous very quickly. But what this revisioning of intersubjectivity implies no less is that marriage could also be the chance of something else: a situation inside which adults will return to the unformed haze of their own childhoods, yes, but only because, given that they *are* now adults, they might yet learn to do things differently this time.

Marriage as Afterlife

11

Divorcing

'Such a marriage can be no marriage.'

John Milton, *The Doctrine and Discipline of
Divorce Restored to the Good of Both Sexes*

Another one of marriage's wedded terms is divorce. The two make
a really convincing couple, in fact, unthinkable, essentially, without
each other. The very vow that makes of marriage a contract unto
death acknowledges that there might emerge such a wish as would
aspire to renege on that contract. No need for a contract otherwise.
Not that a revocation is required to demonstrate how effortlessly
marriage and divorce can cohabit together. For don't they both, in a
way, open upon the same horizon? Yes, marriage arrives on the scene
full of promise, but once the marital deed is done, it's divorce's turn
to step into the breach and promote its own version of a happier-ever-
after. 'Are you *really* happy?' divorce whispers, furtively, into the ear
of each spouse. 'Are you *sure* you're getting everything marriage
vowed to you?'

Why divorce? Because, explained Milton in all simplicity, marital
misery annuls a marriage. As such, divorce isn't so much a subversive
character as a conservative one. Since an unhappy marriage commits
sacrilege against 'God's intention' of providing the nuptial couple
with their portion of paradise on earth, divorce actually has the odd
function of undoing what was never really done – because 'such a

marriage can be no marriage'. To the Church, of course, keen to maintain its jurisdiction over matrimony, Milton's tract did sound pretty revolutionary at the time. Yet Milton was careful to point out that he wasn't saying anything so radical or new. It's there in the Mosaic law that a man who finds he cannot love his wife ought to divorce her. Or when Solomon cautions in *Proverbs* that it's 'better to live on a corner of the roof than share a house with a quarrelsome wife'. Perish the thought. Not to mention that God's matchmaking of Adam and Eve made it perfectly clear from the outset that the couple was created to provide comfort and companionship to mitigate the pains of loneliness and isolation – so the 'sad spirit' who finds they're 'wedded to loneliness should deserve to be freed.' Loneliness is only ever intensified, after all, in the company of the person who has failed to thwart it.

So it was in the seventeenth century that there appeared an essentially moral argument to counter the still-popular opinion that sticking it out in a miserable marriage comprises some sort of moral victory. Marriage as moral victory – could anything *be* less appealing? Milton clearly found that whole concept rebarbative. He thought divorce was something moral, while marriage is existential. Marriage was created for pleasure, divorce for principle. It's a standpoint that has a pleasingly progressive ring to modern ears. And yet taking back one's vows isn't simply the sort of technicality that can elude all moral consequences. One may well live during relatively enlightened times, but when a couple's decision to separate isn't mutual, and often enough when it is, all hell may still be expected to break loose. That there's no pain like the pain of abandonment is something we know in our core – or that we've known ever since we were first put down in our infancy and left as if to fend for ourselves. And that initial shock to our system is likely one whose impact has never entirely vanished. (Few are those for whom the *fort/da* game of loss and symbolic recovery – the game played with a toy reel that Freud famously observed his grandson improvising when faced with the sudden absence of his mother – ended in early childhood.) So if you're the spurned spouse, or the spurning spouse, or even the kind of spouse who believes they made the wrong marital choice without any intention of spurning, you may nevertheless feel, when you leave your marriage, that the ground has given way beneath your feet.

I'm not divorced and hope I never shall be. But I know of course that there's a chance that one day I may be. And I recognize how divorce – the threat of it, the promise of it – plays an unspoken part inside my marital contract. Or more accurately, it's a threat that *has* been spoken aloud on the odd occasion, though rarely and less frequently over time. Before we married, my husband and I did do our fair bit of breaking up; causing hurt and then getting back together again. And we've both experienced what it's like, with each other and with others previous to each other, being abandoned or being abandoning; how truly awful that is. Which may be why, now that the stakes of our relationship have been significantly raised via marriage, shared property and particularly children, we've grown more circumspect about introducing into our quarrels and disappointments an idea that's so drastic. Although the notion that *I don't have to go on like this* remains something that divorce, whether name-checked or not, continually conjures. *I may be married, but I'm still free. He may be married, but he's still free.* It's this that makes divorce, as a structure of possibility subsisting tacitly inside a marriage, alternately liberating and terrorizing.

'One April afternoon, right after lunch,' begins Elena Ferrante's novel *The Days of Abandonment*, 'my husband announced that he wanted to leave me.' Because this novel was my introduction to Ferrante, when I first read that line I wasn't yet used to how quickly she plunges you. Encountering the uncanny composure of an opening sentence narrating a theme of such discomposure, however, I found myself instantly descending into an anxiety about my personal situation; an anxiety that the scene of togetherness I was actually inhabiting at that moment (I was reading the book in bed, my husband by my side) must surely have belied. But then that's the point, presumably. For our narrator, Olga, the trauma this sudden announcement represents is partly due to the way it seems to come at her out of nowhere. 'He was composed, as always', she notes of the man delivering her this life-unravelling news. It's as if he's unaware of the crisis he's so coolly precipitated. And because she can't perceive how he would consider anything wrong with their marriage either, she doesn't quite believe him initially. Can the last fifteen years of her life really have been a lie? As for an explanation, the one he offers her – 'a sudden absence of sense' – is of no help, although later he admits he's fallen in love with another woman.

Soon enough, we join Olga in the earliest days of her marital abandonment and discover that it isn't really her husband who has lost sense, or who has the least inkling of the real terror aroused in a person who *has* lost sense – it's Olga herself whose senses have deserted her. Yet it's Olga too who must strive to be sensible, having been left with their two young children and the family dog to look after. Plus bills to pay and a house and body to clean and maintain. No sooner has she lost her senses, however, than her to-do list suddenly multiplies, as 'responsibilities that had belonged to us both would now be mine alone.' Hers is therefore a perilous situation. Her son has a high fever, her dying dog has diarrhoea, her house is plagued by ants, her daughter is running a premature riot in her mother's adult wardrobe, and even though she knows she must act, she's finding it hard to make herself care about any of these things. She fears she may even forget them. She's at risk of forgetting she has children at all. Aching with love and lust and longing and grief and rage and fear and confusion has rendered her manic. Senseless.

The biggest danger, though, is 'the danger of drowning in scorn for myself and nostalgia for him'. So she tells herself not to appear to the world as someone 'hateful'. 'But I couldn't contain myself', she realizes, as composure and coherence quickly dissipate and she becomes what no man (according to Solomon and Milton) should have to stay married to: a quarrelsome woman. Though she had no quarrel with man or world before. But now it dawns on her that 'I had taken away my own time and added it to his to make him more powerful.' To which authority can she turn and report this theft of her own life?

Meanwhile, as she descends into the hell of senselessness, Olga is haunted by the image of another woman; a woman from the neighbourhood who as a child she used to see wandering the streets, known colloquially as *la poverella* – the poor woman; an abject lesson, the locals warned, of what happens 'when you don't know how to keep a man': 'you lose everything'. She remembers how, even as a child, she'd felt 'ashamed' for this woman. The shame of being left. Of being alone. The shame that mobilizes *normal* people to gather under the protective cover of marriage.

As Olga strives to 'hold the fragments of life together', there also emerges the slow burn of a new understanding: in her terror at being outcast from society, she herself *becomes* a social terror, looming before others as a sort of testament 'to the incoherence of the world' – the very incoherence that marriage is there to hide. So could that mean there's an opportunity to be glimpsed within this crisis? Could a social revolution even be hinged to this vision of the un-hinged woman? There do seem to be certain signs that the breakdown of Olga's marital contract might precede a much wider breakdown of the entire social contract. But in Olga's case, the terror she represents turns out to be relatively short-lived. It ends, in fact, when she falls out of love with her husband – a transition she puts down to his misuse of the term 'absence of sense'; an experience she knows is as foreign to him as it's revealing of her. Although what really keeps a more lasting crisis at bay is the discovery that, love him or not, with him or not, married or not, a marriage can never be entirely retired. 'What a complex foamy mixture a couple is', she muses. 'Even if the relationship shatters and ends, it continues to act in secret pathways, it doesn't die, it doesn't want to die.' If it's marriage itself, then, that refuses to die, marriage must be a structure with intentions of its own: a structure capable of supervening on the intentional relations of its spouses even after their point of severance.

And this, of course, can be a major problem for couples seeking to part ways: divorcing often demonstrates how married they helplessly are. Which it sometimes does by revealing to the couple that they aren't the only ones *involved* in their marriage. Guests at a wedding consenting to bear witness to the marital contract may not have taken seriously their commitment to support the couple in upholding their marriage vows at its inaugural ceremony, but when divorce is entertained, the community frequently find themselves surprisingly invested. Once marriage has removed or partially removed its cover, there's a general demand for reasons to be given, and for evidence to be shown. I've certainly seen divorcing couples who've seldom seemed more married than when they're separating, as if learning only then, and painfully, how acutely exposing the experience of unmarrying must be. The right to privacy conferred on a couple by marriage appears even brutally withdrawn by its annulment. Which sudden violation of their privacy is the sort of rude awakening that a divorcing couple seeking to divide their existences are also, perplexingly, forced to share. Hence why Noah Baumbach's film about a couple divorcing is not for nothing entitled *Marriage Story*. In its portrayal of a couple breaking up, one perceives how, when everything and everyone comes between them, still there's a kind of irrevocableness about their bond that implicates them in the lifetime they originally promised each other, whether or not they spend that lifetime in each other's company.

Marriage, in this context, appears an otherworldly or spectral presence that hovers over any couple that's ever been in one. For the once married, that is, something of the old ways and habits of relating can be uncannily easy to step back into, even after a distance of many years. It's this we observe in American author Elizabeth Strout's novel, *Oh William!*, in which the protagonist, Lucy Barton, finds herself, following the death of her second simpatico husband, in a state of inconsolable grief. At her moment of bereavement, she impulsively harks back in time by reaching out to her first husband, William, with whom she has two now adult daughters. Lucy and William are both suffering an unbearable loneliness due to spouses who have left them in one way or another. As such, they spend a great deal of time together – so much time that their daughters even wonder about the prospect of them remarrying. But that's not on the cards. What is, though, is the evidence that the formerly married are in some fundamental way, when they're around each other, not altogether unmarried. All their familiar dynamics and moods still softly recycle. And even though, with William, little prompts do remind Lucy why she divorced him, he remains, in her most intimate vernacular, not simply William, but 'Oh William!', the exclamation mark reflexively following his name at once marking the exasperated conclusion of their marriage, and yet, by the same token, the ongoing acknowledgement of how profound and fond their relation has never ceased to be.

There's a version of breaking up, then, that can reveal how a couple's marriage may not only outlast their divorce but could even be strengthened by it. Not for all divorced couples, obviously, but nor is this phenomenon irregular. When it happens, it's as if the relations between two people after their marriage constitute the marriage's own afterlife. For these are people who seem to belong on a different plane together; one with different rules of engagement. They may no longer technically be intimates, but they know each other too well to simply be civil. Indeed, theirs is a knowledge so profound that such pretences cannot but feel like just that – pretences. So while they may well enact scenes of courtesy with each other, they both know that they both know how to twist the knife. It's why encountering an ex can be so fraught. And yet presumably such a distinctive situation must have its own distinct possibilities too: the opportunities afforded only to people who know each other's problems but no longer *are* each other's problems. The sort of people, for instance, who might be willing to admit, when they're divorced, the wrongs they each committed but denied when they were married.

So could this be the singular *virtue* of divorce? On the other side of marriage's cover story of a togetherness dependent on the couple's combined efforts at curating a narrative they're happy to share, there lies divorce's refusal to entertain any further compromises or cover-ups. Viewed thus, the married then divorcing couple might appear to have progressed through the veils of nuptiality to something even better: the truth. And in the case of William and Lucy, this allows for a new honesty that renders them, if not closer, then less hurtful than they were in their years of repression. As divorcees, that's to say, there's an implicit pact between them not to lie any more – or not with each other at least – which is the sort of pact that could make of one's ex a surprising source of confidence once the formal part of the relation is over. But then, Lucy and William have been apart for a long time now – long enough to swallow each other's hard truths pacifically. Whereas things between divorcing couples in the imme-diate aftermath of a marriage tend to be more explosive. In that case, the notion of truth unveiled has a very different timbre to it, like a bottled-up veracity finally released and furiously spewing over. In *Marriage Story*, for example, the couple uncensoring themselves into a spitting fury that admits of every cruel or treacherous thing they dared not say before, seem more passionate in their hatred and revul-sion than they may ever have been in their love. But is that because they really do now vehemently hate each other? Or could it be because divorce has liberated them to take out on each other all their discon-tents at the civilization their marriage had symbolized and imposed? If it's marriage itself you're angry with, it's always going to be tempt-ing to lay the blame for that at the door of your spouse.

Anyway, whatever the real reason for their hatred, that take-no-prisoners scene in Baumbach's movie was a hard watch from the vantage of my own presently married situation. It made me shudder to imagine, in fact, if my husband and I were ever to reach such a breaking point, what revision of our own history together we might then arrive at, or what terrible truths we might assume and utter in such a way that they could never again be withdrawn. Because I guess there *is*, buried somewhere inside our wish to be and remain two happily married people, the skeletal structure of the very different marriage story we could still potentially look back on, realize and declare.

If marriage is a cover story, then no one knows that better than the divorcee who finds herself uncovered. And this regardless of whether it was she who sought the cover's removal in the first place. 'Even when Sophie couldn't bear Ezra,' writes Susan Taubes in her 1969 novel *Divorcing*, 'she loved the marriage. It was a many-layered shroud whose weight she relished. To carry it eased, simplified entering a room full of people, it justified her presence in the room. There it was, a costume ready-made for public occasions. Ezra's wife; this was the answer to anyone who wanted to know her . . . It had weight and power: like an impermeable cloak it warded off the inevitable swarm of prying . . . It saved her skin. How not cherish a garment so serviceable?'

Sophie's married name is Sophie Blind, Blind signifying a status that's effectively hidden her from the world, protecting her from its prying swarms. Which is precisely what Sophie loved about her marriage, even when she didn't love her husband. She always liked the fact that she was spoken for. Marriage, with its ready-made cover story, meant no questions needed to be asked of her. In removing the Blind, however, she finds herself instantly exposed to what she's not encountered so directly before: an unmediated collision with reality. In marriage, she inhabited a kind of fiction to which the whole world had given its assent. In divorce, she finds herself confronted by the truth of life in the raw: 'it's terrifying to be this naked, to have given up all personhood, the old wraps and cloaks, some never worn, all burnt up. This nakedness, she knows, can never again be clothed.'

In undoing her marriage, Sophie thus feels herself denuded, as if she now has nothing to hide. There's a hint, therefore, in this act of nuptial unveiling, that it's divorce, not marriage, that could return the innocent bride or groom to the plenitude of a prelapsarian paradise. Divorce as a way of living in the whole truth and nothing but. But is that really possible? You can certainly see the seduction of this idea in the way it seems to animate many people after they first get divorced. In the exhilaration of their liberation to think, say and do whatever they wish. No more bowing to etiquette! No more hypocrisy! No more playing by the rules of a game that has only ever let them down! No more cover-ups! While marriage makes children of us, comforted by illusions and shielded from the brute force of experience at its grittiest, divorce, on this interpretation, is the terrain of those who are prepared to brave the world in all their naked truth.

Or is that just another illusion? What Sophie Blind soon discovers is that her divorce story may not be the sort of story that the world as presently constituted is willing to hear. That world would even have to be completely rearranged for Sophie to make much sense in it. As such, this isn't the world from which she addresses us, as she explains early on in her narration: 'Yes, I'm dead'. It's a dead woman, in other words, who is sharing her tale with us from beyond the grave, the marriage plot having colonized the life narrative so utterly that divorce can only speak from the hereafter. Although it's in that afterlife that Sophie also finds her senses returning: 'I never felt so intensely alive as now'. It was marriage's 'many-layered shroud', after all, that rendered her, when alive, as good as dead. Like Shahrazad, Sophie Blind is another figure of the storyteller who hovers somewhere between life and death, not quite of this world or the next.

Indeed, the formal difficulty of Taubes's highly experimental text is critically related to its aim of dismantling a marriage plot that has structured fiction and reality to the extent of rendering these two so beholden to each other that they've squeezed out any other account. How then to intervene into that plot's seeming intractability? Taubes believed she could do so via fiction in a way that she couldn't in the real world such fictions have helped to forge. A book, Sophie remarks, 'was something really different.' Clearly a book narrated by a dead woman who has never felt more alive is something different. And while *Divorcing*, strictly speaking, is a work of fantasy, it's also, given its barely veiled portrayal of Taubes's own marriage, a work very much married to reality. Yet Taubes's was the sort of different book that would get ignored or critically disparaged when it first came out. A week after its publication, in fact, Taubes committed suicide – motivated to do so, suggested her close friend Susan Sontag, by the bad reviews she'd received. She had hoped to find some sort of afterlife of her marriage through her writing – and it's no accident that the writing itself tells of a suicided woman who addresses us from the afterlife of a life consumed by marriage – yet the reality of that afterlife, it seems, was only achievable posthumously. While today the world does appear readier than it was to receive what Taubes had to share, rendering her book's recent reissue over fifty years after it first appeared both extremely poignant and remarkably vindicating of the faith that a book is 'something really different'.

For all its formal experimentalism, however, the book's originality has as much to do with its heroine's determination to divorce from her marriage rather than adulterating that marriage in the manner of Sophie's predecessors inside the novels of adultery. Indeed, as the daughter of separated bohemian parents and the wife of a man who permits her to take on other lovers, Sophie Blind could not have easily joined the ranks of the adulteress subversives. So it's not the binds of traditional marriage so much as the putative freedom of modern marriage that she feels she's up against. With arranged marriages, whatever their misery, 'it was the objective validity of these marriages that impressed Sophie. As for her parents' marriage, she had never been able to think of it as a true marriage.'

She thus sues for divorce on the basis that her own marriage – made in the mould not of traditional religion, but religion reformulated in the register of Marxism, Freudianism and free love – is not a true one.

Had she suffered inside 'a true marriage' she feels she could have borne her fate. But marriage disguised as a progressive institution? Such a marriage, Sophie believes, is no marriage. As such, Sophie's project is to undo marriage not in the mode of the adulteress – whose rebellion is ultimately a surreptitious effort to escape from matrimony's cauterizing of the soul – but publicly, in a court of law. This she can only do from the vantage of the afterlife, however, where she finds herself at a mock tribunal with her father and husband bearing witness against her. 'Gentlemen', she intones, 'greatly regret, infinitely sorry, unspeakably ashamed of stupidities I got enmeshed in by some particle of belief in your lies . . . When I'm truly dead, my friends, I won't see you standing around me. I will find a way out'. She'll only be dead when she's reached the world of the true marriage and its happy-ever-after; a true marriage that belongs solely to that person who can make of their divorce something final. Whereas in the world as we find it now, Sophie's formal intervention implies, divorce is essentially a metaphysical impossibility.

Hence, in a different but not unrelated way to Olga's state of abandonment, Sophie's intentional act of divorcing is what also seems to abandon her to senselessness. Which is why, anticipating such objections, Sophie pre-emptively rebuffs them: 'Coherent discourse? How do you expect me –? Begin to explain now in my present state of decomposition?' If she's hard to parse, that is, it's because she's neither alive nor dead but decomposing. And what she's decomposing through her writing's incoherence isn't simply herself or her marriage, it's the whole world that rendered her one way on account of the other. As she withdraws her consent from the marital contract, she thus simultaneously withdraws her consent from every other aspect of the social contract in which she's implicated: religion, politics, philosophy, psychoanalysis, the new world, civilization itself. If the marriage plot made that civilization, she figures, the divorce plot must then be called upon by any writer looking to unmake it.

*

In some ways, Taubes's position might be said to resemble Milton's conception of divorce as the procedure needed to annul an untrue marriage. On the question of what constitutes a *true* marriage, however, it's unlikely they'd have found much common ground. In fact, the responsibility for hollowing out the truth of marriage falls, in Taubes's opinion, on the shoulders of the reforming history that Milton, with his tract on divorce, partly helped to initiate. Modernity, she believed, only added further veils to the veiled institution. An opinion one can find broadly echoed in various other reckonings with divorce over three hundred years after Milton first promoted it. According to the American analyst Edmund Bergler's 1948 tome *Divorce Won't Help*, for example, divorce by the twentieth century had morphed into a bastion of false consciousness for the modern subject who doesn't understand her own character. The person 'suing for divorce', he wrote, 'unconsciously wants to get rid of her own inner conflict. Unaware of the very existence of the conflict, she fights with great energy against her partner, upon whom the conflict has been projected.' Since this conflict is really an internal one, however, she will no sooner divorce her spouse than seek another spouse with whom to continue her quarrel. As such, divorce, by marrying her to the marital project even more committedly, could even be symptomatic of her *addiction* to marriage. What divorce really signifies, suggests Bergler, is the alibi of someone for whom marriage is *too* good to be true.

So while Milton saw the situation in relatively simple terms – a marriage should be happy so unhappiness requires divorce – as modern history unfolded, this simple logic no longer seemed to represent the complex nature of social and personal reality. The psychoanalytical claim that there are ambivalent currents residing within such things as love, sex, attachment and happiness, created critical problems for Milton's solution to marital misery. Because what if we *don't* quite grasp what makes us happy? What if we even run away from the things that bring us pleasure? And what if we turn as often to divorce to release us from our joys as our pains?

Late modernity, in other words, has demanded an even more subtle grappling with the question of what constitutes a true marriage, or a true divorce. And that's precisely what we find attempted by Cavell, who wagers that 'only those can genuinely marry who are already married. It is as though you know you are married when you come to see that you cannot divorce, that is, when you find that your lives simply will not disentangle.' He's not talking about coupled lives that won't disentangle for material or pragmatic reasons. While there are of course plenty of those, his theory of entanglement seems less of a physical than a metaphysical proposition. On its basis, a true marriage may be identified when a couple has consented to enter into a state of mutual dependency. What they need to feel is that they can't survive without each other. So, one might surmise, you marry someone if you can't live without them, and you divorce them if you find you can. Which is quite a stance. On this account, a married couple who aren't necessarily miserable together but who could nevertheless exist apart may as well do so – because such a marriage would be no marriage.

Cavell never goes so far as to argue explicitly that one should *divorce if one can*, although the implication for that kind of radical mandate does suggest itself in his writing, I think. And what its clarification also suggests is that divorcing, under such conditions, can be a means of viable resistance to a social order that has sought to keep people married for the wrong reasons – a social order that has made of the matrimonial institution the ultimate bulwark of values and interests that may have very little to do with pleasing the married couple themselves. In which context, we might ask on what grounds campaigns to save or promote marriage have historically been waged. For these are campaigns that have been under way throughout the modern era, expanding into newer and newer fields in tandem with globalization. Right now, for instance, China is noticing an upward trend against marriage in its young people, which trend the government is seeking to redress as a phenomenon it considers harmful to the country's own long-term well-being and survival. In this sense, China's more recent conversion to a market economy seems to be shadowing the social changes that have long since befallen America, where the unmarrying trend (as well as the efforts to combat that trend in the national interest) have an even lengthier history.

'Marriage in America is in disarray, or so they say. Americans, among the marryingest people in the world, are also the divorcingest', is how Jill Lepore begins her 2010 article for the *New Yorker* examining 'The rise of marriage therapy, and other dreams of human betterment'. It's an essay that traces early twenty-first-century campaigns to save marriage from divorce or decline as far back as the 1930s. In particular, Lepore reflects on the pioneering role of Paul Popenoe, 'father of marriage counselling, who is best remembered for the *Ladies' Home Journal* feature "Can This Marriage Be Saved?"'. It's a feature that's still running, as is the family business – David Popenoe, Paul's son, having taken over his father's marriage-saving empire. Which is a large empire. By the 1950s, writes Lepore, Paul Popenoe was the source of numerous marriage manuals, newspaper columns, radio and TV shows. 'People called him Mr. Marriage.' Yet Mr. Marriage didn't aspire to save everyone's marriages, only the marriages of those families whom he considered the most desirable for propagating future generations of Americans. If other marriages fell by the way, so be it. Indeed, as an admirer of Hitler, he held the science of eugenics at the heart of his marriage-saving agenda. 'Divorcees are on the whole biologically inferior to the happily married', he wrote. So by 'saving the marriages of the biologically superior', observes Lepore, 'Popenoe hoped to save the race.' Oh.

We can contrast that *New Yorker* article with 'The Marriage Cure', Katherine Boo's *New Yorker* article from 2003. In Boo's essay, the ideological drive to save America in the twenty-first century *has* come to include an effort to save the marriages of those that Popenoe considered biologically inferior the century before. To see how, Boo goes to Oklahoma City to a public housing project named Sooner Haven, where she gets to know some of the project's residents who are attending a three-day instructional course on how to get and stay married. The course, held at the Holy Temple Baptist Church, sponsors preachers and pastors to teach attendees that marriage is the best way out of the ghetto. The Bush Administration's promotion of marriage as cure to those living far below the poverty line wasn't on account of any wish to propagate or 'save their race', however. Rather, marriage here is spun as a way of limiting the numbers of children born out of wedlock and thus reducing those eligible for government support by combining household numbers and incomes, however negligible these incomes may be.

Noting the degree to which marriage in America has become a relatively middle-class preserve, sociologist Melinda Cooper has more recently tracked how this fact has spearheaded the belief (expressed at both ends of the political spectrum) that marriage must be a marker of social mobility. Yet in tracing the policies that have made 'family values' the cornerstone of neoliberal ones, what looks like social conservatism is actually, says Cooper, a movement for dismantling the social. The anti-State privatizing agenda has accordingly been powerfully aligned with ideological resistance to *any* form of welfare provision. After all, a social order premised on the marital contract effectively lays down the conditions for social reproduction in such a way that there will always be workers to perpetuate the world, but without anyone having to pay for or even recognize their work. The private individuals and family clusters that have been required to take on all social risks and responsibilities may nevertheless imagine that their intimate ties and obligations are simply representative of the traditional world that marriage and the nuclear family has always sustained. However, the reality of the modern nuclear family, as Silvia Federici has pointed out, is that its current arrangements have their roots in the mid-nineteenth century. That was when a modernizing society sought to avert the threat of proletarian revolutions by making the home the centre for the reproduction of labour power.

But the issue is knottier than even this. In Sooner Haven, for instance, marriage promotion isn't limited merely to arguments about social mobility or economic security and advancement. It's also, as the 'Marriage Cure' attendees are told, a means to self-respect. To wit, the few willing participants of the scheme are mostly single mothers eager to figure out a plan for getting a man to marry them and stay married to them in order to attain 'a healthy, wealthy, normal-lady life'. One of these mothers describes her divorce as a 'living death'. There can be no joy, she believes, for those who dwell in the state of the unmarried. And yet the marriage project, Boo finds, is more or less doomed in the housing project. Marriage cannot be prevailed upon to cure all social, economic and political ills and injustices. What we perceive instead, in her article's shattering depiction of lives lived without opportunities, is how many other conditions would need to be in place before anyone thus afflicted could be expected to make a good fist out of marriage.

Of course, not every marriage-saving scheme has been instituted simply to protect the interests of a nation, economy, race or (let's face it) patriarchy, although any established method for bringing people who are finding it hard to *be* together *back* together will invariably have its reasons for wanting to save marriage; much as the therapist in each case will have their own reasons too. It's interesting, for instance, that two of the best-known contemporary couples' therapists, Esther Perel and Orna Guralnik, both descended from Holocaust survivors, understand the intergenerational transmission of trauma and conflict in such a way that this adds a palpable dimension to their practice – a practice in which you can perceive how histories might be unconsciously acted out and then worked through in the therapeutic engagement of individuals within their marriages. Although the therapeutic approach is trickier when the sort of background conflicts and traumas that can get displaced into private relations aren't so much a historical legacy as a description of the therapeutic subject's ongoing social reality – like the reality of life in Sooner Haven. In that situation, the marriage promoted as redemptive is so unreachable as to make the lack of it feel that much more damning and, as a consequence, harder. As such, places like Sooner Haven beckon us to imagine a different social contract *not* founded upon marriage. For in a situation where marriage can't and won't bind the social world, we have to ask – what will?

In Sooner Haven, despite the infrequency of successful marriages, there remains a critical dependence upon the family unit, particularly in the case of single mothers relying on kids who will eventually flee their nests. But while these family networks and relations are vital, they're not viable over the long term. That fact makes hardly a scrap of difference, however, when marriage and the nuclear family are the talk of the church and the town. If marriage is what's being preached, literally, as the source of both personal and social salvation, it can be hard to come up with any alternatives. Though there is, in Boo's article, the odd glimmer of other possibilities, such as when yet another town bus swerves to avoid picking up Kim Henderson, a young woman who can't get home otherwise. Left stranded, Kim eventually finds a woman who will stop for her because 'I know, I used to have to take the bus, too.' And there are other small signs of a torn-apart and barely surviving community pitching in together to share in each other's sufferings and responsibilities. In such forms of recognition, sympathy and solidarity there are thus intimations of alternative ways of imagining and organizing a society that would offer (or at least agitate for) rights, opportunities and structures of contact and support that *aren't* contingent on one's family situation.

Not that you need to be in the state of economic abandonment that marks the lives of those whom marrying has left behind in places like Sooner Haven, or even in the state of marital abandonment into which Ferrante's Olga suddenly finds herself plunged, to wonder whether there might be alternatives to a social contract founded on marriage and the nuclear family. In the most rudimentary sense, this search for alternatives could be the very thing that best characterizes progressive as opposed to conservative thinking. In his 1998 essay 'Against Monogamy', for example, the critic Leo Bersani laments the acceleration of a popular movement amongst homosexual couples looking for security and recognition by gaining entry into the very institutions from which, historically, they've been viciously excluded. The pursuit of legitimacy via marriage and its sexual norms, he even charges, amounts to a moral and political failure. And equally an aesthetic failure. For whoever pursues 'normality' relinquishes the utopian hope that homosexual lives and histories might be sources of imagining 'new ways of being together' – new ways, that is, of enlarging the compass of the human group by shedding light on the matter of 'how we become social beings and not merely familial beings'.

To take up this challenge in resistance to the drive that would seek to straighten out the singular into the coupled, the promiscuous into the monogamous, and the queer into the straight, Bersani turns, if ambivalently, towards Freud and psychoanalysis, finding in Oedipal theory both a source of the problem and a source of the insights that can be summoned to resolve it. For it's true, on the one hand, that there exists a psychoanalytic framing which, based on Oedipus, assumes all sexual desire is nostalgic for the attachments first formed in infancy. On this version, putatively new objects of interest are really an attempt to recover old objects – so there can be no real movement beyond the realm of the family, which the subject is always implicitly seeking to reconstitute in veiled form. Hence, if one cannot escape the family and the past, social progress cannot be founded upon the erotic. It's this argument, invoking an idea of desire as in some sense inimical towards progress, that we've already considered in previous chapters. So it's to counter that more conservative interpretation, therefore, that Bersani identifies an alternatively progressive desire (not his term – my clunky one) taking root in the same early dynamics of the family set-up. He notes, for instance, that Freud's pre-Oedipal infant is actually a curious character, subject to multiple roving impulses and attractions, and that it's this very curiosity that the social order will soon enough seek to commandeer and constrain. Indeed, subsequent demands on the child will require them to choose a parent to identify with in an effort to resolve the havoc that might otherwise be caused by their essential promiscuity. By thus aligning the child with an adult signifying a particular (genital-based) affiliation, this developmental theory is one that tends towards the politics of identity in lieu of the politics of emancipation. Although Bersani goes further still, critiquing Oedipal theory in a slightly different way to the approach taken by Jessica Benjamin mentioned earlier. For even in the *post*-Oedipal situation, he notes, it's possible to read the role of the father in this intimate drama not as an authoritarian figure necessarily, but as someone who very promisingly leads the infant away from their sheltered home life into a world of new and unlimited possibilities. Thus the 'father' (or whoever enacts the role of introducing the child to the world) is the guide to a perpetually expanding horizon from which the child may never wish to look back. On this account, then, the family unit is rejected in favour of a less hermetically sealed idea of the social group, albeit a group still bound by a questing that's rooted in the erotic.

Having tried it, Taubes didn't agree that free love was the solution that some of her contemporaries imagined; it was just another way for patriarchy to play the same old games, she thought, but in progressive clothing. Still, even if 'free love' hasn't always been as good as its word, nor is it a dream that's easily relinquished. There's the bathwater and there's the baby, and most of us, presumably, would wish to be able to love who we happen to love freely, without censorship, coercion or constraint – hence the vital importance of knowing there's such a thing as divorce when one chooses to get married. Although as a politically inflected dream, free love has remained mostly associated with a particular decade, the 1960s, as the banner of a protest movement seeking liberation from the bourgeois complacencies of marriage and the nuclear family, not via the divorce that Taubes invoked in a

1969 work that doubled up as a damning verdict on the hopes and aspirations of that decade, but via the sex and sexuality that leads, in the first place, beyond the family and the settled home.

In Tessa Hadley's recent novel set in the 1960s, *Free Love*, we're introduced to Phyllis, the ultimate figure of the upper-class housewife so familiar to the history of the novel. And here too, it's Phyllis whose story we follow as she takes it upon herself to abandon both her children and her smart, decent and forbearing husband – not because she's suffering any great hardship, but because her married life is somewhat listless, and her home life feels as if it's being lived inside a mausoleum. The trigger for her departure is her captivation by a young man with whom she falls helplessly in love; a youthful rebel who claims that marriage is a capitalist conceit and that 'civilization was an appalling error'. It's his body more than his ideas that first attracts her. As her story develops, however, his luminosity somewhat dims as she finds that she has indeed recommitted to a new way of life – one not without its precarities, but whose alternative vision of community and housing invokes a utopianism she can at least believe in. Hence, for all the uncertainty she's willingly embraced, and for all the suffering she's unintentionally caused, she is not destined to meet with the sort of tragic ending that her famous literary precursors – bourgeois heroines such as Anna Karenina and Madame Bovary – could find no means of escaping. Phyllis's fate and her future remain, at the end, a much more open horizon of possibility. In that sense, Hadley's novel, by rejecting the virtuous marriage plot, isn't so much a late addition to 'the novel of adultery' as it's an alternate vision of the divorce plot – if we allow divorce's meaning to get fully stretched to the point wherein Cavell invites us to think of it: for Phyllis chooses to leave her marriage on the basis that she can – and because such a marriage would be no marriage. Indeed, in abandoning her husband, Phyllis doesn't pursue another marriage. What she's pursuing instead is the idea that life and love *after* marriage might be lived and enjoyed even more fully, and more truthfully, than they were before.

One paradox of Phyllis's narrative is that she should find herself led into her adulthood by a youth and a youth movement that her earlier more conventionally adult life gave her no real access to. And this, it seems, isn't simply because she's leaving her cocoon of upper-class privilege, but because marriage had been for Phyllis what it was for Sophie – a sort of blind. In theorizing his ethics of promiscuity, Bersani quotes the psychoanalyst Christopher Bollas's 1992 work *Being a Character*. In a chapter entitled 'Why Oedipus?', Bollas describes marriage as a commitment to one's own regression – a regression wilfully pursued in order to escape two complexities: that of one's own mind (one's individual character) and that of group diversity. It's a regression marriage is said to uniquely enable by evoking the bodies of the pre-Oedipal mother and father 'before the solitary recognition of subjectivity grips the child.' As such, marriage may be considered a means not only of narrowing one's horizon, but also of defacing one's character altogether – which, when you consider what's out there, or what's in there, is certainly one way to go. But there are, of course, those who would prefer to go the other way – by expanding their horizon and by facing their character.

Real Estate, the third slim volume of Deborah Levy's 'living auto-biography' representing the realities of its author's life after marriage and separation, is written in the wake of her newly 'empty nest', her two daughters having grown up and left home. In this volume, Levy is on the hunt for the 'female character' who's been 'disappeared' from so much cultural history. Having sought release from the patri-archal institutions that have traditionally claimed the body of woman as their own real estate, is it possible that she could herself be this missing character? Her vocation as a writer is certainly a critical part of this venture, but she engages no less committedly in other forms of truth-seeking and other kinds of non-married and non-parental relation. Could this character be discovered, for instance, within alter-native configurations of the social or indeed the familial? Levy certainly finds inspiration in cooking for her daughters and their female friends, in whose occasional company an exhilarating sense of feminist community and possibility seems, as if organically, to emerge. Likewise, she relishes opportunities for engaging others in unflinchingly honest conversation, especially with colleagues and the various female friends whom she visits or who visit her during an increasingly itinerant period of her life (Levy for the most part names the female characters in her book, leaving the men unnamed). Yet, gesturing towards her 'empty nest', her 'best male friend' insists that what she really needs is a new lover – someone to share her home, life and future with. And she does entertain that possibility, although she isn't sure it's the solution. This friend is himself someone who seems to need constant companionship; someone who, we might speculate, is unable to be alone because he cannot tolerate the solitary recognition of his own subjectivity. He's not only the marrying type, in fact, but something of a marrying addict. Currently on his third marriage, to Nadia, when he visits Levy in Paris he begins an affair with yet another woman. Soon, we can guess, his marriage to Nadia will be over. But even as he lines up wife number four, he feels himself to be no less abandoned than abandoning. Is he doomed, therefore, to a life of fickle faithlessness that will keep him lonely precisely because of the backfiring ways in which he seeks to mitigate his own loneliness? Not necessarily. For he *is* at least enduringly faithful in his friendship with Levy, whom he seems to follow around the world, and to whom he pours out his heart, as we note in one scene where Levy listens to her best male friend's romantic turmoil, tears, confusion and long silences on the phone. 'After a while my best male friend asked me if I was still there. I told him I was still there. In this sense, he and I were attached to each other for better, for worse, for richer, for poorer, in sickness and in health.' Though one may well abscond from the traditional frameworks of the family in favour of alternative arrangements, marriage's fundamental structure of relation *doesn't die, it doesn't want to die.*

*

'The wish to be alone is never an original wish', writes Bergler in his cautionary tale against the divorcee who imagines she can leave marriage and enter the realm of nothing but the truth. 'Such a wish simply does not exist. What is clinically observable is a stubborn refusal to acknowledge defeat sustained in the battle of marriage. The defeat is denied by the compensatory claim that nothing was lost.' Despite their differences, this is a point upon which Bergler and Milton might have agreed. Milton approved of divorce, but he didn't doubt that divorce is testament to a major defeat. Marriage was created, after all, because of man's existential need for companionship. The original wish isn't to be alone, it's to be in contact with others. Although the other side of this creation story is that marriage is what comes along not only to resolve but to intensify the sense of loneliness – whether because the marriage itself is as isolating as a prison cell, or because there are few things more guaranteed to make a person feel lonely than the proliferation of long-term couples enacting the role of 'normal people' everywhere around them.

Writing in the *Guardian* about what can be experienced as persecuting for so many living in the world of 'the couple-norm', Sasha Roseneil notes that the marginalization that comes with living one's life outside of a couple has rarely attracted the attention bestowed on various other forms of marginal identity. And this even though the couple, for all it may be the norm, isn't necessarily all that normal. Certainly huge swathes of people are living alone or in alternative forms of community, with friends, comrades, extended family, pets and other animals, including alternative (non-romantic) couplings. Which is why, for Roseneil alongside her fellow researchers of a book contesting the 'tenacity of the couple-norm', it's high time governments and civil societies caught up with the historical transformations that have already taken place so as 'to move beyond couple normativity': 'We propose a rethinking of the welfare state to be more "single-person friendly", and to start thinking about how international human rights conventions might be extended to place the right to a fulfilling single life alongside the right to family life. The time has come to release the tenacious grip of the couple-norm, for the benefit of us all – currently coupled or not.'

The cruelty of a system that has relegated single people to the margins of a society that has barely thought about the reality of their needs at all was brought home with particular viciousness during the Covid pandemic when, especially during the first mandated lockdowns, a single person could find themself almost entirely cut off from the social world. And this was during a period when their friends or relatives with spouses and/or children had never had their hands fuller or their time less available. That said, for many people living alone, 'the new normal' wasn't so different to their old normal either. In one newspaper article that really shook me, the journalist Claire Bushey describes her existence as a single woman living alone during lockdown as little more than an accentuation of what she already recognizes as her lot in life. Loneliness, in her view, is not best described as an 'epidemic' but as a 'famine'. 'I am lonely as the body is hungry three times a day,' she writes, 'hollowed again and again by an ache that does not ease except with the sustenance of connection.' It needn't be a lover, in other words, that's required to ease this constant ache, it could just as well be a friend. For what the real issue is here is the lack of *any* lastingly meaningful contact or connection, leading towards a terrible 'gnawing sadness' that's only exacerbated by the tenaciousness of a couple-norm that forces her to feel, on top of this sadness, also 'the shame of loneliness' – which shame isolates her all the more, for loneliness is hard to admit of when others may consider it as a sign not of one's misfortune, but of one's fault.

Bushey writes beautifully on such a painful subject, her words rendered still more searing for being so unusually open about a common yet rarely depicted reality. Nor does one need to live alone to recognize their accuracy. We all know *something* of what loneliness (as opposed to solitude) can feel like, and the acute sense of desperation it can sometimes arouse. One of the reasons I felt so moved when I first read her piece was down to my own familiarity with that terrible ache and gnawing sadness, notwithstanding that these moments of familiarity are relatively short-lived in the course of my mostly shared and hectic day-to-day existence. And I say this as some-one who of course frequently feels – and who felt especially keenly during lockdown – that she would do pretty much anything to get some time alone. I mean, who doesn't need that semi-regularly? Although I'm conscious too that if I'm given very *much* time alone, I unravel remarkably fast. Left to my own devices, I'm soon enough nothing *but* my vices, reverting to various forms of self-destructive and addictive behaviour. In fact, the speed with which I seem to *fort/ da* myself into not so much mastery as oblivion is sufficient to make me wonder sometimes if I might be using marriage's cover story mainly in order to keep me away from who it turns out, when left alone, I really am. Hence why, in a society predicated on marriage, the loneliness famine should surely set alarm bells ringing. As Bushey points out regarding the real dangers sometimes posed by discon-nected people whose social life exists entirely online, these are often the conditions of a turn towards extremist politics. The world from which you're excluded, after all, is the world you may be inclined to drop out of – or burn.

A critical question to be asked, therefore, of the civilization whose social contract is rooted in the marriage contract, is whether marriage has sufficient latitude to be capable of enlarging itself in such a way as to bring into its fold *all the lonely people*. It's a question that the British director Mike Leigh seems to be asking in his 2010 feature, *Another Year*. In this remarkable film, we spend most of our time in the home of a long-term happily married couple, Tom and Gerri. We meet this couple in late midlife playing occasional host to numerous waifs and strays, as well as their only child, Joe, who is himself on the lookout for someone he wishes to settle down with. Their single guests, Mary, Ken and Ronnie, are all implicitly infantilized in their company, as emphasized by their temporary lodging in Joe's childhood bedroom. It's the middle-aged but far from grown-up Mary (played stunningly by Lesley Manville), though, who appears as the most desperately in need of the married couple's attention, and who shows up in their house and at their table with every passing season. Mary is a divorcee whose life has not gone according to plan. She seems lost and she frequently *gets* lost. She is, it's plain to see, achingly lonely. Yet she tries to put a brave face on it. And she tries to persuade herself that she's on an equal footing with her friendly hosts, giving as much as she's taking. She also, if deludedly, tries to persuade herself she could be a love match for their son, Joe.

Clearly not every single woman of a certain age is such a car crash of a character. The film, as a consequence, might appear to be pathologizing the single woman, or indeed the single man – since Ken too is another car crash, and a coronary case waiting to happen. But Leigh isn't in the business of condemning individuals. Rather, he meticulously situates individuals in the social world that has made their lives more or less possible. So it's the nature of the social contract which he's really exploring. On which basis we can see, for instance, that a happy marriage *is* as good as its word for those who happen to be so fortunate. In their own little version of the Miltonic idyll, Tom and Gerri garden together, cook what they've gardened together, and tell tales of going on holiday together – the happy holidaying of people who know where home is. And they also drink, but not to excess. And eat well, but not to excess. They don't smoke. Meanwhile, Mary, Ken and Ronnie, who do not garden or cook or holiday, all drink and smoke far too much. They have what some would call addictive personalities – personalities that make a stark contrast to the happy couple looking out for them.

But what do we really think of Tom and Gerri? Some critics have taken against them as smug marrieds, identifying a conceitedness within their happiness and citing evidence of something cruel in the knowing glances they occasionally dart at each other when one of their guests is having a pathetic moment. Nor is it hard to notice that all their most open communication takes place with each other and with other happy people. With their unfortunate friends, they seem more akin to managers or therapists, as if this part of their personal life was really an extension of their professional life (Gerri actually *is* a counsellor, for the NHS). I'm not sure that this critique of them holds up, however. For these are clearly kind and hospitable people; people with social consciences who are always looking for ways to help the have-nots in their midst. And they evidently feel duty bound to open up their home and share their happiness, as if experimenting with the idea that their own marital fulfilment could or should somehow be socialized. So if you still can't stand them, then that's a sign, surely, that there's not much they could do to make this social solution one that could work for everyone. Indeed, though they strive to make of their own good fortune a resource for others, they'd lose their happiness if their marriage was altogether diverted into its welfare state; as, indeed, we observe clearly towards the end of the film when Mary shows up uninvited, having been somewhat frozen out by Gerri after how badly she reacted upon first meeting Joe's girlfriend. Desperately in need of her friend, Mary begs for forgiveness and for a return to their former fellowship. And Gerri does forgive her, but in doing so she also explains where the line between them is drawn: 'This is my family, Mary. You've got to understand that.' Mary may have been welcomed back inside her friends' happy home, but that word 'family' is a slammer firmly shut in her face. It's a heart-rending moment. During all her earlier appearances at their dinner table, Mary couldn't stop talking, but now she's mostly silent, no longer quite capable of wearing the brave face that she keeps in the jar by the door. Still, the camera ends with a long, extremely affecting and I think loving shot of that face; as if to remind us that, though this may be Tom and Gerri's house and Tom and Gerri's family and Tom and Gerri's home-grown and home-cooked food, it's Mary's story that we're really watching, and Mary's predicament that we're really being invited to feel.

That a story always finds its pulse not in the group but in the individual, no matter how marginal the individual character may look to be, brings to mind other films, including the Japanese director Yasujirō Ozu's 1953 masterpiece, *Tokyo Story*. It's a film in which we get a rather more brutal depiction of a modern world whose rapid transformations have made the consolations of the family an increasingly poor resource for whoever finds themselves situated on the outside of its protections. And Ozu was certainly concerned, especially in the traumatic aftermath of the war, with what becomes of people and the ties that bind them when traditional frameworks break down in the shift to urbanized and liberalized economies. For that reason, he was sometimes accused by critics of a cultural conservatism bordering on the reactionary. I don't think that's a fair representation, though, of films that are never really polemical so much as they're scrupulously attentive to the intimate changes that take place in conjunction with broader social and historical ones. In *Tokyo Story*, for example, the film follows an aged couple who decide, for the first time as they near the twilight of their days, to leave their seaside town and visit their grown-up children who are trying to keep up with their middle-class lives in the capital city. But their children, busy with demanding jobs and demanding families, do not offer their parents a warm welcome. Their parents, indeed, come to feel very quickly that they're unwanted guests – more of a burden than anything else to children who cannot easily accommodate non-instrumental relationships within their tight schedules. Or that's the case with their own children anyway. With their daughter-in-law Noriko, the war widow of the son they have already had to lose and mourn, they do find a more hospitable reception. She even seems as familiar to them as the children they raised have become alien. Familiarity here having less to do with bloodlines than with timelines, or temporal wavelengths. Living alone in the wake of her marriage, Noriko has the feeling and time for her in-laws that their own children lack. Indeed, living on after her marriage, she has the feeling and time that Tokyo itself perhaps lacks. Worried for her, her in-laws urge her to remarry and begin another family, but she has no interest in re-entering that fray. Removed from the demands of family life, she alone (and seemingly, *because* she's alone) can perform the traditional virtues of her elected kinship, thus making of her marriage, in its residuum, a continuance of her love story – which love story, if her sister- and brother-in-law's marriage is anything to go by, may well not have continued had her husband remained alive.

Noriko is a character who haunts me. I remember watching *Tokyo Story* for the first time and feeling how acutely my sympathies lay with hers. And I remember thinking, too, that I would like to resemble Noriko and behave as she does. I imagined myself liberated into a solitary existence free from the demands of family life. In this fantasy, I wasn't a liability when left alone. On the contrary, I was an angel, fully present with everyone, generous with my time and attention. But even as this fantasy took hold of me, I guessed who I must really resemble with my constant complaints about my never-ending to-do list: the middle-class family on the make; the family who can cause even those they love most to feel squeezed into a schedule, like just another item they have 'to do'.

Still, for all that my daily reality may resemble not Noriko's but her sister-in-law's, it's Noriko who engages my sympathies because the story of the passions belongs to the solitary figure, not to the group and not even to the couple. Which is what, in a moment of bleak humour, the undertaker who met my mother, brother and me (when we went to see her about arranging a tombstone for my father) must surely have meant when she cautioned us against the temptation of the double gravestone, which some couples choose, she said, 'romantically but foolishly', since it denies death's great truth 'that we all have to enter and leave this world alone'. A statement as simple as it's undeniable. And since my father died, I have never felt more conscious of its stark reality. It's the overwhelming fact of her left-aloneness that has assailed my mother in the grief of her loss. Although what our undertaker (also a widow) was intimating, I think, was something still more fundamental about an existential solitariness that precedes even one's bereavement. Some of my most intense and sublime experiences have been in the presence of my husband, for example. Just as some have been without him. But whether they've been with, without or even *about* my husband, these are experiences so intense or sublime that they felt intensely mine in a way that could not have led to their easy translation into the sense of another, even if he was going through what appeared to be the same thing at the same time.

In Christopher Isherwood's singular novel *A Single Man*, we find ourselves with another bereaved spouse, although George's grief at being left alone is enveloped in the even greater isolation that befalls a man who has lost his life's great love and companion, but who does not even have the permission to name his loss given the taboo surrounding homosexuality in the American suburbs of the early 1960s. At the start of the book, in his seeming antipathy towards the world and everyone in it, one wonders if he'll ever recover his will to live, or mingle. But over the course of the novel, he is won back over to the side of life. Not, as one might expect, because he's now able to speak of his loss or share his story. No, it's the erotics of actually living that reignites him: '*I am alive*, he says to himself, *I am alive!* And life-energy surges hotly through him, and delight, and appetite.' Like Ferrante's Olga, and Taubes's dead heroine, Sophie, George is finally, on the other side of his widowhood, returned to his senses. And curiously, one aspect to this recovery is his reconciliation with the idea of his singleness not as a new fact marked by his sudden bereavement, but as his most basic and enduring fact. Hence when Charley, his good friend, seeks to remind him that they understand each other, he marvels at this 'absurd and universally accepted bit of nonsense . . . that your best friends must necessarily be the ones who best understand you'. In registering this absurdity, he realizes it's his singular senses and not any sort of common sense that's recovered him.

Indeed, the consolation of his friendship with Charley, he reflects further, isn't down to her good sense but rather her lack of it: '. . . how could I have gotten through these last years without your wonderful lack of perception? How many times, when Jim and I had been quarrelling and came to visit you – sulking, avoiding each other's eyes, talking to each other only through you – did you somehow bring us together again by the sheer power of your unawareness that anything was wrong?' Thinking these private thoughts in sympathetic company, he's enjoying himself again. And he's enjoying, in particular, his own illegibility for another who cares for him and would earnestly seek to know him. Which present moment also recalls an earlier, happier time, when his lost love was still alive and with him. But what was the nature of that espoused happiness?

Quarrelling with one's partner and being ill-perceived by one's friend doesn't sound like the ideal community. But maybe it is. For it isn't so much that George, in his bereavement, misses being fully known. If he and Jim had been of one mind, with no quarrels, what would have been the point of their relationship? Such a marriage would be no marriage. What his most significant others have given him, rather, is the solace of feeling himself tantalizingly unknown, and unknowable, even for those who really do care to know him. So the memory that returns gladly to him here, of a fulfilment made up of the perfect sum of the three it takes to make a couple, is one that doesn't forgo either the complexity of group life or the complexity of individual consciousness. It does, however, depend on real connection and contact with loving others, of whatever relation, without whose doomed efforts to know us we might forfeit any connection with the infinitely complex character we're really looking to discover, who ought never to disappear – the lifelong companion we must all learn to become, unto death, for ourselves.

12

Obscenes from a Marriage

'Few women do not feel cheated when the bride's day is over and they find themselves in front of a dirty sink.'

Silvia Federici, *Revolution at Point Zero*

Happy Days

When Covid lockdown eased for the first time in the UK and public spaces and entertainment venues cautiously reopened, my husband and I went to the theatre to watch Samuel Beckett's *Happy Days*. First staged in 1961, it's a play featuring a married couple dwelling in a kind of wasteland, with the wife, Winnie, buried up to her waist in a dirt mound, while the husband, Willie, spends most of his time burrowed down below in a hole out of which he occasionally, though rarely, pokes his head. For theatregoers coming out of lockdown and blinking into the light, this was surely the right historical moment to stage that particular production. Especially for theatregoing couples who'd spent the previous period tied exclusively to each other, seeing barely any other adults, other than via Zoom, the online platform that demands we make our upper body presentable, while what lies beneath our waist may be a squalor that grows and grows until it threatens to take over the whole. And if that wasn't resonant enough, this symmetrical topography was further reinforced by the layout of the theatre, whose socially distanced seating meant our twosome did look as dismayingly hitched to each other and nobody else as did the pair we had come along to watch.

My husband (my Willie) has a chronic pain condition and can't sit for long without succumbing to terrible pangs and aches. So we don't go to the theatre often. But when we do, as soon as the lights dim, he straight away starts figuring out how to make his situation more comfortable. He often lies on the floor, or the stairs, or else he finds a seat with a free chair in front to put his legs on. On this occasion, he grabbed another free-standing chair and lay down low on his own (sitting upright is back-breaking for him) and then lifted his legs on to the chair he'd nabbed. Whenever he does stuff like this, a few other paying customers tend to stare over huffily at the man with the invisible disability. So what I usually try to do is look as if I am nothing whatsoever to do with him. What I want my fellow audience members to imagine is that I just happen to be seated next to this total stranger – a disruptive presence who is bothering me more than anyone else. But when the seating plan requires that everyone sit together only with those they already live with, there's no hiding the fact that we are indeed each other's significant others. And on this outing, it felt doubly exposing because of how much he and I eerily mirrored the action onstage. Just as Willie, buried down low in his hole, occasionally emits the odd grunt of pain, so there were, from our corner, intermittent grunts emanating from my husband splayed awkwardly on his bed of chairs. Meanwhile, the more he betrayed what life was like below the waist, the more I sought, like Winnie, to keep up appearances above. Should anyone happen to be looking over in our direction, there I was, just as she was, denying the pain, keeping things chirpy, thanking my lucky stars. Happy days!

Why *Happy Days*? Can that really be the best way of describing such a barren wasteland? Well, perhaps, if what we're beholding is a landscape situated not only in space but in time, as in the postnuptial wilderness of the happy-ever-after that ensues once the marital deed is done, leaving the couple tied together with little else to accomplish besides surviving until death doth them part. So what should we make of a space and time that's been emptied out of anything like a narrative drive? Wouldn't such featureless monotony necessarily imply that the existences of those who subsist on the other side of the marriage plot must be empty of meaning also? To marry is to affirm something – it's to say, 'Yes, I do.' But in a stagnation of gathering dirt, what *are* a couple doing exactly? How are they supposed to spend, in the exclusive company of each other, all of their remaining happy days?

Ground Zero

The principle of marriage is 'obscene', claims Simone de Beauvoir in her acerbic takedown of the institution in *The Second Sex* (1949). For girls, 'marriage is the only way to be integrated into the group, and if they are "rejects," they are social waste'. However, if girls are considered waste products outside of marriage, their conjugated lives don't look to be much less wasted either. A wife may well be tasked with perpetuating the species, but she has no real access to the future she's busily forging. Not only is marital happiness far from guaranteed to her – it's guaranteed to no one – but marriage actually 'mutilates her; it dooms her to repetition and routine.' And this because her conjugal labours – housework, care work, emotional work – are unending: 'Few tasks are more similar to the torment of Sisyphus than those of the housewife; day after day, one must wash dishes, dust furniture, mend clothes that will be dirty, dusty, and torn again. The housewife wears herself out running on the spot.'

Marriage is consequently quite a pivot for the young girl turned wife, says Beauvoir, who alights on the example of a romantically inclined bride who marries a poet, but then 'the first thing she notices is that he forgets to flush the toilet'. Marriage, in other words, as the dawning realization that there's just so much shit to deal with. Which is why the postnuptial bride finds herself possessed of a new 'reverie': 'the dream of active cleanliness, that is, cleanliness conquering dirt.' It's this dream of conquering dirt that the housewife wages unto death, dirt being the mundane matter that threatens to inform on her by hinting at the waste of insignificance that she, or her life, really is.

But what then of the bourgeois housewife who employs others to do her housework? She too is mutilated by her marriage, says Beauvoir. As the overseer of other women's labours, she's transformed into a character cruel and shrewish, blaming those she considers beneath her for the emptiness her own married existence has imposed. Or if she avoids this corruption of her soul and finds alternative ways to keep herself occupied, still, as the critic Sara Ahmed remarks of Mrs Dalloway, there's so much sadness revealed 'in the very need to be busy. So much grief expressed in the need not to be overwhelmed by grief. It is hard labour just to recognise sadness and disappointment, when you are living a life that is meant to be happy but just isn't, which is meant to be full, but feels empty.'

Housework, the 'Wages for Housework' campaigner Silvia Federici once claimed, is 'the work in which the contradictions inherent in "alienated labour" are most explosive, which is why it is the *ground zero* for revolutionary practice, even if it is not the only ground zero.' Ground zero, in other words, as the ground upon which one's connection to the wider world gets severed, is also the ground upon which new connections might be made. For it's here that one finds the scraps and dregs of society – all those whose meanings and motivations have been discarded or discounted. Including wives, alleges Beauvoir, whose diminishment via marriage is the result of the marital sum that can make two into one only by assuming that the positive integer comes wholly from the husband's half of the equation. Or, as co-authors S. Pearl Brilmyer, Filippo Trentin and Zairong Xiang put it in their 2019 article 'The Ontology of the Couple: or, What Queer Theory Knows About Numbers', 'If sexual difference is the difference through which two become one, this is because the second one is actually *none.*' Beauvoir hoped to elude that erasure of her own figure by committing to a man outside of the institutional framework performing its negation. But since, contracted or not, a couple must wrangle with the social significance of their coupling, despite her best efforts to negate the marital negation, 'in this lifelong relationship of supposed equals,' observes the writer Lisa Appignanesi of Beauvoir's alliance with Sartre, 'he, it turned out, was far more equal than she was.'

So what the authors of 'The Ontology of the Couple' are aiming at is a vision of the coupled relation that doesn't bolster the values of a patriarchal system that's relegated many more than just wives to the status of 'nonbeing, nothingness, void'. Rather than overturning these negative ascriptions with positive ones, however, they wonder if it might be worth our first considering if there's any value to be disinterred from *within* the experience of negation. Such a move would require us to seek for significance where we've been taught there's none, by questioning, for instance, the plus and minus values of a social contract mapped on to the body's male and female genitalia. In order to found an alternative social contract, we'd even likely need to look elsewhere on the body, towards an anatomical feature that signifies something other than sexual difference. Whence, notwithstanding its negative cultural associations with 'dirt, stench, and death', it's to the anus that these authors suggest we return to find a symbol of our common humanity – which symbol, precisely insofar as it excludes no one, makes of the rectum not 'a grave', but the source of a renewed and radical affirmation of life. (Yes, that's what I just said. Please bear with me.)

In 1967, London's Royal Albert Hall censored a screening of Yoko Ono's art film *Bottoms* on the grounds of obscenity. The film was first shown in the venue fifty years later, on 3 May 2017, which I happen to know about because I was invited (by the feminist curatorial group

Bird's Eye View) to speak after the screening. So this was the moment when I first began to think seriously about bottoms. Think seriously? About bottoms? Yes, I found myself thinking seriously about bottoms after watching, with a fascination that surprised me, Ono's close framing of hundreds of buttocks and upper thighs walking on the spot. And I soon discovered that I wasn't alone in these posterior ponderings. For floating over the film's parade of bums, one can hear snippets of dialogue between various pontificators engaging in an ongoing 'But is it art?' conversation. The words of these pontificators are sometimes political, sometimes moral, and sometimes aesthetic or philosophical. And yet for all their sophistication, it's the dialogue in this feature that strikes the truly bum notes. Everyone seems to be talking out of their arses. Bottoms, Ono clarified when interrogated about her choice of subject, possess an honesty and innocence that faces lack. So for Ono too, it's via our fundaments that she identifies our fundamental humanity, as well as our fundamental vulnerability. For however padded our backsides, the fact that they're out there behind us without our knowing who may be sizing them up, also makes of our bottoms a symbol of our essential dependence on others. We always have to trust that someone has got our back. That, you could even say, is our first lesson in life. As infants, we need others to clean up our shit. And this 'rearing' can be a profoundly bonding experience; the ground zero of all our subsequent relations of love, care and intimacy. However, it can also be, and perhaps particularly for those who've suffered too many humiliations and punishments in the course of their potty-training, an experience to make one develop in such a way as to be less attuned to the pleasures of ingestion and excretion. The messy pleasures of creation. So perhaps the real question we should be putting to *Bottoms*, I pontificated (then as now), isn't 'But is it art?' so much as 'Is this where art comes from?' Not from our minds but from our behinds.

It's a thought to remind one (again) of Bottom the Weaver, Shakespeare's comical figure for the artist as dreamer and amateur actor, who could also be the bard's foremost representative of true love. For unlike two alternative Shakespearean figures for the artist as nobleman – the blocked Prince Hamlet and the blocking Duke Prospero – it's the lowly Nick Bottom whose bare-faced cheek allows him to move freely between the upper and lower worlds, mixing with everyone and muddling all categories and hierarchies in the process. In fact, it's precisely on account of his being a bit of an ass that Bottom becomes the character with the power to reveal how, upon ground zero, we might yet see emerging the conditions for the art of real, revolutionary social change.

Happy Days

The great thinker of negative values was the Marxist critic, psychologist and musicologist Theodor Adorno. In 1955, looking upon the wasteland of the world post-war, he ascribed zero value to pretty much all of Western civilization, hence his notorious dictum that poetry after Auschwitz is barbaric. Around a decade later, however, he did partially retract that statement, acknowledging that 'perennial suffering has as much right to expression as a tortured man has to scream.' And he also acknowledged certain exceptions to the impossibility of culture continuing. In music, for instance, he favoured the anti-aesthetic avant-garde minimalist compositions of Arnold Schoenberg. While in literature he recommended Beckett as the quintessential writer to understand that culture can only proceed under the conditions of its own erasure, by going on when one can't go on.

'We are affirmed by happiness', writes Sara Ahmed, 'we go along and get along by doing what we do, and doing it well . . . Happiness involves here the comfort of repetition, of following lines that have already been given in advance.' So happiness not only affirms us, it affirms, *via* us, the social logic that has granted us such happiness. A failure to 'go along' or repeat those lines, on the other hand, is to become what Ahmed terms 'an affect alien'. She notes, for example, how those who've been typecast as 'feminist killjoys, unhappy queers, and melancholic migrants' have all found themselves variously excluded from or alienated by the cultural promise of 'happy families' – a promise which is no less an injunction. But what then are we to make of those who *do* go along with this promise of happiness – even when they can't go on, and even when they may be perennially suffering throughout what they're doing so well. What are *they* affirming?

With Beckett's *Happy Days* we're back in the ambit of *One Thousand and One Nights*. Admittedly, the high-risk conditions that characterize Shahrazad's nights are not the most obvious comparator for the distinct lack of intrigue that marks Winnie's days. Yet both are wives who abide in the intimate vicinity of what threatens to take their lives too soon – Shahrazad by her husband's decree, Winnie by the possession of a gun that she keeps temptingly by her side. And they're both also wives who opt for the same method of holding off that fatality. For in a play comprised almost entirely of her monologue, Winnie presents us with another vision of a wife whose talking is undertaken for the sake of continuance – for the sake of survival. Winnie, indeed, is a wife who goes on even when she can't, knowing, just as Shahrazad knew, that words, her prime resource, are at risk of running out. 'Cast your mind forward,' she tells herself, 'to the time when words must fail'. Yet words are pretty much all she has left at her disposal. For they really are at rock bottom, Winnie and Willie. Nor do they have many objects with which to distract themselves, though Winnie does what she can each day to entertain herself with the few things she still keeps in her bag. Meanwhile, Willie isn't exactly the most invigorating company. In fact, he's hardly what you'd call company at all. They may be wedlocked, but these two hardly ever lock eyes. Finding them thus stranded in a scene of postapocalyptic dereliction, you can't but wonder if there's *anything* here worth saving. *But no. No no* . . . as Winnie corrects herself (repeat-edly) when moved to banish despair with a resolute look forwards in affirmation. So, though she may not summon a 'Yes' in the spirited way her rather more at liberty (and equally monologuing) compa-triot Molly Bloom summons a yes, Winnie's double negative musters no less positivity out of the limits of her world. How she braves the eternal return of her days could even bring to mind the efforts of those various existentialist philosophers who took up intellectual arms against nihilism. 'One must,' professed Albert Camus, 'imagine Sisyphus happy'.

Yet despite their surface similarities, said Adorno, Beckett's char-acters don't really belong to the existentialist 'creed'. Adorno dubbed this creed that of 'the permanence of individual existence'; a way of affirming the self over and against the fundamental meaninglessness of the world, implying there's no society to speak of, nor time or history to contend with either. Whereas, for all that Winnie's days are repetitive, time *does* change things, as evidenced by the dirt that steadily accrues, reaching up to her neck by the second act. If Win-nie's double negative (her *No no*) affirms her commitment to the continued promise of marital happiness, therefore, then hers is an affirmation that comes much closer to the affirmation Levinas describes as the 'secret of angels': the angel as the one who says 'yes' even without knowing what changes a yes could bring. Moreover, despite the sorry spectacle of isolation Winnie's solo presence on the stage suggests, she doesn't relinquish her commitment to the social either. She's not talking to herself, after all, but to Willie, who, if she's lucky, occasionally grunts in what may or may not be acknowledge-ment. They occur rarely, these grunts, and decreasingly over the years, but they're all that's necessary to motivate Winnie in her daily exertions. A grunt from Willie occasions a sort of celebration from Winnie: 'Oh this will have been a happy day!' A happy day is a day when Winnie has had it affirmed that Willie is still there. For the thing Winnie says she truly can't bear is the thought of being entirely alone.

Which is why, even on those numberless days when she gets no response at all, she tells herself, 'something of this is being heard, I am not merely talking to myself'. Indeed, by the time Winnie finds herself almost entirely deluged by the dirt, the belief in Willie's company has become an item of faith. So though she's not heard a pip out of him in years, still she goes on talking to Willie as a matter of necessity: 'I say I used to think that I would learn to talk alone. [*Pause.*] By that I mean to myself, the wilderness. [*Smile.*] But no. [*Smile broader.*] No no. [*Smile off.*] Ergo you are there. [*Pause.*] Oh no doubt you are dead, like the others, no doubt you have died, or gone away and left me, like the others, it doesn't matter, you are there.'

But then, would you believe it, Willie *is* there! Suddenly he appears from around the mound, dressed as if for his wedding day. To which 'unexpected pleasure', Winnie, who mostly avoids quarrels, finally admits to some of the pains she's been covering up with her determined cheerfulness: 'Where were you all this time? [*Pause.*] What were you doing all this time? [*Pause.*] Changing? [*Pause.*] Did you not hear me screaming for you?'

Is it really possible that what Willie has been *doing all this time* is *changing*? And could this hidden-away husband's changing (into what? a better-presenting husband?) have anything to do with what Winnie has been *doing all this time*, namely talking? But how can her talking possibly have changed him? If Winnie's words have merely been covering for her perennial suffering or muffled screaming, what is it that Willie can have heard within his wife's incessant chatter that hasn't rendered her talking, to his ears, essentially senseless – void?

Ground Zero

In a scene not so dissimilar to the one inhabited by Winnie and Willie, Austrian director Michael Haneke's 2012 film *Amour* also features two married characters, Anne and George, both of whom are retired music teachers in their eighties. Though with Anne and George we also meet a couple still in the flow of good and sensuous communication, and still very much in love. Indeed, the film begins when they attend a Schubert concert and seem near enough ecstatic about the music upon returning home. George also tells Anne that she looks particularly pretty that night. But then, change. Anne has a stroke that paralyses one side of her body. She feels there's little left to live for with her mobility so reduced, but George cares for her admirably, as if his body was an extension of her own. She wishes never to return to the hospital, she tells him. Following her second stroke, therefore, he keeps her at home, albeit now his duty of care is 24/7 for she can do nothing for herself – her physical and mental capacities have disintegrated, and so too has her capacity for speech. Mostly what she expresses is a continuous echolalia. Or whenever George – now engulfed by endless care and housework – leaves her momentarily to deal with something in another room, he hears very quickly the sound of Anne screaming for him, summoning him back to her side.

Haneke clearly wants his audiences to train their eyes on the parts of reality that most people would rather not see, or which we tend to sugar-coat with sentimentalism and happy endings. But while this is a film that does, as it were, continue to emit the underlying scream uniting his various movies, I don't assume the film's title to be a cynical one. This, he's saying, is Amour. This is what it means to love someone unto death – and even to love them enough to want to end their suffering by executing that death yourself. Indeed, Haneke's is a film that could rightfully claim to belong to the romance genre, by revealing how the very end of the marriage plot shares a strange symmetry with the plot's romantic beginnings. If romantic lovers are those who begin, like outlaws, in pursuit of a love that leads them to transgress the rules of the social order to which they normally adhere, then something of this young love is curiously repeated, under dramatically altered conditions, in old age. That isn't, of course, to say that the apartment George and Anne share, which, as the daily task of survival takes its toll, they seem increasingly intent on keeping others out of, is an obvious image of the grove. Nonetheless, if romantic comedy tells of a love that discovers itself in the secrecy of the grove before re-entering the social world whose sanction this love requires, then senescence is a period during which that wider world can often appear to beat another retreat, leaving the couple back alone together in the secrecy of their twoness. As George explains to their uncomprehending daughter, after describing in painstaking detail the naked truth of what her parents' intimacy now involves: 'none of that deserves to be shown.' Haneke, though, *does* show it to us – although not entirely. Some things are still left to the viewer's imagination. And so when we see this husband tenderly changing his wife's incontinence pants, the horror, if we feel it, is ours, not his. For while it's true that he's suffering, just as she's suffering, he makes no grimace. For him, when it comes down to it, this is simply the labour of love, akin to that of a mother tending to her newborn child.

Marriage, I can affirm, is a whole lot easier in health than it is in sickness. And George, though he loses his temper once or twice, is surely as good as a spouse gets – a kind of angel on our screens. His example certainly shames my earlier confession of how, when we go to the theatre, I try to make out that there's a sharp distinction between my own body and my husband's in its chronic pain. Which isn't because I'm oblivious to my husband's pains, any more than he's oblivious when I'm overrun with my own symptoms. Sometimes, like Winnie, or like George talking to occasional visitors, my spouse and I each perform the part of a public chirpiness in order to cover up the other's sufferings. But I'd be lying if I didn't admit that we're not always as attentive to each other's torments as we could be. I often wonder if that's because we experience each other's pains as our own referred pains, and so react to them less charitably, as if they're being inflicted upon us. When one of us is on our back, after all, the other has more work to do: more housework, more care work, more emotional work. Although there's more to it too than just logistics. And when I pause to reflect on what that 'more' could be, I think it's perhaps that we feel these suffering parts of each other and ourselves are the future that awaits us; as if it's these very parts that we're truly married to, committed to, devoted to; as if caring for each other's bodies as they move through time is what our marriage ultimately is, or means.

If it's strenuous work caring for the shittiness of failing bodies, when minds fail then that work can begin to seem not only thankless but hopeless. American author Amy Bloom's *In Love* is a memoir about caring for her husband, Brian, following his Alzheimer's diagnosis. And this care includes, upon his request, committing to help him realize his wish for a self-chosen death (at the euthanasia centre Dignitas in Switzerland). What Alzheimer's destroys, Bloom explains, is 'connection within and without, first in the entorhinal cortex and hippocampus (the part of the brain devoted to memory) and then in the cerebral cortex (language, processing, and social behaviour).' As neurological connections break down, so social connections likewise break down, leaving the person there, but nothing that feels personal. Memory goes, language goes, conversation goes, and by these processes relations of intimacy go too. And if this was hellish for Brian, it was no less hellish for Bloom, who was left feeling 'even worse' than alone, she says; not only forgotten, but uprooted from her husband's interior landscape, as if she'd never been there at all. Hence, in the torment and stress of his gradual loss, she began mirroring some of Brian's symptoms, as if in losing him, she was bound to lose herself as well. So suddenly she was no longer a safe driver, no longer an adequate cook, no longer bothered to tend to appearances, and no longer even happy to pick up the litter that fell on a floor accumulating dirt that had never been allowed to tarry there before.

Meanwhile, as it became harder for Amy to leave Brian safely on his own, his constant physical presence was also a stark reminder of his interior absence, and though she did have trusted confidantes to talk to, the implicit transgressiveness of assisted suicide also imposed its own additional atmosphere of social isolation on the couple. Her memoir thus details a state of developing disconnectedness that presents a remarkable counterpoint to Beckett's Winnie, who really *is* on her own in the barren landscape of her marital dwelling, and yet who sustains within her own interior landscape all the forms of relation and connection that Bloom witnessed eroding day by day in Brian, and which also seemed at times to threaten her own sense of self too. In a marriage, Bloom came painfully to understand, there can be no real tomorrow if there was no yesterday. So it would be wrong to underestimate the vital work Winnie is doing when, locked down in the present tense, she daily revisits her fading memories, her half-recollected lines of poetry, and her proverbs in the 'old style'. To perpetuate the ground zero of a world that still has the power to connect people, Winnie takes it upon herself to roll the boulder of history up the hill that's slowly engulfing her. And she continues to roll that boulder bit by bit and more and more each and every darkening day.

Happy Days

Elizabeth Strout's Olive Kitteridge is the protagonist of two novels, *Olive Kitteridge* and *Olive, Again*, set in the small town of Crosby, Maine (a town whose social contract is as conspicuously tied to the marriage contract as it is in Eliot's *Middlemarch*). And Olive is another inveterate talker whose talk appears a dynamic and connecting force within her coastal community – although Olive, always intent on speaking the fullness of her mind, isn't such a diplomat as we find with Winnie. What she says includes the things you're not really, in polite society, supposed to say. Yet sometimes it's this, her capacity for directness, that allows her to get to the heart of things. After Henry, her husband of many years, dies in the first novel, Olive encounters another man, Jack, whose own wife has also recently left him widowed. 'Then, you're in hell', Olive sympathizes. 'Then, I'm in hell', he agrees. Soon after, Olive tells her friend Bunny about meeting this fellow among the bereaved. In doing so, she detects that Bunny, though her own husband 'had driven her nuts for most of her married life', had now come to appreciate the simple fact that he was 'still alive': 'Olive thought Bunny could see what it was like, her friends losing their husbands and drowning in the emptiness'.

In *Olive, Again*, Olive commits to marrying Jack. This exasperates her adult son:

> 'I don't get this, Mom. Why are you getting married?'
>
> 'Because we're two lonely old people and we want to be together.'
>
> 'Then be together! But why get married? Mom?'
>
> 'Chris, what difference does it make?'
>
> He leaned forward and said – his voice sounded almost menacing – 'If it doesn't make any difference, then why are you doing it?'
>
> 'I meant, to you. What difference does it make to you?' But horribly, Olive now felt a niggling of doubt. Why was she marrying Jack? What difference did it make?

Why marry? What difference does marrying make? Marrying is something Olive infers she needs, and it's something Jack infers he needs too. Perhaps in order to recover through each other the connection to the world they both felt they'd lost with their original spouses. Although if she still feels it's marriage that retains the peculiar power to promise her happier days, then this decision of her later life is one that the usually forthright Olive doesn't quite have the wherewithal to articulate or defend before her irate son.

Much later and with other people, however, Olive does begin to make sense of her ongoing orientation towards marriage as her chosen way through all the stages of her life. When a younger woman, Cindy, asks her how long she's been married to Jack, she replies, 'Coming up to almost two years, I guess. Imagine at my age, starting over again . . . But it's never starting over, Cindy, it's just continuing on.' So marrying Jack isn't Olive's way of getting over Henry. It's her way of keeping her relationship to Henry alive too. Marriage, indeed, is how she *stays* related, not only to others, but to herself. Hence in *Olive, Again* we meet marriage again as a means of continuance; with marriage's formal shelter looking a lot like survival to those who've been widowed: 'Jack thought of their large old bodies, shipwrecked, thrown up upon the shore – and how they held on for dear life!'

Ground Zero

One of the most moving weddings I've ever attended was also the smallest. It was in a registry office and just the bride and groom, their two adult kids and the kids' spouses were in attendance. I was one of the kids' spouses. The wedding couple had already been together for over thirty years and so the decision to formally tie the knot was only made after the groom had been diagnosed with cancer, and though he'd done well with his treatment, it made legal sense at that point to ensure their two estates were married lest the worst should happen and the government refused to recognize what they'd long since shared. As the previously divorced author of *Simone de Beauvoir* amongst various other books exposing the deleterious impact of patriarchal institutions on the second sex, Lisa Appignanesi (the bride) had few romantic illusions about what marriage offered women. Still, despite the practical nature of the arrangement, on the day itself it struck me that they both were – I think we all were – surprised by how deeply romantic the occasion felt. After the ceremony, over lunch, everyone was exhilarated, exuberant, jubilant. It really was a celebration of marriage – and marriage seemed to signify something in excess of what any of us could quite grasp. Indeed, this long-established couple, who had already suffered some wretchedly painful hitches over the course of their history together, now that they were *formally* hitched, appeared to carry themselves off with enviable erotic flare, like young lovers, but also like so much more than young lovers.

But subsequently, the worst did happen. 'Day Zero', explains Lisa in *Everyday Madness*, her memoir of the inward psychic collapse she suffered following the death of John Forrester, was 'the apocalyptic name given to the day when the harvested stem cells had gone back into his chemically cleaned system'. This cellular cleaning process was the radical new treatment the hospital had chosen to implement with regard to his cancer, and he seemed so strong and so ready for it, there were high hopes of its success. A truly deep clean – the deepest of cleans – was what was meant to cure him. And Lisa was optimistic. 'I'm a terrible and impatient nurse', she admits, but 'I was a star Pollyanna.' So the treatment's failure to cure came as an even more brutal shock.

When John died, Lisa felt she couldn't go on, but she went on. A star Pollyanna, no less accomplished than Winnie at keeping the world ticking even when she'd never felt more radically lost or at risk of dissociating, she kept up appearances, saying all the right things, remaining a good-enough mother, a good-enough friend and a good-enough widow. What she was really suffering, though, was the terrifying and isolating condition which her book diagnoses as a madness whose passions and torments are extreme but whose ordinariness is so everyday that even those with whom one is most intimate might fail to hear within the chatter the underlying scream. I remark this with some embarrassment given that I was there at the time, but it was only much later when I read her book – one of my most visceral reading experiences – that I found out what agonies she'd really been living through.

At John's funeral, Lisa spoke of how his loss was also, for her, the loss of her life's key interlocutor. When he died, it seemed as if conversation and language had died a sudden death too. What she didn't add in that funeral oration was how much of her agony since his death had been to do with the last spoken communication she and he had shared together. It's a cruel irony that it should have been the last given that not so long before he'd been thanking her for her constant presence by his side. But this was the moment when the situation had grown graver and he was evidently becoming desperate. When Lisa had to briefly dash home to grab a few things, he told her to take his pyjamas with her to wash and return to him. She went into the bathroom to locate the PJs, but finding them completely sodden with diarrhoea, she told him she'd bring him back a new pair instead. He only wanted this pair, he insisted, they were his favourite pyjamas:

> I go back into the toilet, not allowing myself to breathe, and realize I simply can't lift the squelch of body and other materials. I feel defiled. I will dissolve, liquefy into the stench. My body is turning to waste, mirroring his, yet I'm being called upon to be mother to this ageing toddler.
>
> 'That's all you're good for,' I hear him shouting. 'Cleaning shit.'
>
> That was the last sentence he uttered to me. It hit me with the force of a body blow and mired me. Engulfed.

As I said, it's a visceral reading experience. And one made all the more so for me, perhaps, because I hadn't the least inkling of how, during the various days and weeks and months that followed his death, John's last words had played themselves over and over again in her head, making her feel that that 'was his final estimate. After all those thirty-two years together, that was what I was good for. Cleaning shit.' This on top of the zeroing of her personhood that her bereavement had also automatically implied – as she observes a little later in the book when noting how the 'archaic "viduity", meaning widowhood, chimes with *vide* or "empty"'. It's not for nothing that viduity is the word that Beckett's character Krapp, upon hearing himself utter it on an old tape, has to go and look up again in the dictionary in an act evoking the sort of forgetting that can so quickly envelop those subject to the viduous experience. A sense of social erasure bound to age and viduity was indeed something that Lisa felt sharply encroaching in the wake of John's loss. Though it was really John's final sentence that became the focus of the unrelenting mental torture she experienced after he died. These were the words that sprang into her mind every time others stepped forward to express their condolences. And while she did go along with things, carrying off her duties, smiling gratefully and responding appropriately, on each occasion she was forced to battle the Furies – the hurt, rage and turmoil – secretly undoing her within. Latterly, however, when her emotions had somewhat calmed, it dawned on her what was likely the real reason for all the anger she'd found herself feeling towards a man whose final words she knew, deep down, to be the sign of extreme distress at his own loss and abjection rather than hers: 'If he were back . . . I could kill him. And we could make up.'

Happy Days

Prior to her famous viduity, Yoko Ono was already pictured in the popular press as a sort of black widow. When I recently watched *Get Back*, Peter Jackson's engrossing three-part documentary film of the Beatles recording, in 1969, their final album and public performance together, I found myself thinking about what she must have suffered on that account. Not that suffering was anything so new to her. She was a woman who had sheltered with her family in a bunker when Tokyo was bombed during the war and then, at risk of starvation, had gone with them to beg for food once the bombing was over. Her father, whom she only met for the first time when she was two years old, was subsequently placed in a concentration camp in Saigon. And she'd also been married twice and spent time in a mental institution for clinical depression before she met Lennon.

In Jackson's documentary, we feel we're privy to an extraordinary intimacy with the world's most celebrated band as we spend a month with them in the recording studio watching on as they make music that's now so familiar it seems strange that there was ever a time when it wasn't already composed. And throughout that period of the recording, we also watch Ono sitting pretty much constantly by Lennon's side. 1969 was the same year Ono and Lennon, after divorcing their previous partners, got married. In the studio, she isn't a disruptive presence at all. She says almost nothing and does barely anything. But her silence within the inner sanctum of the pop group in the full creative flow of their combined genius does strike one as uncanny, as if she's mutely composing another kind of music, or sounding through her person John Cage's *4'33"*. Besides, as quiet as she is, her presence was by then making a lot of noise outside the studio. In the papers, in language as racist as it's misogynist, she was being held preemptively responsible for breaking up the band of boys and then preying on their remains. Sometimes, during recording breaks, the band read aloud such gossip pieces for their ridicule and amusement, although when Ono and Lennon are out of the room, we also find some truth to the idea that she features amongst the tensions that were then taking over the fab four. If John was forced to choose between Yoko and the Beatles, McCartney predicts at one point, he'd go with her. But what the film actually demonstrates, Ono has argued since it came out, is the spuriousness of the idea that she was the one to kill off the Beatles. And watching it, that's what I felt too, that she's really in the studio to keep John there, who seems to be holding on to her, as Jack holds on to Olive Kitteridge, for dear life.

Yet we know too, of course, that Ono was also a creative inspiration for Lennon (she had by then already been making her own music, including her collaboration with the avant-garde jazz artist Ornette Coleman). And there *are* moments during the documentary when we do hear her voice. In the time-outs of the band's recording breaks, we even see her with the microphone. But she doesn't speak or sing into it – she makes peculiar screams. I say peculiar because that's how her naked noises sound to me, notwithstanding that the Beatles' repertoire was similarly punctuated by various types of screaming. It's one of the fascinating facets of pop songs, in fact, that though these are musical pieces that tend towards high-octane blasts of cheerfulness sustained by the stabilizing promise of the hooks and repetitions, they also tend to register all sorts of other sounds and furies within their wider arrangements. Could those be the sounds of the repressed returning? While a pop song can be about any number of things, part of its signifying structure, very often, is the way it can so forcefully interrupt itself with a howl, shout or counterpoint chorus that heads off in another direction entirely. In the opening verse of 'Dig a Pony', for instance, Lennon expounds sagely upon our freedom to celebrate whatever the hell we want. But then the chorus kicks in with something much more emphatic and personal, as all he really wants, it turns out, is *YOU*. (Nor is it hard to guess who the 'you' is here.) So when one takes that all in, it's as if a celebration is what we do to veil a crisis, or to veil what feels critical precisely insofar as it's existential. Because no matter what one may appear to be singing about, even ponies, doesn't a song's interruption by shouts and screams suggest that its real addressee is always, and somewhat desperately, the beloved?

'The Ballad of John and Yoko' effectively got started when Lennon first encountered Ono at her art exhibition in 1966. He'd been particularly impressed by her famous *Ceiling Painting/Yes Painting*. Visitors were invited to climb a stepladder and then look through a magnifying glass into a framed black canvas to discover that the white dot in the centre was the word YES. In subsequent interviews, Lennon claimed to have found this piece the perfect antidote to the post-war nihilism then gathering momentum in the arts. And this boldness of affirmation is what came to characterize his public relationship with Ono after they got together and collaborated in making their own art and music too. After receiving a deluge of racist hate mail about his new lover, he actively sought out the press to tell them, in no uncertain terms, 'I'm in love with her.' And then of course, famously, they invited the press to join them on their week-long bed-in on their honeymoon in the Hilton Hotel Amsterdam as they endeavoured to raise out of their conjugal situation the awareness necessary for world peace. Their utopianism was such that they even seemed to imagine – Imagine! – their marriage could bypass the institution's bourgeois connotations and family values to inspire a political revolution. This invitation to everyone to join them under their matrimonial covers is what's implicit, for instance, in the naked portrait of the two of them standing together like a prelapsarian Adam and Eve on the cover of *Two Virgins*, their avant-garde album – influenced by Schoenberg and Cage – which includes the sound of their yelling 'yes' back and forth at each other before lots of strange and strained screaming takes them over. And it's implied no less by the paraphernalia surrounding their *Wedding Album*, whose boxed offering incorporated wedding photos, a copy of their marriage certificate, and a picture of a slice of the wedding cake. Happy days indeed.

Ground Zero

But not, as we know, happy ever after. And given that the whole world was invited to derive its greatest political hope from this singular couple's spin on marriage, it's perhaps not surprising that Ono and Lennon's marital fidelity began to fray when they lost faith with what was happening to world history. It was when Nixon was re-elected that John, purportedly, gave up on political radicalism and on his recent conversion to feminism, becoming very publicly unfaithful to Yoko, whose own somewhat Beckettian response, as reported to the *New York Daily News*, was that 'when something like this happens, each one of us must go on.' And they did both go on,

for a while apart (with Ono actively sourcing for Lennon his substitute lover – talk about devotion!) and then, before Lennon's
assassination, together again. It was just before that assassination
too that the photographer Annie Leibovitz took her iconic picture
of a fully clothed Yoko on a bed with a gut-wrenchingly vulnerable
and naked John lying in a foetal position by her side, his leg strad-
dling her body, his lips kissing her cheek. It was a photo to show, the
historian Simon Schama has remarked, that Ono had become 'not
just wife and lover but, unmistakably, mother too.' His own mother
had abandoned him early in life and so until he met Ono, adds
Schama, he 'felt somehow homeless. Apple was not home. The
Beatles were not home. She could see the red demon deep inside,
listened to him and sent him to someone who told him to scream.
They screamed together. *Waaaoooooo.*'

Happy Days

Words as we meet them in Beckett's theatre appear denuded, as if
shorn of all content. Content, but not sense. Instead they seem to
expose something fundamental; something about how inextricably
bound we are to each other, thereby evoking a state of relation whose
best metaphor could well be the marital one whose meaning reveals
itself incrementally, although not via the outward quality of the
exchanges. So what is this meaning? Recalling Levinas again, what
Beckett reveals can perhaps be envisaged as the 'saying' within the
'said' – that which allows us to hear the underlying murmur or scream
of whatever it is that continually beckons us within the other person.
For that, in the end, is what also seems to summon Willie back to
Winnie. After all her perpetual chattering, he returns to her as if he's
returned from the dead. Her marital word can hardly be deemed void,
therefore. With her words, Winnie is someone who can transform
monologue into dialogue, physics into metaphysics, and small talk

into the largest talk there is. And she does this by going on – and on and on – even when she can't go on.

But that's just her spoken word. The word Winnie sings is a whole other matter. To sing, she needs Willie to no longer be hiding his love away. So it is that, at the end of *Happy Days*, when we find Willie on his knees as if intending to propose to his wife again, Winnie is finally roused to sing her song – a love song in the old style from *The Merry Widow*, the operetta by Franz Lehár that was once the very essence of pop:

> Though I say not
> What I may not
> Let you hear,
> Yet the swaying
> Dance is saying,
> Love me dear!
> Every touch of fingers
> Tells me what I know,
> Says for you,
> It's true, it's true,
> You love me so!

Is it a swansong? The play doesn't reach that conclusion. But at the end of her song, this locked-down and wedlocked couple do at last lock eyes:

> Smile off. They look at each other. Long pause.

EPILOGUE

Because we time-travel into the future
at a blistering sixty minutes an hour,
I ask you to sit down and write me
one beautiful sentence I might carry
in my pocket on the journey when I go,
and in the window of the train unfold

O you were the best of all my days.

Nick Laird, 'Incantation'

One Beautiful Sentence

'This world of couples.' That's a single sentence in Luce d'Eramo's short story, 'Life as a Couple'. *This world of couples.* What does it conjure for you? For me, there's something about it that's vaguely comical, but also something that's enigmatic, and then too there's something about the terseness of the phrase that makes it feel monolithic, obdurate, even tyrannical. For our narrator, what it provokes are reflections on the vicissitudes of her own coupling: the way she and her partner are at home, where 'we receive visitors together, but we have distinct roles', and the way they are when visiting friends, where 'we lose sight of each other, then bump into each other by chance. But when a discussion starts up, you just have to join in, you get heated, and then it's hard to avoid ending up shoulder to shoulder, presenting a united front, which isn't very nice. Or else you get into an argument you might as well be having in private.' So it's a quarrelsome world, this world of couples. Couples unite to fight against others, or they divide to fight between themselves. Such quarrels are as unfortunate as they're inevitable: 'Why must I always wake him up with some tiresome reminder?' But between the lines of these dull and predictable repetitions, of arguments, frustrations and resentments, there are also bursts of something else, something that's a bit harder to parse, such as the laughter that occasionally erupts in the heat of a furious battle, which may be all that's necessary for the couple to shift gear, initiate a joint trip to the refrigerator, and enter upon the shared pleasure of appetites recovered and a midnight snack. And then there's the curious way in which some couples who aren't getting on don't necessarily want to part:

'Don't leave the cups around,' I yell after him, 'put them in the sink.'

I go back to the study. He looks at me, dragging on his cigarette, he follows me with his eyes around the room. 'Stay,' he says, as I'm about to withdraw (my presence doesn't bother him, it's part of him).

They can't really be apart from each other because they *are* a part of each other.

In Nick Laird's 'Epithalamium', a poem to celebrate a marriage, he and his wife are represented by a series of improbable metaphors, from the tactile ('I am menthol and you are eggshell'), to the caustic ('If I'm iniquity then you're theft'), to the epic ('and I am Trafalgar, and you're Waterloo'). The sheer pace and proliferation of all these metaphors would render them absurd if it wasn't for the fact that they do seem to make a strange sort of sense because of the way they gather all their meaning from their proximate relation to each other. And then there's the poem's final metaphor:

and frequently it seems to me that I am you,
and you are me. If I'm the rising incantation
you're the charm, or I am, or you are.

Spouses, it winds up, are metaphors for each other. This is a very different sort of metaphor, though, to the one that says *my presence doesn't bother him, it's part of him.* That too is a marital metaphor, but here, via a mutual dependency that at times hinges close to interchangeability, the metaphor of the marital relation never settles itself into anyone's possession. Rather, spouses are rendered not just as a series of metaphors, but as metaphor itself. As metaphors for each other, spouses are even metaphors for metaphors. I know, it hurts the head to try to think it. What even is a metaphor? It's not 'merely decorative', explains Laird in an essay on the subject, 'it's an agent of transformation'. And what metaphor transforms isn't so much things in themselves as the space between things: the space of relationships. A metaphor, in fact, is what *allows* for relationships, for what the metaphor does is bring together things or ideas that, prior to the poet's intervention, may have seemed utterly *un*related to each other. So metaphor is a conjugal term; a means of marrying together different histories, identities and experiences.

Indeed, it's because metaphor 'relies on what has been experienced before', the American author Cynthia Ozick writes, that 'it transforms the strange into the familiar', whence 'strangers can imagine the familiar hearts of strangers.' Note that, for this to work, all must be acknowledged, in the first place, as strangers – nor does the metaphorical conjoining of strangers ever entirely eliminate that fact. But by means of metaphor, something more intimate nonetheless enters into the distances between us so that we come to share even those things we can't share, or can't share straightforwardly. In Laird's poem 'Talking in Kitchens', for example, he and his wife are at home one evening with a friend:

> When Michael has left we head upstairs
> and the baby's asleep and we've talked ourselves out
> and we feel as we feel every day of the year

like nobody knows how we feel and it's fine,
because our secrets live near the secrets of others,
and our wants are not so mean.

There's the kind of talking you can do with your spouse and your friends in kitchens, and then there's the other kind of language that belongs between just the two of you as you head back upstairs into the realm of your one thousand and one nights. And that language, eschewing the frothy exchanges of conversations and debates as held forth in kitchens, moves towards the quieter, stealthier language of poetry and metaphor – the sort of language that can create such connections as aren't always on the table for the party committed to talking themselves out. What it brings back to my mind is Maurice Blanchot's rising incantation, that the 'experience of strangeness may affirm itself close at hand as an irreducible relation', and that 'by the authority of this experience, we might learn to speak.'

For Laird, this type of conjugal talking – or this way of learning to speak – is best done when alone, or when writing. Hence why the 'one beautiful sentence' that he and his wife write and hand over to each other in an ongoing relay is what they only allow themselves to unfold when they've already embarked like Odysseuses upon separate voyages. It's a tone they set down for their life as a couple early on. In 'Aubade', a paean to the wish to spend some time as the sole occupant of one's bed, the poet explains to his then new lover what use he makes of distances: 'know removed is how you're loved.' And it's this method of love that we're also privy to in 'Use of Spies', where we find the poet on a plane at night flying back long-distance to his lover, who is now his wife. Watching dawn rising over the clouds through the window, the sky's spectacular setting appears to him 'like some fabled / giant wave'. But then alongside that thought comes another: 'I thought I'll have to try and tell you that.' Which is how the poem concludes. What exactly is it, though, that he, or the poem, wants to try to tell his wife? Is he trying to tell her something about the metaphor of the cloud transformed into a wave 'that people travel years to catch'? Or is the cloud as wave already shapeshifting into another metaphor, as conveyed by that final line: a metaphor to suggest how every impression he makes in solitude contains within it the kernel of his unrelenting desire to conjugate his own life, mind and experiences to hers?

I've been reading these poems in *The Beautiful Sentence*, a limited edition of Laird's poetry that collects together a selection of earlier poems written over several years. One is entitled 'To the Wife', but pretty much all the poems selected seem to have this same addressee in mind. So if you begin the book by supposing 'The Beautiful Sentence' must be a metaphor for poetry, by the end you've gathered that it's no less a metaphor for marriage. Both marriage and poetry are imagined as beautiful sentences, with all the pleasure and punishment, expansion and restriction that phrase implies. Although in *The Beautiful Sentence*, the comparison of marriage and poetry is also one that weds the two terms: thus poetry becomes a metaphor for marriage, and marriage becomes a metaphor for poetry. In 'Mixed Marriage' and 'Adultery', for instance, it's not marriage but poetry that's the subject, albeit it's striking how much the poet's words for the special language of poetry in the latter ('In the mind of the language is the dream-life / you hope to re-enter at night, intent on a scene / of revelation that cannot be found in words –') resemble those he uses (in 'To the Wife') for the special language of marriage ('all of the tunes are inside us and wordless'). As if both poetry and marriage find inspiration for their own future horizons upon the ground zero of a similar kind of wordlessness; a wordlessness that leads both the poet and the spouse to reach into the darkness in the belief that there's no pause or silence or punctuation that isn't also an invitation towards acts of further and further conjugation. 'It seems to me that metaphors come down to a certain idea of interconnectedness', Laird has stated elsewhere, 'that everything relates to everything else. Metaphors don't believe in autonomy. And in the end, perhaps that idea of interconnectedness is a moral position.'

The Key to All Mythologies

'It sounds fantastic. The whole thing.'

Mrs Palm in *Scenes from a Marriage*

It's during the lifestyle interview in *Scenes from a Marriage* that Mrs Palm tells Johan and Marianne how fantastic their marriage sounds. She doesn't seem to catch the irony pervading her choice of word – the way fantastic connotes what's too good to be true – but we can catch it, as can Johan and Marianne, who are both supremely conscious of the problems they risk inviting by appearing before the world as the very apogee of marriage's cultural ideal. 'A life like ours always has its dangers. We're well aware of that,' signals Marianne, in the vain hope that showing awareness of something – such as privilege – can inoculate you against its blindnesses. Meanwhile, interrogated as to what conditions their marital bliss, Johan dutifully lists the fundamentals their life as a couple has nailed down: 'Security, order, comfort and loyalty. It all has a suspiciously successful look.'

In the initial stages of my research for this book, I was a bit like Mrs Palm. When I went out, I often asked the people I met what their reasons were for getting married. And since, much as parents don't own children, spouses don't own marriage, I also asked unmarried people what they thought people got married for. No matter who I asked, the question, I noticed, bordered on the triggering, and was as quick to generate shame, solemnity, laughter and cynicism as anything resembling thoughtfulness. Although it was generally the unmarried who were the happiest to reach into the dark and hazard the guess that marriage might be one possible consequence of love. Whereas the question seemed to acutely embarrass the married, and even, I sometimes sensed, anger them. But why? My hunch both then and now is that marriage is a source of perplexity for many married people. In the secular world especially, few people have the full measure of why they want or do it, and so their answers sound, to their own ears, unconvincing. I mentioned at the start of this book the theory that marriage is what you can only do if you don't allow yourself to think too much about it. Because if you do give it much serious thought, you'll find that *it sounds fantastic. The whole thing.* I definitely didn't think it over much before I got married, and not much afterwards either. For the sake of this book, however, I've now thought about marriage a lot. And I've really enjoyed thinking about it. I've found it a rich, fascinating and bottomless subject, one that's led me in countless directions I never expected to go. I wonder if that was Eliot's joke throughout *Middlemarch.* It's not that there isn't a key to all mythologies, it's that the key to all mythologies is marriage, and so the book Casaubon was unable to write is the book that Eliot did write.

If that's Eliot's joke, then it's one I sort of feel I'm in on. But maybe I'm not, because having thought so much about marriage, the truth is that I still don't know what I think about it. Pretty much all the positions I've encountered on the subject seem to me to have a great deal of validity. Indeed, the one constant I've noticed that marriage does seem unusually good for, both in theory and practice, is playing host to contradictions. So perhaps that's why it's an institution that attracts someone like me, who can take the immense step of committing to marriage, but then can't seem to commit to any idea *of* marriage. Besides this one: that marriage, not necessarily as a legal contract, but as the metaphor for a certain structure of meaning and relating, still has a lot to tell us about how we might come to know love.

That said, I don't recall any married person I asked in those early impromptu interviews telling me they'd married for love. Not, I think, because love had nothing to do with it. I suspect, rather, that the way I represented myself as some sort of grand marital inquisitor made them feel that love was the wrong answer. Or that claiming to have married for love would make them look like fools. Or maybe it was just that they wanted to protect the secret of their love life from the prurience of my interest, using marriage as a cover. So what mostly came back at me when I canvassed for opinions were variations on Johan's list of what gives a marriage a suspiciously successful look. Security, comfort, certainty, and so on. The very things that, in *Scenes*, make of the marital ideal we're first confronted with something that does turn out to have been too good to be true. Although that's not where *Scenes* ends. In forsaking the marital ideal, Marianne and Johan do not forsake marriage. Their marriage story continues even after it's broken and even after its knot is formally untied. Indeed, what emerges by the end of *Scenes* is a couple who've been able to invent for themselves another kind of marriage, which marriage, shorn of norms, ideals and great expectations, sees them alone together in the middle of the night learning to speak to each other anew. Isn't that fantastic?

For obvious reasons, I share Marianne's fears that there may be an inherent hubris in the act of modelling one's marriage before the world. Not because modelling an ideal marriage is what I've been doing in this book – I hope! – but still, I have to assume that any celebration of marriage that one can identify beneath these covers (if indeed one can) must come back to the dreams I have for my own. So I hate to look ahead and imagine myself, like Marianne, waking up from what I thought was my dream to discover that it was actually my nightmare. I find myself wishing instead to protect my own union by sounding knowing about what lies in store. *A life like ours has its dangers. We're well aware of that.* But of course, the dangers I'm anticipating can't all be foretold. No matter what secret discontents we may knowingly conceal behind our marital cover, be these shared or not, celebrating one's marriage in public is liable to be as much of a cover story for what we haven't been able to face. And then, too, there's just the fear of the future itself as the night into which we must all venture forth. Is celebrating my marriage a cover for the fact that, more and more, I feel I'm holding on to my husband, as Olive

Kitteridge holds on to hers, for dear life? If so, then it all sounds rather desperate. Or perhaps that *is* a cause for celebration. I'm married to someone who, for better or for worse (and we've definitely sampled both), I don't wish to let go. I'm married to someone I feel I can't live without. Could that even be what this book is up to in the end? Was writing it my way of trying to tell someone that? Which doesn't mean I've concluded via my own very narrow experience that marriage *itself* is for better or for worse. What I have though (for better or for worse) concluded is this: that marriage, for all the rising and fading of its historical fortunes, is an institution that continues to shape and carry our human story, and so on that basis, if on no other, we're likely to see it remaining with us long into the future, until death do us part.

ACKNOWLEDGEMENTS

It was my great good fortune to have been raised under the roof of my parents' long, lively and loving marriage, the most beautiful example of a workable romance I could have wished for. This project would undoubtedly have had a very different flavour to it had I not felt such gratitude for that stroke of formative luck. Thank you too to my mother, Shirley Baum, for the real wisdom you've shared with me through your practice both as a spouse and as a counsellor. I was bereaved of my beloved father, Geoffrey Baum, in the course of researching this book. It has been written in his blessed memory.

Deep gratitude also goes to my mother-in-law, Lisa Appignanesi, for your always invaluable support, direction and insight. Just to think, had I not married your son, I might never have known the wonder of those things!

Thank you to my dear friends Poppy Sebag-Montefiore and Nicole Taylor for inviting me to speak upon your wedding day. I suspect it was your wedding rather than my own that first got me thinking seriously about marriage. And thank you to Katrina Forrester and Jamie Martin, sister-in-law and brother-in-law, for extending to me one of my life's most extraordinary honours: officiating at your nuptials. I think that was when my astonishment at marriage as an undertaking properly hit me.

An almighty thank-you goes to Simon Prosser for not only editing my work so perceptively, but for ingeniously proposing marriage to me in the first place as a subject at once ubiquitous yet strangely occluded. And my thanks too to all those at Penguin who've helped the project along, including Ruby Fatimilehin, Ellie Smith, Anna Ridley, Chloe Davies, and Mary Chamberlain for her consummate copy-editing.

Thank you to Sigrid Rausing for inviting me to publish an earlier version of the chapter 'What Do Women Want?' in *Granta*.

Thanks really aren't enough for my brilliant agent, Tracy Bohan, after whose initial response to the unfinished draft of this book my whole world seemed changed for the better.

I'm extremely grateful as well to some exceptional early readers of my manuscript, particularly Peter Boxall, Stephen Frosh and Anouchka Grose. And this work is also happily conjugated with numerous others who've offered me their inspiration, or instruction, or both – especially Adam Andrusier, Chloe Aridjis, Philip Baum, Josh Cohen, Yehoshua Engelman, James Jordan, Nick Laird, Nikita Lalwani, Darian Leader, Nicky Marsh, Diana Matar, Hisham Matar, Will May, Rachel Miller, Stephen Morton, Chris Oakley, Adam Phillips, Abigail Schama, Vik Sharma, Zadie Smith and Marina Warner.

Thank you to Manny and Isaiah, the true amazement of my life and the daily proof that my marriage has opened up so much of the future for me.

Josh, this whole book is an acknowledgement of you, but it also doesn't even begin to acknowledge you. I think it might actually frighten me to recognize my indebtedness to you in all areas, including in my writing. So I can't quite bear to admit how dependent on you I am, or how much help you give me, or how desperately I feel I need you. Still, I can thank you for your unique take on husbanding. Not every wife would go for it, I'm sure. But I do. I really do.

PERMISSIONS

BIBLIOGRAPHY

Theodor W. Adorno, 'Trying to Understand *Endgame*', trans. Michael T. Jones, *New German Critique*, No. 26, Spring–Summer 1982
—*Negative Dialectics*, trans. E. B. Ashton (California: Continuum, 1981)
—'Freudian Theory and the Pattern of Fascist Propaganda', *The Culture Industry: Selected Essays on Mass Culture*, ed. J. M. Bernstein (London: Routledge, 2001)
Sara Ahmed, *The Promise of Happiness* (North Carolina: Duke University Press, 2010)
Hanan Al-Shaykh, *One Thousand and One Nights* (London: Bloomsbury, 2011)
Louis Althusser, *On the Reproduction of Capitalism: Ideology and Ideological State Apparatuses*, trans. G. M. Goshgarian (London: Verso, 2014)
—*The Future Lasts a Long Time*, trans. Richard Veasey (London: Vintage, 1994)
Yehuda Amichai, 'Instructions for a Waitress', *The Early Books of Yehuda Amichai*, trans. Yehuda Amichai and Ted Hughes (New York: Sheep Meadow Press, 1988)
Josh Appignanesi, 'Netflix might dominate our viewing, but cinema brings us another sort of pleasure', *Guardian*, 24 December 2019
Josh Appignanesi, Devorah Baum, Hisham Matar, 'The New Man', *Granta*, February 2017
Lisa Appignanesi, *Simone de Beauvoir* (London: Haus Publishing, 2005)
—*Everyday Madness: On grief, anger, loss and love* (London: 4th Estate, 2018)
Jane Austen, *Pride and Prejudice* (London: Penguin, 2003)
—*Emma* (London: Penguin, 2003)
J. L. Austin, *How to Do Things with Words* (Connecticut: Martino Fine Books, 2018)
Julian Barnes, *Levels of Life* (London: Vintage, 2014)
Roland Barthes, *Roland Barthes*, trans. Richard Howard (London: Vintage, 2020)
—*A Lover's Discourse: Fragments*, trans. Richard Howard (London: Vintage, 2002)

Isaac Bashevis Singer, 'Gimpel the Fool', trans. Saul Bellow, *Collected Stories* (New York: HarperCollins, 2004)

Simone de Beauvoir, *The Second Sex*, trans. H. M. Parshley (London: Vintage, 1997)

Samuel Beckett, *Happy Days* (London: Faber, 2010)

Jessica Benjamin, *The Bonds of Love: Psychoanalysis, Feminism and the Problems of Domination* (New York: Pantheon Books, 1988)

Edmund Bergler, *Divorce Won't Help* (New York: Hart, 1948)

Ingmar Bergman, *The Marriage Scenarios*, trans. Alan Blair (New York: Pantheon Books, 1988)

—*The Best Intentions*, trans. Joan Tate (London: Vintage, 2018)

Leo Bersani, 'Against Monogamy', *Is the Rectum a Grave? and Other Essays* (Chicago: University of Chicago Press, 2009)

Maurice Blanchot, *The Infinite Conversation*, trans. S. Hanson (Minnesota: University of Minnesota Press, 1992)

Amy Bloom, *In Love: A Memoir of Love and Loss* (London: Granta, 2022)

Roberto Bolaño, *2666*, trans. Natasha Wimmer (London: Picador, 2009)

Christopher Bollas, *Being a Character: Psychoanalysis and Self Experience* (London: Routledge, 1993)

Katherine Boo, 'The Marriage Cure: Is wedlock really a way out of poverty?', *New Yorker*, August 2003

S. Pearl Brilmyer, Filippo Trentin, Zairong Xiang, 'The Ontology of the Couple: or, What Queer Theory Knows About Numbers', *A Journal of Lesbian and Gay Studies*, Vol. 25, no. 2, April 2019

Taffy Brodesser-Akner, *Fleishman is in Trouble* (London: Headline, 2020)

Claire Bushey, 'Loneliness and Me', *Financial Times*, 21 November 2020

Albert Camus, *The Myth of Sisyphus*, trans. Justin O'Brien (London: Penguin, 2005)

Angela Carter, *The Bloody Chamber* (London: Vintage, 1995)

Raymond Carver, *What We Talk About When We Talk About Love* (London: Vintage, 2009)

Stanley Cavell, *Pursuits of Happiness: The Hollywood Comedy of Remarriage* (Massachusetts: Harvard University Press, 1981)

Michael Chabon, 'Nick Laird', *Interview* magazine, June 2017

Clare Chambers, *Against Marriage: An Egalitarian Defence of the Marriage-Free State* (Oxford: Oxford University Press, 2017)

Josh Cohen, *The Private Life: Why We Remain in the Dark* (London: Granta, 2013)

Peter Coleman, *Christian Attitudes to Marriage: From Ancient Times to the Third Millennium* (London: SCM Press, 2004)

Stephanie Coontz, *Marriage, a History, from Obedience to Intimacy: Or, How Love Conquered Marriage* (New York: Viking, 2005)

Melinda Cooper, *Family Values: Between Neoliberalism and the New Social Conservatism* (New York: Zone Books, 2017)

Luce d'Eramo, 'Life as a Couple', trans. Howard Curtis, *The Penguin Book of Italian Short Stories*, ed. Jhumpa Lahiri (London: Penguin, 2019)

Jacques Derrida, 'Force of Law: The "Mystical Foundation of Authority"', *Acts of Religion*, trans. and ed. Gil Anidjar (London: Routledge, 2002)

—*Learning to Live Finally: The Last Interview*, trans. Pascale-Anne Brault and Michael Naas (New York: Melville House Publishing, 2007)

Chitra Banerjee Divakaruni, *Arranged Marriage* (London: Black Swan, 1997)

Lee Edelman, *No Future: Queer Theory and the Death Drive* (North Carolina: Duke University Press, 2004)

Maria Edgeworth, 'An Essay on the Noble Science of Self-justification', *Letters for Literary Ladies* (Michigan: Gale ECCO, print editions, 2018)

Luise Eichenbaum and Susie Orbach, *What Do Women Want? Exploding the Myth of Dependency* (California: CreateSpace Independent Publishing Platform, 2014)

George Eliot, *Middlemarch* (London: Penguin, 1994)

Buchi Emecheta, *The Joys of Motherhood* (Edinburgh: Heinemann, 2008)

Ralph Waldo Emerson, *Selected Journals 1841–1877* (New York: The Library of America, 2010)

Nora Ephron, *Heartburn* (London: Virago, 1996)

Diana Evans, *Ordinary People* (London: Vintage, 2018)

Silvia Federici, *Revolution at Point Zero: Housework, Reproduction, and Feminist Struggle* (Oakland: PM Press, 2020)

Elena Ferrante, *The Days of Abandonment*, trans. Ann Goldstein (New York: Europa Editions, 2006)

Helen Fielding, *Bridget Jones's Diary* (London: Picador, 2016)

Gustave Flaubert, *Madame Bovary*, trans. Geoffrey Wall (London: Penguin, 2003)

Sigmund Freud, *Introductory Lectures on Psychoanalysis, The Standard Edition of the Complete Psychological Works of Sigmund Freud*, Vol. 3, trans. and ed. James Strachey (London: Vintage, 2001)

—*The Psychopathology of Everyday Life*, Vol. 6

—*A Case of Hysteria, Three Essays on Sexuality and Other Works*, Vol. 7

—*The Joke and its Relation to the Unconscious*, Vol. 8

—*On the History of the Psychoanalytic Movement, Papers on Metapsychology and Other Works*, Vol. 14

—*Beyond the Pleasure Principle, Group Psychology and Other Works*, Vol. 18

—*The Future of an Illusion, Civilization and its Discontents and Other Works*, Vol. 21

William Godwin, *An Enquiry Concerning Political Justice* (Oxford: Oxford University Press, 2013)

Johann Wolfgang von Goethe, *Elective Affinities*, trans. R. J. Hollingdale (London: Penguin, 2005)

Anouchka Grose, *From Anxiety to Zoolander: Notes on Psychoanalysis* (London: Routledge, 2019)

Thom Gunn, 'Thoughts on Unpacking', *Collected Poems* (London: Faber, 1994)

D. D. Guttenplan, 'An Interview with the Most Hated Man on the Internet', *The Nation*, 16 October 2016

Tessa Hadley, *Married Love* (London: Vintage, 2013)

—*Free Love* (London: Jonathan Cape, 2022)

John Halkett, *Milton and the Idea of Matrimony* (New Haven: Yale University Press, 1970)

C. J. Hauser, 'The Crane Wife', *Paris Review*, July 2019

G. W. F. Hegel, *Elements of the Philosophy of Right*, ed. Allen W. Wood, trans. H. B. Nisbet (Cambridge: Cambridge University Press, 1991)

Lisa Hopkins, *The Shakespearean Marriage: Merry Wives and Heavy Husbands* (London: Macmillan, 1998)

Tera W. Hunter, 'Putting an Antebellum Myth to Rest', *New York Times*, 1 August 2011

Eva Illouz, *Why Love Hurts* (St Ives: Polity, 2012)

Christopher Isherwood, *A Single Man* (London: Vintage, 2010)

Henry James, *The Portrait of a Lady* (London: Penguin, 2011)

—*What Maisie Knew* (London: Penguin, 2010)

Fredric Jameson, 'The End of Temporality', *Critical Inquiry*, Vol. 29, no. 4, Summer 2003

Tayari Jones, *An American Marriage* (London: Oneworld, 2018)

Immanuel Kant, *Groundwork of the Metaphysics of Morals*, trans. Mary Gregor and Jens Timmermann (Cambridge: Cambridge University Press, 2012)

Søren Kierkegaard, *Either/Or: A Fragment of Life*, trans. Alastair Hannay (London: Penguin, 1992)

Esther Kinsky, *Grove* (London: Fitzcarraldo Editions, 2020)

Laura Kipnis, *Against Love: A Polemic* (New York: Vintage, 2004)

Julia Kristeva, *The Kristeva Reader*, ed. Toril Moi (Oxford: Wiley-Blackwell, 1991)

Julia Kristeva and Philippe Sollers, *Marriage as a Fine Art*, trans. Lorna Scott Fox (New York: Columbia University Press, 2016)

Nick Laird, 'Author, Author: Like a Prayer', *Guardian*, 30 May 2009

—*The Beautiful Sentence* (Banholt: Bonnefant, 2021)

Darian Leader, *Stealing the* Mona Lisa: *What Art Stops Us From Seeing* (London: Faber, 2002)

David Lehmann and Batia Siebzehner, 'Power, Boundaries and Institutions: Marriage in Ultra-Orthodox Judaism', *European Journal of Sociology*, 'Jewish Institutions and Practices', Vol. 50, no. 2, 2009

Jill Lepore, 'Fixed: The rise of marriage therapy, and other dreams of human betterment', *New Yorker*, March 2010

Harriet Lerner, *Marriage Rules: A Manual for the Married and Coupled Up* (Wyoming: Gotham Books, 2012)

Emmanuel Levinas, *Totality and Infinity: An Essay on Exteriority*, trans. Alphonso Lingis (Pittsburgh: Duquesne University Press, 1969)

—*Otherwise than Being: or, Beyond Essence*, trans. Alphonso Lingis (Pittsburgh: Duquesne University Press, 1999)

—'The Temptation of Temptation', *Nine Talmudic Readings*, trans. Annette Aronowicz (Indiana: Indiana University Press, 1990)

Deborah Levy, *Real Estate* (London: Penguin, 2022)

Alison Light, *A Radical Romance: A Memoir of Love, Grief and Consolation* (London: Penguin, 2019)

Javier Marías, *A Heart So White*, trans. Margaret Jull Costa (London: Vintage, 2003)

Karl Marx, 'The Eighteenth Brumaire of Louis Bonaparte', *Marx Later Political Writings*, ed. Terrell Carver (Cambridge: Cambridge University Press, 1996)

Hisham Matar, *The Return: Fathers, Sons and the Land In Between* (London: Penguin, 2017)

—*A Month in Siena* (London: Penguin, 2020)

Rebecca Mead, *The Road to Middlemarch: My Life with George Eliot* (London: Granta, 2014)

John Stuart Mill, *'On Liberty' and Other Writings* (Cambridge: Cambridge University Press, 1989)

D. A. Miller, *Jane Austen: Or, The Secret of Style* (New Jersey: Princeton University Press, 2003)

John Milton, *The Major Works*, ed. Stephen Orgel and Jonathan Goldberg (Oxford: Oxford University Press, 1991)

Wesley Morris, 'Rom-Coms Were Corny and Retrograde. Why Do I Miss Them So Much?', *New York Times*, 24 April 2019

Alice Munro, *Hateship, Friendship, Courtship, Loveship, Marriage* (London: Vintage, 2013)

Anna K. Nardo, *George Eliot's Dialogue with Milton* (Missouri: University of Missouri Press, 2003)

Maggie Nelson, *The Argonauts* (Minneapolis: Graywolf Press, 2015)

Friedrich Nietzsche, *Human, All Too Human*, trans. and ed. Marion Faber and Stephen Lehmann (London: Penguin, 1994)

Kathleen Nott, 'Is Rationalism Sterile?', *Objections to Humanism*, ed. H. J. Blackham (London: Constable, 1963)

Emily Nussbaum, 'How Jokes Won the Election: How do you fight an enemy who's just kidding?', *New Yorker*, January 2017

Cynthia Ozick, *Metaphor and Memory: Essays* (New York: Knopf, 1989)

Grace Paley, 'Wants', *The Collected Stories of Grace Paley*; introduction by George Saunders (London: Virago, 2018)

Esther Perel, *Mating in Captivity: Unlocking Erotic Intelligence* (London: HarperCollins, 2007)

Adam Phillips, *Monogamy* (New York: Pantheon, 1996)

—'The Uses of Desire', *One Way and Another: New and Selected Essays* (London: Penguin, 2018)

—*In Writing* (London: Penguin, 2019)

—'Politics in the Consulting Room', *Granta*, February 2019

Plato, *The Symposium*, trans. Christopher Gill (London: Penguin, 2003)

Adrienne Rich, 'Sources', *Your Native Land, Your Life* (New York: Norton, 1986)

Sally Rooney, *Normal People* (London: Faber, 2019)

Phyllis Rose, *Parallel Lives: Five Victorian Marriages* (New York: Knopf, 1984)

Sasha Roseneil, 'It's time to end the tyranny of coupledom', *Guardian*, 14 November 2020

Sasha Roseneil, Isabel Crowhurst, Tone Hellesund, Ana Cristina Santos, Mariya Stoilova, *The Tenacity of the Couple-Norm: Intimate Citizenship Regimes in a Changing Europe* (London: UCL Press, 2020)

Norman Rush, *Mating* (London: Granta, 2013)

—*Mortals* (London: Granta, 2003)

Peter Salmon, *An Event Perhaps: A Biography of Jacques Derrida* (London: Verso, 2020)

Simon Schama, *The Face of Britain: The Nation through its Portraits* (London: Viking, 2015)

William Shakespeare, *The Complete Works* (London: Arden Shakespeare, 2020)

Elaine Showalter, '*Fiddler*, Tevye's Daughters, and Me', *New York Review*, July 2019

Zadie Smith, *Intimations: Six Essays* (London: Penguin, 2020)

Marie Carmichael Stopes, *Married Love; or, Love in Marriage* (Moscow: Dodo Press, 2009)

Elizabeth Strout, *Olive Kitteridge: A Novel in Stories* (New York: Simon & Schuster, 2011)

—*Olive, Again* (London: Penguin, 2020)

—*Oh William!* (London: Viking, 2021)

Tony Tanner, *Adultery in the Novel* (Baltimore: Johns Hopkins University Press, 1979)

Susan Taubes, *Divorcing* (New York: New York Review of Books, 2020)

Jia Tolentino, 'I Thee Dread', *Trick Mirror: Reflections on Self-Delusion* (London: 4th Estate, 2019)

Linn Ullmann, *Unquiet*, trans. Thilo Reinhard (London: Hamish Hamilton, 2019)

Giambattista Vico, *New Science*, trans. David Marsh (London: Penguin, 1999)

David Foster Wallace, '*E Unibus Pluram*: Television and US Fiction', *A Supposedly Fun Thing I'll Never Do Again* (London: Hachette, 1998)

Edith Wharton, *The House of Mirth* (London: Penguin, 2012)

—*The Children* (London: Virago, 2016)

Oscar Wilde, *The Picture of Dorian Gray* (London: Penguin, 2003)

—*The Importance of Being Earnest and Other Plays* (Oxford: Oxford University Press, 2008)

D. W. Winnicott, 'Hate in the Countertransference', *Through Paediatrics to Psychoanalysis: Collected Papers* (London: Routledge, 1975)

—*Playing and Reality* (London: Routledge, 2005)

Mary Wollstonecraft, *A Vindication of the Rights of Women* (London: Penguin, 2004)

Virginia Woolf, *Mrs Dalloway* (London: Penguin, 2000)

—*A Room of One's Own and Three Guineas* (Oxford: Oxford University Press, 2015)

Slavoj Žižek, 'Hegel on Marriage', *e-flux journal issue #34*, April 2012

FILMOGRAPHY

Lenny Abrahamson, *Normal People* (miniseries), BBC Three, 2020
Josh Appignanesi and Devorah Baum, *The New Man*, CreativeLife, 2016
—*Husband*, Dartmouth Films, 2022
Noah Baumbach, *Marriage Story*, Netflix, 2019
Ingmar Bergman, *Scenes from a Marriage*, Sveriges Radio, 1973
George Cukor, *The Philadelphia Story*, MGM, 1941
Lena Dunham, *Girls* (first season), HBO, 2012
Asghar Farhadi, *A Separation*, Filmiran, 2011
Victor Fleming, *Gone with the Wind*, MGM, 1940
Michael Haneke, *Amour*, Les Films du Losange, 2012
Joanna Hogg, *Exhibition*, Fugu-Filmverleih, 2014
Peter Jackson, *Get Back*, Walt Disney Pictures, 2021
Norman Jewison, *Fiddler on the Roof*, United Artists, 1971
Mike Leigh, *Another Year*, Momentum Pictures, 2011
Richard Linklater, *Before Sunrise*, Sony Pictures Entertainment, 1995
—*Before Sunset*, Warner Independent Pictures, 2004
—*Before Midnight*, GEM Entertainment, 2013
Kenneth Lonergan, *Manchester by the Sea*, Amazon Studios, 2016
Sam Mendes, *Revolutionary Road*, DreamWorks Pictures, 2008
Yoko Ono, *Bottoms*, Joko, 1967
Ruben Östlund, *Force Majeure*, Alamode Film, 2014
Yasujirō Ozu, *Tokyo Story*, Shochiku, 1953
Donald Petrie, *Mystic Pizza*, Samuel Goldwyn Company, 1988
Rob Reiner, *When Harry Met Sally*, Columbia Pictures, 1989
Phoebe Waller-Bridge, *Fleabag* (two seasons), BBC Three, 2016–19
Billy Wilder, *The Seven Year Itch*, 20th Century Fox, 1955